EMPOWERING A PEASANTRY IN A CARIBBEAN CONTEXT

Chinakuruk Falls, Essequibo. *Source:* Fernandes 1990

EMPOWERING A PEASANTRY IN A CARIBBEAN CONTEXT

The Case of Land Settlement Schemes in Guyana, 1865–1985

Carl B. Greenidge

The University of the West Indies Press
Barbados ● Jamaica ● Trinidad and Tobago

The University of the West Indies Press
1A Aqueduct Flats   Mona
Kingston 7 Jamaica

05 04 03 02 01   5 4 3 2 1

CATALOGUING IN PUBLICATION DATA
Greenidge, Carl.
Empowering a peasantry in a Caribbean context : the case of land settlement
schemes in Guyana, 1865–1985 / Carl B. Greenidge.

p.cm.

Includes bibliographical references and index.

ISBN: 976-640-068-7

1. Land settlement – Guyana – History. 2. Land tenure – Guyana – History.
3. Land grants – Guyana – History. 4. Agriculture and politics – Guyana.
5. Guyana – Economic conditions.
I. Title.
HD540.3.G74   2001   333.31   -dc20

Set in 11/14 Adobe Garamond with Gill Sans display
Book and cover design by ProDesign Ltd, Red Gal Ring, Kingston
This book has been printed on acid-free paper

Printed in Canada

To

Liz
Stella
Vony
Nenzie Olga

Grandmother, Mother, 'Other Mother' and Godmother,
respectively, in acknowledgment of the sacrifices so
selflessly and often cheerfully borne in order to nurture
and encourage their 'sons' and 'daughters'.

CONTENTS

ILLUSTRATIONS

FOREWORD

Almost every facet of the plantation system in the Caribbean has been extensively studied. Slavery, indentured servitude, the sugar and other primary producing industries, revolts and social protests, the labour movement, the assertion of nationalist aspirations and the multiple issues that constitute the plantation legacy account for much of the social science literature on the region as a whole. Among the topics that are less examined as a regional phenomenon are land settlement schemes. In 1951, W. Arthur Lewis undertook the first comprehensive examination of Caribbean land settlement schemes in an article, "Issues in Land Settlement Policy in the Caribbean", that appeared in the *Caribbean Economic Review*. Any expectation that this pioneering effort would be followed by a plethora of similar regionwide studies on land settlement schemes has remained largely unfulfilled. The concern has been with the broader issue of land reform in terms not only of the redistribution of property or rights in land but also of supplementary measures to promote productivity such as credit, extension services, changed forms of agricultural organization and institutions such as cooperatives and tenancy reform. In any event, whether they are limited to land settlement schemes or encompass the wider concept of land reform, the studies have tended to focus on specific countries and, less frequently, on the subregion of the Eastern Caribbean states.

Carl Greenidge's book is in this tradition of national studies. While he draws comparisons with other Caribbean countries, the setting is Guyana. It is the country in the region that has the greatest potential in terms of its physical size and the variety of its economy. At the same time, in terms of internal social and political cohesion, Guyana is the least prepared for addressing these vital concerns. While present day changes are summoning the region to policy responses appropriate for the next century, Guyana finds itself mired in racial politics, the legacy of the plantation life of the nineteenth and early twentieth centuries, unable as yet to turn its attention adequately to the needs and challenges of the twenty-first century.

It is a function of the spirit of community and of regional unity being forged in the Caribbean that the problems of Guyana are also those of the entire region. It is more than simply a question of solidarity, the rest of the region needs a strong, unified Guyana. Even if the region chooses to be indifferent, Guyana's problems would nonetheless press themselves upon its attention.

Although the evolution and empowering of the peasantry in Guyana is analysed in a Caribbean context as the title indicates, this book is clearly not written with Caribbean politicians in mind. But if Caribbean politicians delve into this book, they, like its mainstream readers, will be rewarded. For Guyana's problems today cannot be properly understood except with reference to its colonial and plantation history – the dynamics of the relationship between the Colonial Office in London and the administration of the former colony, the convergence between the interests of the local administration and the planters, and the emergence of factors that were completely alien to British Guiana or the Colonial Office, all of which had an impact on the country's land settlement schemes. The understanding and even appreciation of these issues is necessary for the formulation of a viable solution to Guyana's problems.

A considerable body of literature on land settlement schemes in Guyana exists. But none of these studies is as comprehensive as Greenidge's or as thoroughly and rigorously researched. Greenidge's work convincingly refutes the orthodox view that land settlement schemes in Guyana have, in general, not worked. Such an orthodox view is the outcome of a static approach to history. Whatever might have been their original purpose, Greenidge argues, land settlement schemes operated in a dynamic setting, and their objectives changed according to the need to be served at varying points in time. Because the objectives were periodically revised, land settlement schemes were not simply the by-product of the sugar industry but also a strategic element of it. Greenidge contends that, judged in terms of specific objectives, land settlement schemes were, in general, a success story.

The heavy hand of the local colonial administration, often in tactical alliance with the planter class, is felt through much of Greenidge's account. In fact, in this work, the sugar plantations of pre-independent Guyana are the setting for a long, drawn-out and vicious two-sided battle. On one side there was European capital, dedicated to maximizing and maintaining profits from sugar sales, exerting control over the supply and price of labour and limiting its bargaining power. On the other was newly liberated African labour dedicated to exercising the options that were available to it and to use effectively its potential bargaining power.

Land settlement schemes were much more than a strategy of economic organization. They were also strategies of social organization, which when put into
effect, together with the growing of sugar, planted the seeds of what would be
decades of mistrust and hostility between the country's two major races, which
continue to polarize the country to this day. Lest the wrong signals were sent to
the powerful antislavery lobby, following the end of slavery, the European
planter class was reluctant to import African labour. The hiring of indentured
labour from elsewhere, and overwhelmingly from India, was the technique
utilized by the planter class to minimize the cost of labour for producing sugar.
The indentureship contract allowed the planters to hire labour as needed. Those
contracts provided for repatriation of indentured labour at the end of five years.
However, as the number of persons eligible for repatriation began to grow and
particularly in the middle of the depression of the 1870s, the local administration sought to avoid the high repatriation costs by offering the labourers land in
lieu of return passages.

The social and economic consequences of this policy were manifold, far-
reaching and long term. First, the policy constituted the genesis of the land
settlement schemes primarily related to agriculture and characterized by government sponsorship and financial support. Second, in emphasizing permanence of
abode to indentured labour, land settlement schemes completed the destruction
of the African bargaining power which indentureship had precipitated. Third,
while the number of Indians was steadily increasing after the 1940s, the same
was not the case with the Africans. Fourth, the land settlement schemes fortified
the colonial administration in its policy of withholding financial and infrastructural support from the villages which were sugar estates that the liberated
Africans pooled their savings to purchase and communally owned. Instead of
providing assistance to these villages, the colonial administration taxed them
punitively to ensure their failure and the consequential return of the Africans to
the sugar labour market. Notwithstanding the enormous odds against them, the
liberated slaves persevered with their village movement and today there are
villages that bear the hallmark of their tenacity and industry.

The undermining of the village movement, coupled with the establishment
of the land settlement schemes for Indians under the aegis of the colonial
administration continued to tip the scales against Africans. Greenidge recognizes that the Africans also contributed to the decline of their bargaining power
and their fortunes in relation to those of the indentured labourers. As Africans
encountered difficulties with their communal ownership of lands and,
frequently, with establishing their title to these lands as these were progressively

partitioned, they adopted a less forward-looking attitude towards their holdings. This outlook certainly facilitated the squatting by indentured labourers who, while appealing to the colonial administration for land on which to settle, had begun to penetrate the African villages. Squatting usually constituted the first phase in the transfer of African land to Indians; the first step in the assertion of ownership which the sugar interests encouraged. And as Indian hunger for land continued to assert itself, notwithstanding the multiplication of land settlement schemes, Indians began purchasing the land, in addition to squatting, as the more orthodox form of appropriation of African lands.

As we contemplate present-day relations between the two major races in Guyana, the pieces begin to fall into place, and the scene begins to be set. The social division of labour on the plantation at the time that land settlement schemes were established was such that management was white and labour non-white. The system of indentureship was a complicating factor, in that it added a new subdivision of labour by ethnic group. This, in turn, further complicated and exacerbated relations between Africans and Indians.

It is not only in his discussion of racial issues that Greenidge touches on the relations between the political economy of land settlement schemes and the social structure of the society. He also opens the window on several other aspects of life in pre-independent Guyana, including conflicts among the various classes in the society and, more particularly, the development of socioeconomic differentiation among the occupants of the land settlement schemes. The book describes the emergence of landlords, merchants, moneylenders, including usurers, agrarian capitalists and large farm holders. Rice cultivation provided the break towards a better economic life and social standing in the land settlement schemes and the rural communities in general. Greenidge illustrates the ways in which rice cultivation was once held hostage by the sugar industry. Such cultivation was supported only when its demands on labour and land resources were not in conflict with those of the sugar industry. For example, it was following the closure of the Cane Grove Sugar Estate that the existing land settlement scheme, based on rice production, was established in that area. But this support for rice production, as Greenidge observes, kept alive allegations of racial bias in the establishment and administration of these schemes.

Today, rice is one of Guyana's leading exports and contributors to its gross domestic product (GDP). Its principal beneficiaries – large farmers, rice millers, extensive property owners and landlords – progressively lost their feeling of identification with the labourers on the land settlement schemes as they gradually joined the ranks of the country's middle class that was occupationally varied and racially mixed. A peasantry was very much in the process of being empowered. The outcome was complex. Class solidarity cut across racial lines and there were occasions when African and Indian workers made common cause against the capitalist interests.

In the debate that the racial conflict and the competition among political leaders for power in the closing years – the early 1960s – of colonial rule in Guyana stimulated between the cultural pluralists and the structural functionalists in the Caribbean, the latter argued that the socioeconomic differentiation overrode the cleavage between the major races, and that an analysis of Guyana's political economy in terms of class was more appropriate. Greenidge does not allow either the racial or socioeconomic framework of analysis to overpower the other. Indeed, one of the great merits of Greenidge's book lies in the deft manner in which it establishes vital relationships between a number of variables which, prima facie, might be thought to be independent, if not in contradiction. His use of both analytical frameworks in an eclectic manner distinguishes his work from previous studies.

Of the 120 years, 1865–1985, that the study covers, twenty of them belong to the postindependence period. Many of the features of land settlement schemes that originated in the colonial period persisted during these two decades and continue to do so. To this day squatting, which has extended to urban areas, is a sensitive issue for governments of whatever racial or ideological complexion and one that has to be handled with the greatest of delicacy. Often, such delicacy demands that squatters' rights be respected. But this outcome has increased the incidence of squatting especially when the government, as will be illustrated later, does not take decisive action to dispel the notion that its actions are conducive to this form of appropriation.

Likewise, agricultural development may seem to be a natural and innocuous exercise for developing the potential of a country and enhancing its economic development. But in a country such as Guyana where key industries are predominantly controlled by one or the other race, agricultural development becomes a coded word. Other problems that arose in the colonial era, such as those of absentee farmers, nonsettlement of plots, lack of coordination among governmental agencies, nonexistent facilities for community development including schools, community centres, adult education and other necessary accoutrements of country life, were carried over into the postindependence period.

To these old dimensions, other primary dimensions were added during this latter period. One of these was party politics. Another was a socialist ideology and the third was the widening of the scope and purpose of land settlement schemes. Indeed, these added dimensions had begun to emerge during the advent of independence.

If state involvement in land settlement schemes was a colonial legacy, it was reinforced by the socialist outlook of the two major political parties, the People's Progressive Party (PPP) and the People's National Congress (PNC), during the period that the book covers. Since both parties rely mainly on Indians and Africans, respectively, for their support, the state involvement favours supporters when their party is in office. During the tenure of the PPP in the late 1950s and early 1960s, land settlement schemes, of which Black Bush Polder was the prime example, were associated with rice production; an emphasis or bias that benefited its supporters. At the same time, modernization of the industry was forcing out the small farmers whose interests it was ideologically incumbent upon the PPP government to protect against the burgeoning power and influence of the larger farming and milling interests. This protection of Indian small farmers, however, provided little comfort to their African counterparts who felt that they were being overlooked. A policy that was ideologically defensible therefore became racially explosive.

With "Land to the Tiller" as its rallying call, the PNC, during its tenure in office from 1964 to 1992, undertook widespread land reform, including reform on the sugar estates following the nationalization of the sugar industry in 1976. It also established a major drainage and irrigation scheme – the Mahaica-Mahaicony-Abary Scheme, a facility that is generally vital to economic life in the low-lying coastal land of Guyana. Additionally, the PNC government concentrated on new land settlement schemes in the hinterland and on establishing housing schemes whose beneficiaries were principally Africans in both rural and urban areas.

The programme of hinterland development planned to populate selected areas by moving people from the coastland and encouraging immigration from the Caribbean region, more so as small communities of West Indians already existed in the hinterland. But this introduction of a new Caribbean population was readily interpreted as an effort by the PNC government to augment the number of Africans and thereby adjust the racial balance rather than to increase the small size of Guyana's population relative to its physical size and its great economic potential. The plan was adversely affected in its infancy by economic difficulties in the late 1970s.

It is, however, the housing schemes that sustain Greenidge's argument that land settlement schemes were in general successful. Declaring Guyana committed to cooperative socialism and to a trisectoral economy – public, private and cooperative – the PNC government organized these schemes on aided self-help and collective bases. The emphasis on cooperatives drew much of its inspiration from the postemancipation period when the ex-slaves pooled their resources to purchase lands and created the village movement in order to assert their independence of the sugar plantocracy. This form of social and economic organization appealed more to the Africans in the postindependence period than to the Indians whose economic initiatives remained family based. As one of the legs of the sectoral tripod of the economy, cooperatives lagged behind the other two just as they did in their relationship with state involvement in the land settlement schemes and the expansion of the private sector during the colonial period. The limited role of cooperatives in the development of the economy, in particular agriculture, has raised the question of whether they are a viable strategy of economic organization.

Although the two decades of postindependence that the book covers are close in time and one in which he participated as a prominent PNC government figure, Greenidge does not depart from his scholarly analysis in the final chapters. On the contrary, the study benefits from his being an insider. He has brought his public policy perspective to his account of the challenges that modernization of agriculture poses for the land settlement schemes and of ills attributable to a lack of coordination and/or integration of efforts expended on these development schemes. Above all, however, the contribution of this book resides not only in the physical research undertaken but in the dramatic qualities of the analysis.

The year 1985 is a convenient date for Greenidge to end the period that the book covers. In August of that year, an era came to a close with the untimely passing of Forbes Burnham, the founding leader of the PNC and the president of Guyana. Although Burnham was known for his racial balancing act during his twenty-one years in office, it was his successor, Desmond Hoyte, who made observers highly confident that the spectre of racial division was finally being put to rest, and that a period of racial healing, if not indeed of reconciliation, was at hand. With a profound understanding of the strength of the race factor in Guyana's politics, Hoyte knew well that racial politics in the country could not be wished away. He knew that it required bold, full-blooded and deliberate policies which assured the two major racial groups and enhanced conditions for their participation, on a more equal footing and with more equitable rewards, in the nation building effort. In this endeavour, Hoyte often found himself out on a limb in relation to some of his own supporters who believed that he was bending too far backward to satisfy Indian desires and concerns, including those relating to land ownership.

It may be too soon to judge whether the extremists or the moderates in the PNC were correct, but the mandate of the PPP that began in 1992 under Cheddi Jagan and the national election of 1997 that has kept this party in office, this time under Janet Jagan, is instructive. The PPP pursues policies that reveal that the ghost of racial politics was anything but laid to rest and that the more things changed, the more they remained the same, or became worse. The PPP government's land policy bears eloquent testimony to this contention and has added practical relevance to Greenidge's work for our time.

This policy confirms that land not only is a valuable political commodity for the major political parties and that it is more so for the PPP since its supporters are more wedded to the land and consider it a gut issue, but also that its allocation can be racially charged. The PPP government pursues its land policy on a scale, pace and intensity that have never been experienced during the PNC tenure. A glaring and recent example was its decision to appoint to a land selection committee for the country's largest and most populous region which the PNC won in the 1997 national election and whose administration the PNC controls, persons of PPP affiliation which effectively excluded PNC representation. Compounding this selection is the fact that all the named members are Indians. Such action is seen as creating a nonconstraining milieu in which PPP supporters have embarked on the practice of trespassing on the land of non-PPP supporters, tying up landowners in the courts with injunctions and proceeding to cultivate the lands. The PPP land policy and the action of its supporters of targeting the lands of non-PPP supporters have drawn charges from the PNC that the political and racial composition of the Land Selection Committee was in keeping with the government's thrust to monopolize all political, economic and cultural space in the country. Such controversies recall the way in which the political economy of land settlement schemes evolved and operated in relation to the social structure.

This book deserves recognition in its own right. But coming at a time when, in the distribution of land, it appears that the most distant past is in danger of being repeated; when the economic power that the appropriation of land confers on its holders arouses or instils fears of dispossession in those that consider themselves denied by questionable policy and action; when emotions and racial feelings surrounding land ownership have soared to an unprecedented high or when, from a different perspective, the contemporary style table which replaced the colonial one at independence has merely turned, it is essential reading not only for academics, policy makers and national stake-holders of every political hue but also for anyone who has an interest in Guyana.

Cedric Grant
Clarke University
Atlanta, Georgia
November 1998

PREFACE

So close was this past here, it was as if the landscape wore many masks
and the spirits of the past still lived here, especially here in the forest
where even the silence echoed. He said, "Driving across a flat land, you
get the feeling you're going nowhere . . . Endless, endless space. Lord, the
country is really empty, the end of civilization."
   "As you know it," she commented.
Janice Shinebourne, *Timepiece*

In the polity of Guyana, things are rarely as they appear. The story of land
settlement is no exception. The country's pattern of land settlement is itself an
anomaly. In a country generously endowed with land resources, the population
is crowded into some 10 percent of the total area. Not only is the population
density very high on the coastal strip but the distribution of that land across
sectors is also surprising. This pattern owes its origin entirely to the social relations of production rather than to any physical imperative. The remainder of
the country, with its very low labour–land ratios and most of the country's
known mineral reserves, is the home of the spectacular Kaiteur Falls (seen on
the cover of this book) and the stunningly picturesque Chinakuruk Falls. This
potential wealth underlies the perception of a hinterland at once fecund and
dangerous, beautiful and menacing. The dark side of this paradox is attributable
to the challenge of developing the physical space. This duality of consciousness
is well captured by Harris whose work Jonas [1990: 30] describes as using "the
hinterland/coastal opposition – particularly rich in connotation for a country
geographically facing Europe from its narrow, cultivated (mask-like) coastal
strip, yet facing inland across vast regions of unchartered terrain, full of potential wealth and danger in its southward visage toward an antithetical continent".
This dichotomy is reflected in the works of other authors, such as Edgar
Mittelholzer, who gives special emphasis to supernatural aspects notably in *My*

Bones and My Flute [1955]. In her first novel, *Timepiece*, Janice Shinebourne also makes reference to this spatial and psychological/cultural link. But, most striking of all is, perhaps, the following passage from Pauline Melville who invokes a rich range of indigenous (Amerindian) mythology in illustrating her stories:

The intentions of those who designed the canals and kokers – which looked like guillotines – who attempted to measure the tidal gradation of rivers were insidiously confounded and the capital city seemed to have been stretched out beyond its ideal size to keep at bay the citizen's terror of the land mass at its back. [Melville 1997: 36]

We shall return to this analogy.

The cover photograph captures very effectively the majesty as well as the aura of foreboding, bordering on the supernatural, to which reference is made. In a way the story of land settlements is similar, a story of promises and disappointments, reality and mirage – the elusive quest for em-powerment.

Developing states are for the most part characterized by a heavy dependence on their agricultural sectors for output, incomes and employment. Consequently, the state of agricultural productivity is of great importance to their economic as well as political well-being. A major preoccupation of those who have attempted to modernize the Caribbean economy has been to increase the productivity of the smallholder sector and to establish a viable peasantry.

And yet, judging from much of the literature, not only have they failed to attain their ostensible aims regarding the peasantry but they have also enjoyed an abiding popularity over time. The prerequisites for the success of such schemes and for the maintenance of a viable peasantry remain elusive. If the reasons for promoting a peasantry have been the same over this time then it is necessary to explain how and why the efforts have been so frequently and easily derailed. If those objectives have not been the same, we need to know how they have changed and why. This raises the question of whose goals and the position of the intended beneficiaries in the process of goal formation and attainment.

In a sense it can be argued that a crucial requirement for successful land settlement is the mechanism for ensuring an identity of goals between the promoter of the schemes, the state, and the actors intended to pursue the goals, the farmers. The exploration of such issues requires us to venture well beyond the traditional staples that are the remit of studies on settlement schemes – incomes, output and employment.

The idea of a paper on this subject was first conceived during the course of a seminar on "Income and Production of Guyana's Rural Farm Households" as long ago as 1980. The first outline of the paper may well not have gone further had the work on my thesis at Birkbeck College, University of London, not revived interest in the matter. This served to spur me on to prepare the paper for a wider audience. This book is a revision and expansion of a working paper entitled "Land Settlements in the Caribbean: Policies, Problems and Prospects" (January 1982), prepared in 1982–83 during my sabbatical leave at Birbeck College. Somehow, not only did the preliminary draft grow inexorably, in spite of my best efforts, but the demands of public service hardly permitted concentrated and sustained work on such an exercise. In a way, the delay may not have been wholly unproductive for recent academic research and political events in this area, and in Guyana in particular, should serve to provide a keener audience. Recent research on the Caribbean has provided new material on which I have been able to draw.

ACKNOWLEDGMENTS

An endeavour of this magnitude could not have been concluded over such a long period without substantial assistance, tolerance and understanding from a host of colleagues and friends. In the preparation of this book, I have received such direct and indirect assistance from several persons. Inevitably, the influences and forms of assistance cannot be comprehensively acknowledged. With this apology, I wish to record a debt of gratitude to the following persons for their assistance and support in the manner mentioned.

For reading and offering extensive comments on the earliest drafts of the paper: Dr Adam Fforde, formerly of Birkbeck College, and Dr Cedric Grant of Clarke University, Atlanta, Georgia, USA.

For reading and kindly providing additional material and/or extensive written comments: Gavin Kennard, CCH, former director of agriculture and subsequently minister of agriculture, Guyana, inter alia; Sita Ramlal, formerly of the National Archives and currently registrar of the Supreme Court, Guyana. I am also grateful to Jean Craigwell of the Organization of American States Library for providing most of the photographs used.

A special word of thanks is reserved for Sita Ramlal whose unstinting contribution of time in locating and summarizing some of the archival material and whose encouragement contributed immeasurably to the completion of this task.

For preparing additional material for some of the tables and the unearthing of additional archival material on the Guyana National Service (GNS) and Youth Corps schemes in particular, former GNS students, Alleyne and Nurse, at the University of Guyana.

Finally, I should like to thank my two former secretaries, Sharon Macey and Marcelle Bennett, without whose enthusiasm, patience and dexterity with word processing and typewriting facilities this effort would never have been completed. To them I also offer my sincere gratitude for the spirit in which they received the innumerable 'slight' corrections or 'minor' additions and amendments. Additionally, special thanks are due to Pat Goodwyll, my current secretary, on whose very broad and expert shoulders rested the retyping of the text.

Naturally, none of those good enough to have lent of their time, skills or goodwill in the manner indicated above is responsible for any inadequacies which remain in the paper. I do hope, however, that they find the completed text worthy of their invaluable contributions.

INTRODUCTION

Land settlement schemes (LSSs) have been a very important part of land and labour policies in the Caribbean for over a century. These schemes have been the subject of many studies. Those studies of schemes in Guyana have been limited in number, scope and perspective. This study, by setting these schemes in the context of the problematic and often turbulent evolution of the wider political economy and land policy in particular, highlights the underlying objectives and consequences of land settlement.

One test of the efficacy of LSSs is their impact on the relevant land, labour and commodity markets. Although there may of course have been other objectives, including some that may have been incidental, the ostensible objectives of the LSSs usually, in one way or another, encompassed these ends – land, labour and commodity markets.

It is argued in this book that the stated objectives of the schemes, namely the empowerment of a peasantry, have been, for most of the period under consideration, a façade. The actual objectives shifted over time in response to evolving circumstances which reflected the changing needs of the dominant modes of production and more especially the relative power of labour and external forces. The schemes have actually played an important role in providing access to land and in mediating the relationship between the dominant 'mode of production' and the smallholders.

Until the most recent phases, that is, 1965–80 and 1981–85, the schemes were employed to restrain the geographical mobility of rural wage labour. During the late colonial and postcolonial periods (1948–85), land policy was directed to extending the cultivable margin, and labour policy was directed to land occupation for employment and strategic reasons. Indeed, it may be said that the policy was intended to hinder rural-urban drift. These were objectives reflected in the location and administration of the subsequent LSSs.

This study examines the factors giving rise to the establishment of these schemes, their administration, evolution and consequences. It is argued that, properly understood, the schemes have served the ends for which they were intended. Initially they enabled the sugar interests to enjoy what was in effect a transitional 'mode of production' between slavery and capitalist agriculture. They have, without a doubt, helped to shape the development of the rural labour market. In this regard LSSs were one of many tools employed in a complex process involving the moulding of wage labour, the expansion of small farming and the protection of sugar interests.

The story of why and how the dominant interests influenced policy also needs to be understood if the picture is to be complete. This examination highlights how the objectives evolved as the composition of the dominant groups changed over time. From time to time, fractures in the alliances that made up these dominant groups gave rise to paradoxes and changes in policies. Some exploration of the resolution of these fractures and paradoxes is also undertaken. The study not only suggests that policies were reasonably coherent relative to the objectives of the dominant social interests but that the range of policies employed to achieve those common objectives was relatively comprehensive.

At the same time, the capacity of the peasant/smallholder sector to handle or profit from the changing environment would be of interest. Faced with institutional arrangements which were frequently, but not always, of the making of the dominant groups, the challenge was to find a form of organization, which would provide some semblance of countervailing power. This challenge could not always be adequately met. The vehicles of organization, such as cooperatives, whilst having some social strengths, often proved to be inadequate.

The search for associative forms of production was influenced and, in turn, affected by developments external to the peasantry. These developments were both domestic and international. The study seeks therefore to weave into one work, all the relevant elements that could contribute to a holistic vision of the story of LSSs.

NOTE ON CURRENCIES

All references to dollars ($) prior to 1965 pertain to the British West Indies (BWI) dollar which was equivalent to four shillings and two pence sterling (4s.2d). Subsequent references are to Guyana dollars (G$) unless otherwise noted.

Between 1839 and 1941 a number of currencies coexisted as accepted legal tender in Guyana. These included pounds sterling, Dutch guilders (1.3–1.5 shillings), stivers and BWI dollars. The European currencies and those of the neighbouring states were gradually phased out after 1900 and 1939. In 1941 the currencies of Trinidad and Tobago as well as Barbados were also accepted. In 1951 Guyana became a member of the British Caribbean (Eastern Group) Currency Board. As with the Sterling Exchange Standard, £1 was equivalent to G$4.80 [Thomas 1965; Danns 1990].

The value of the Guyana dollar changed as follows in relation to the US dollar and the pound sterling:

	US$1	£1	
1838–1967	G$1.74[a]	$4.80	
Nov. 1967	$2.00	$4.80	14.3 percent devaluation of sterling
Dec. 1971	$2.00	$5.2114	G$ devalued against sterling
Oct. 1975[b]	$2.55		US$ new intervention currency
June 1981	$3.00		Devaluation of G$
Jan. 1984	$3.75		
Oct. 1984	$4.12		G$ pegged to a basket of currencies and moved as the US$ floated against that basket

a – June 1967

b – The G$ floated with the £ from July 1972 to October 1975 when it was tied to the US$ and sterling ceased to be the intervention currency.

ABBREVIATIONS

ASCRIA	African Society for Cultural Relations with Independent Africa
BBP	Black Bush Polder
BG	British Guiana
BGLU	British Guiana Labour Union
BWI	British West Indies
CARDI	Caribbean Research and Development Institute
CARICOM	Caribbean Community
CCH	Cacique Crown of Honour
CDW	Colonial Development and Welfare
CO	Colonial Office
CPI	Consumer Price Index
CSO	Central Stationery Office
DCCB	District Cooperative Credit Bank
D&I	Drainage and irrigation
FCH	Feed, clothe and house (the nation)
FITUG	Federation of Independent Trade Unions of Guyana
GAPC	Guyana Agricultural Products Corporation
GAWU	Guyana Agricultural Workers' Union
GCC	Guyana Credit Corporation
GDC	Guyana Development Corporation
GDF	Guyana Defence Force
GDP	Gross domestic product
GIWU	Guiana Industrial Workers' Union
GLU	Guyana Labour Union
GMC	Guyana Marketing Corporation
GMWU	Guyana Mine Workers' Union
GNS	Guyana National Service
GOG	Government of Guyana
GRB	Guyana Rice Board

GRC	Guyana Rice Corporation
GRDC	Guyana Rice Development Corporation
GSO	Government Stationery Office
HMSO	Her (or His) Majesty's Stationery Office
IAG	Immigration Agent General
IBRD	International Bank for Reconstruction and Development
ICJ	International Commission of Jurists
ICOR	Incremental Capital Output Ratio
IDB	Inter-American Development Bank
IICA	Inter American Institute for Cooperation in Agriculture
IMF	International Monetary Fund
LAB	Latin American Bureau
LDD	Land Development Division
LSS	Land Settlement Scheme
MARDS	Mahaicony Abary Rice Development Scheme
MMA	Machaica-Mahaicony-Abary
MOA	Ministry of Agriculture
MPCA	Manpower Citizens' Association
NAACIE	National Association of Agricultural, Commercial and Industrial Employees
NARI	National Agricultural Research Institute
NWD	North West District
OAS	Organization of American States
PNC	People's National Congress
PPP	People's Progressive Party
PTAP	Peoples' Temple Agricultural Project
RAC	Rice Action Committee
RMB	Rice Marketing Board
RPA	Rice Producers Association
SILWF	Sugar Industry and Labour Welfare Fund
TNC	transnational corporation
TUC	Trades Union Congress
UF	United Force
USAID	United States Agency for International Development
WPA	Working People's Alliance
WCB	West Coast Berbice
WCD	West Coast Demerara

MAPS OF GUYANA

Map 1 Detail from a map of British, French and Dutch Guiana, 1863, by J.W. Lowry, FRGS.

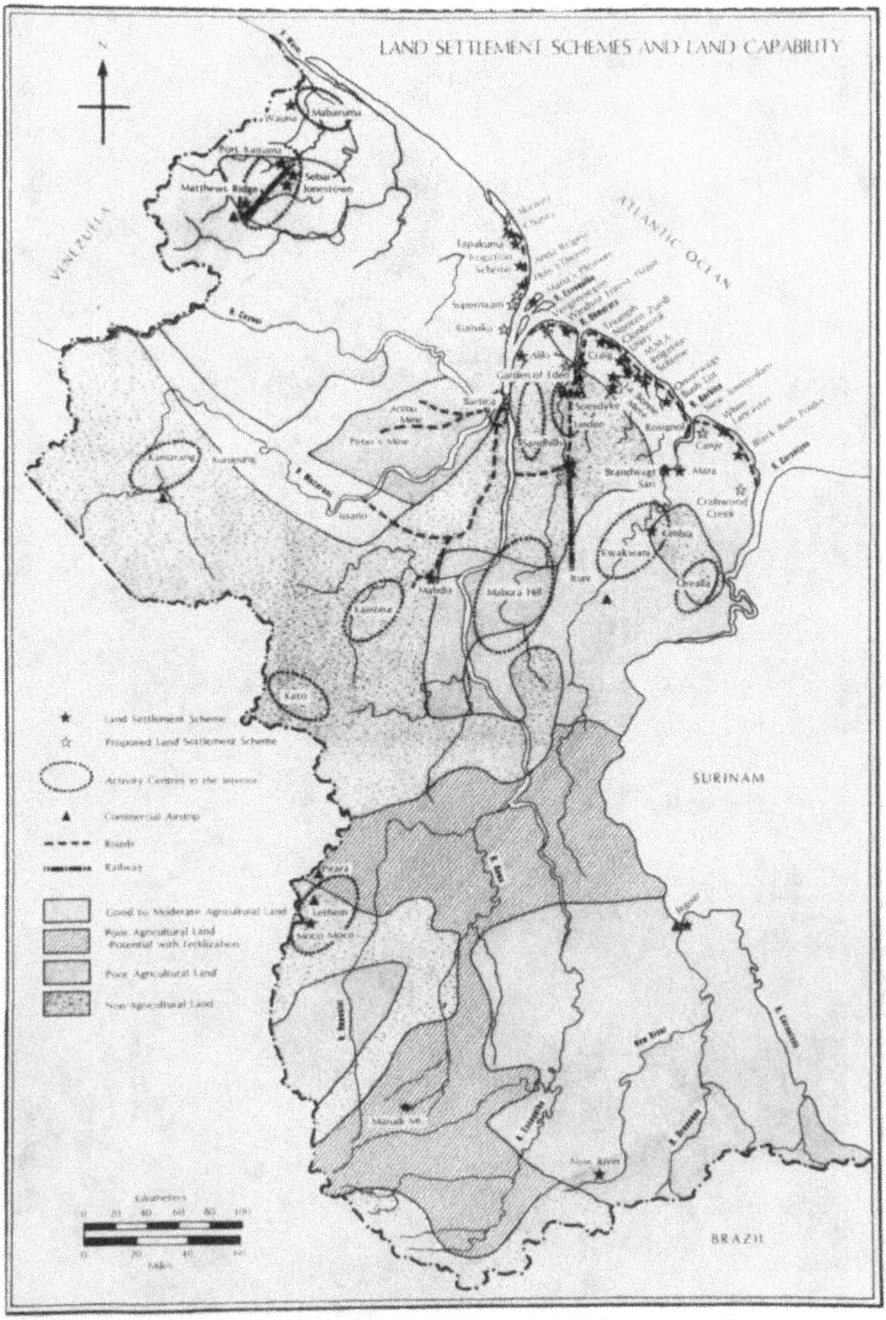

Map 2 Sites of the main schemes.

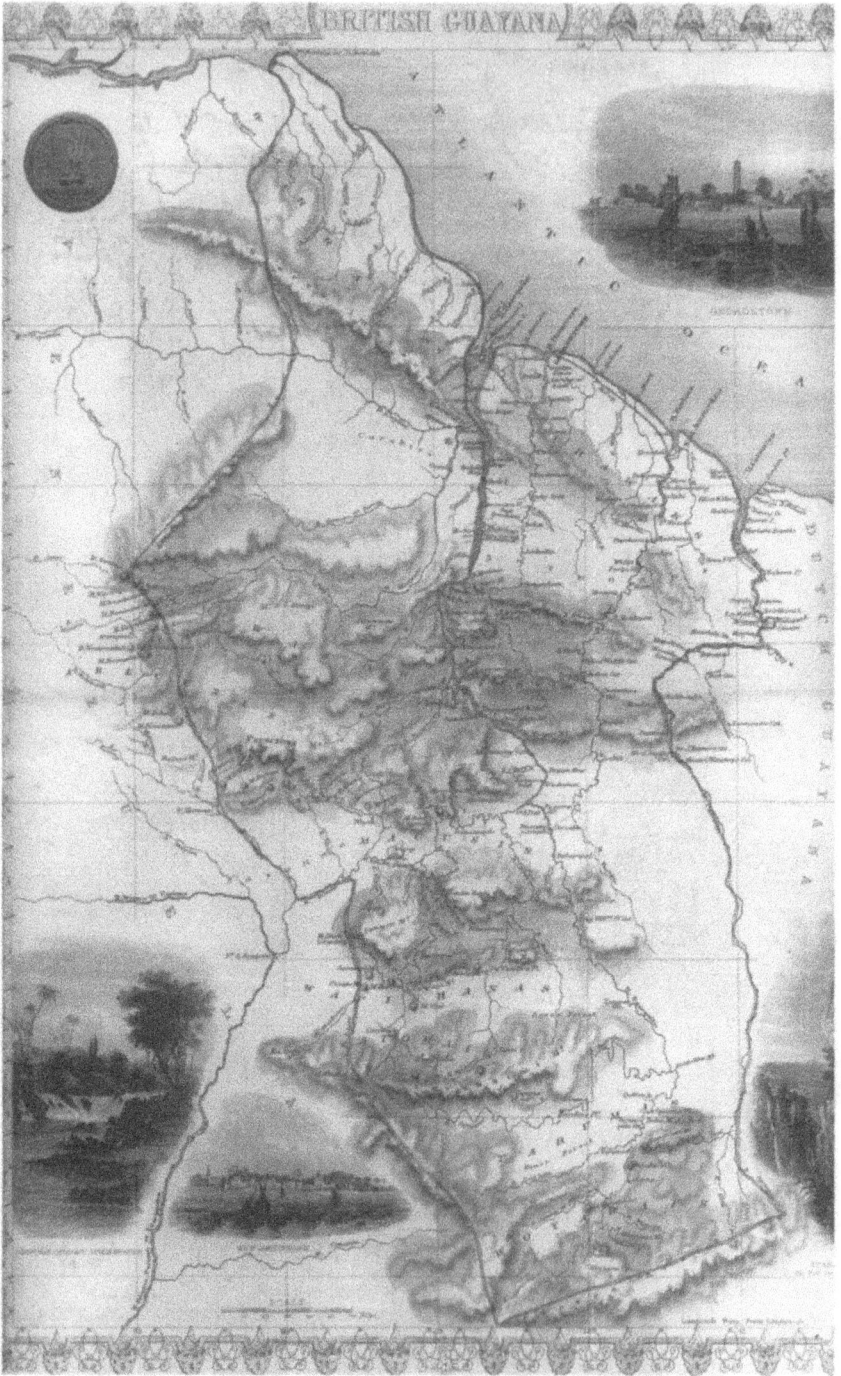

Map 3 Map of British Guiana, 1851. *Source:* Drawn and engraved by
J. Rapkin with illustrations by H. Winkles.

CHAPTER I

SCOPE OF STUDY
AND DEFINITION OF LAND
SETTLEMENT SCHEMES

*In New Amsterdam they would not be taken seriously; they were
too close to the past, to India and Africa where labour came from,
to the sugar plantations where labour went to, and to the forest
where the ex-slaves and Amerindians still lived. But because the
past was so real in Pheasant, the future could only be entirely a
fantasy. The motor cars and American films which came to the
area had a magical appeal more powerful than visiting magicians,
and so you had to entirely invent the future before you could go
forward to meet it. Not so in New Amsterdam.*

Janice Shinebourne, *Timepiece*

Introduction

Land settlement schemes (LSSs) are important in the context of Guyana[1] for a
variety of reasons. First of all, they played an integral part in the formation of a
market in rural wage labour. Second, they were instruments through which land
policy was implemented. In this sense, land settlement has been a factor in the
evolution of the coastal/hinterland, plantation/peasant dichotomy that has
characterized development in Guyana. Third, the schemes have been one
dimension through which the political and economic links with the metropolitan centre, the UK, were manifested. A study of LSSs therefore brings into sharp
relief the role of the state, the development of socioeconomic classes/ strata, the
evolution of Guyana's factor and commodity markets, and domestic responses
to international political changes.

It is timely to revisit these LSSs at this point in time, some 160 years after the
abolition of slavery and the commencement of East Indian indenture.[2] The
evolution of LSSs is closely bound up with both these events. In addition, there

has recently been renewed interest in LSSs centring on the reasons for their popularity and the scope for improving their performance.[3]

The study of LSSs in Guyana is a neglected area compared with say Africa, [Chambers 1969; de Wilde 1967; Fosbrooke et al. 1960; Clayton 1964-65] or Sri Lanka[4] [Dunham 1982; Amerasinghe 1973]. In most cases insights into LSS are the by-product of wider studies [e.g. Young 1958; Potter 1975; Rodney 1981a, 1981b; Moore 1987]. In spite of their titles, most of the studies specifically on LSSs in Guyana have been restricted to single schemes. The most popular of these is the Black Bush Polder, established in 1959. These studies have focused almost exclusively on the question of migration and, have been primarily concerned with the benefits, or rather the lack thereof, accruing to East Indian communities [Sukdeo 1978; Standing et al. 1977; Nath 1950 and Potter 1979a, 1979b].

In focusing on these issues, the opportunity to trace the interrelationships between the historical evolution of the mode of production in the wider economy and the changes in LSS (developments) has been missed. In effect, a large number of studies merely catalogue the problems of LSSs thereby giving the impression that the causes are basically exogenous or external to the LSSs, or indeed, to the entire economy.

One consequence of this approach is an abundance of misconceptions about LSSs. Changing or hidden objectives, for example, are hardly reflected in the literature and as a result there is a consensus that all but two of the schemes have been failures [e.g. Mandle 1977]. In this context, many authors assume that the schemes were intended to promote, or ought to have promoted, the establishment of an idealized, undifferentiated peasantry. Such an outcome was regarded as being both desirable and possible. This study seeks, inter alia, to avoid this pitfall by addressing the development of LSSs within a structural/historical framework – in the sense used by Harriss [1982: 18–26], and for the same kind of reasons.

Definition

An LSS may be defined in a variety of ways [Warriner 1969; Ali 1974; IBRD 1978]. Some definitions turn on the extension of the cultivable margin [Tuma 1968: 2; Ali 1974: 25], but it can be argued that this focus on physical expansion is unnecessarily restrictive and certainly inappropriate in the context of Guyana's experience. Generally speaking, settlement need neither involve new areas of land nor the opening up of land that is not utilized. Indeed, it may

1.1 Water Street – Georgetown's main commercial centre at the turn of the century. *Source:* Crookall 1898.

involve the reallocation of land to an additional, alternative or larger population. For the purposes of this study, and in keeping with the experience of settlement in Guyana, we have employed an historical and therefore relatively broad definition which encompasses the wide variety of forms taken by land settlements over the years [Dorner 1972].

In Guyana, the extent and nature of the state's involvement in implementation has varied over time. In some areas, it has been restricted to the acquisition of land on behalf of settlers, whilst in others, the state has been responsible for the provision of management, marketing and infrastructure.

The organizational forms of the schemes have also varied: they have ranged from individual cultivation to state farms. Similarly, agricultural systems associated with the LSSs have included irrigated as well as rain-fed systems. Finally, areas of settlement have ranged from abandoned plantations to virgin land and near-operational entities.

An LSS involves the planned movement of persons mainly, but not exclusively, to areas of under- or unutilized agricultural potential, ostensibly for the purpose of undertaking small- to medium-scale farming under private ownership. The definition does not include the unsponsored movement of persons and requires some degree of involvement by the state in the planning or implementation of the schemes. Although urban land settlements may properly be considered to be relevant to our study, they have, with one important exception, been largely excluded in the interest of clarity of focus.[5]

3

CHAPTER 2

AN AFRICAN 'PEASANTRY' IN UNFREE LABOUR AND LAND MARKETS

In Pheasant, the sense of the past and future was different. Here, you could not forget the past, could not escape from it. It was not a fiction or fantasy. The cane fields, the factory, the English overseers, were very real, so were the Amerindians and the freed slaves who still lived in the forest, still afraid of being recruited into plantation labour.

Janice Shinebourne, *Timepiece*

This chapter examines the factors affecting the establishment of smallholder/peasant agriculture and the ethnic genesis of the LSSs. Whilst the early villages do not fall within the definition of LSSs it is important to understand the process of their establishment in order to appreciate the manner in which LSSs were employed and the purposes to which they were put. It highlights the underlying political and social alliances and their influences on land and labour policies in particular and the relevance of sugar to their alliances and policies.

Saccharine Despotism

The first land settlement, or colonization schemes as they were called prior to 1940, was approved in 1865. Almost three decades after the abolition of slavery, it represented in part the colonial government's continuing efforts to respond to some of the changes occurring in the aftermath of the emancipation of African labour.[6]

In retracing the story of these schemes we need to be cognizant of the poles of interest and influence as well as centres of power and decision making. In this chapter we study these interrelations as they were unfolding just prior to the establishment of LSSs. The centres of power and decision making have been carefully set out in various studies [Moore 1987; Will 1968].

These centres were, in summary:

  i. metropolitan government
  ii. civil service of the colony
  iii. local legislature
  iv. propertied planters and representatives of sugar interests
  v. agrarian labour
  vi. mélange of interests present in the urban areas

The objectives and interests of these centres were often distinct and when they coincided did not do so permanently. Subsequent to the abolition of slavery the main objective of the metropolitan state vis-à-vis the colony was "to ensure the special application of the values and ideology of English bourgeois society; it had less to do with the modernisation of Guyana than with the maintenance of a particular class structure" [Smith 1977: xiii–xiv].

The interests of the metropolitan government were pursued by the Colonial Office, mandated to control the colony with as few disruptions as possible, and with a concern to protect, at the same time the interests of the metropolitan capital and the colonial power, the UK. Their task was to overview the administration of the colony and to ensure that in the execution of these functions the interplay of the various vested interests did not give rise to too many threats to the interests of the UK or demands on the time of British ministers and officials. As with the preceding Dutch administration, their most consistently pursued aim appeared to be the protection of the interests of the sugar industry.

We acknowledge that the Colonial Office was not a monolith with a single brain, as it were, but for purposes of analysis it is convenient to recognize some general tendencies. In fact, the direction of the Colonial Office was from time to time strongly influenced by individuals [Lobdell 1988: 195–207]. It also needs to be stressed that the views of the Colonial Office and those of other elements within the metropolitan community often diverged, sometimes radically.

The local administration, the colony's civil service, was responsible for some policy formulation but its primary task was to refine and elaborate the policies handed down by the Colonial Office and to execute such policies. The refining included the preparation and enactment of local legislation as well as the elaboration of policies. Nineteenth century Guyana enjoyed a unique constitution within the British Empire. Basically, the Dutch constitution of 1803 was maintained until 1891. This constitution provided for civil service representation in the legislature, the Court of Policy and in the Combined Courts. The latter body exercised control over financial matters through control of the budget including the salaries of the local civil service.

2.1 The Public Buildings, later to become the National Assembly. *Source*: Bayley 1909.

Until 1891 the constitution provided for propertied and income representation in the legislature, the Court of Policy and the Financial College. Propertied planter representation assured control over the local budget by virtue of a statutory majority over the civil servants in the Combined Courts. In that sense it was the most independent of the legislatures in the British Caribbean colonies. That local legislature was dominated by sugar planters and their representatives.[7] Fraser gives us an insight into the basis and exercise of their dominance [Fraser 1981: 26–28] and Rodney contends that "planters remained firmly in control of the postemancipation legislature and were confirmed in the ownership of all property except slaves" [1981b: 331–51]. Additionally, sugar dominated the economy and this economic hegemony reinforced the influence of the planters on the executive [Will 1968; Adamson 1972; Moore 1987: 96]. Fraser has pointed out that public officers frequently retired into plantation service and that officials, such as medical inspectors, who reported unfavourably or were critical of conditions on plantations were often sanctioned [Fraser 1981].

Moore argues that "subject only to the authority of the Imperial Crown, the state became the political will of the planter class, through which they were able to institutionalize social and political inequalities designed to preserve and perpetuate their dominance in the colonial society" [1987: 216]. But the interests of the imperial Crown did not deviate very far from those of the sugar planters.

Whilst it would not be accurate to portray the colonial state and the planters

2.2 A view of Georgetown. *Source*: Crookall 1898.

as having a complete unity of interests in this setting, it is true that the areas of overlap were formidable [Shahabuddeen 1983: 112–13]. The well-known planter influence over the colonial state was based on absentee planter control of UK parliamentary boroughs, the transfer of property rights to UK-based persons and entities, and the well-organized pressure group, the West India Committee [Taylor 1984: 70, 76–77; Shahabuddeen 1983: 91–92, 347]. In this way the planters exerted considerable influence over the metropolitan colonial government and its executive arm, the Colonial Office, in most matters affecting Guyana. This close connection between the local planters and the interests of metropolitan capital provides a practical illustration of the concept of the "articulation of modes" (à la Rey) of production at work across national borders [Bottomore et al. 1983: 335–37; Taylor 1979; Hindess and Hirst 1975].

The agrarian labour market was severely constrained after the abolition of slavery. The primary concern of agrarian labour appeared to be to escape the handicaps of the market by acquiring land and/or by selling its services in areas where it would enjoy some degree of anonymity and therefore some protection from noneconomic coercion.

It has been correctly observed that, "when capitalism was shaped by imperialism, class relations were distorted by racism" [Graham et al. 1977: xi, xii]. In his formidable history of the colony, Dalton asserted that the question of colour has been too much mixed up with that of class [Dalton 1855: 312]. The reality was of course that race was the primary basis of social segmentation and stratification in Guyana. Occupational specialization resulted from deliberate policies which sought to exclude first Africans and later East Indians and other immigrants from certain occupations and positions in government, the civil service, plantation and commercial management as well as the professions and the Christian church. These functions were concentrated in the hands of a small number of Europeans whose share of the population never exceeded 3 percent in post-eighteenth century Guyana. The local representatives of the imperial government were, like the 'planters', European (preferably British born).[8] Africans and those partially African were, initially at any rate, to be relegated to agriculture, unskilled labour, domestic service and the like. East Indians and other indentured immigrants were initially destined for a similar fate. But over time Portuguese and, later, Chinese immigrants were allowed to enter the retail trades, shopkeeping and the like, and eventually forestry.

The Africans constituted, for all practical purposes, the agricultural labour force immediately on the abolition of slavery. Their ownership of property and own-account farming awaited the change in the legal status of slaves from property to human beings. Even with that change in status, however, various devices, legal and social, were employed to deny this ethnic group representation in the legislature [Moore 1987]. More specifically, the African peasantry, which was not the beneficiary of LSSs provides a useful point of reference when we come to examine the impact and objectives of the LSSs.

These alliances between planters and metropolitan interests, mirrored in an identity between colour and class (economic interests), provided a basis for both the exercise of planter supremacy and white dominance [Moore 1987: ch. 3]. It has been said that in recognition of the disenfranchisement of the Africans, from time to time the Colonial Office tried to temper the excesses of the whites, "to facilitate protection, instruction and guidance of the unrepresented classes" [Smith and Kemper 1971]. But white dominance was employed to blunt or divert Colonial Office intervention and was the source of some major confrontations. As the century drew to a close, both white supremacy and planter dominance came under attack from centres other than the Colonial Office. The attack was given added momentum by the crises of 1884, 1885 and 1894–97, which heightened working class consciousness.

Since the power of the planters rested in part on the economic dominance of the economy by the sugar sector, persistent and severe difficulties in that sector could undermine the position of the planters. During the crises of the sugar industry in the 1880s and 1890s, the special political influence wielded by the planters was openly questioned by the Reform Movement [Fraser 1981: 28–30; Moore 1987]. Although a variety of factors restricted a collective response by the various classes and strata, the separate reactions of middle class "coloureds" and Portuguese (by way of the Reform Movement) on the one hand, of immigrant East Indian and Chinese labour (work stoppages in the 1870s and 1880s) and of African villagers (rates war) and urban protoproletariat (Reform Movement) were eventually sufficient to force the pace and direction of change. A debate about the viability and the advisability of continuing the economy's heavy dependence on a single crop eventually emerged as a national issue by 1891 [Greene 1974; Adamson 1984]. There were calls for assistance to be extended to the existing peasantry and non-plantation non-sugar agricultural sector [Shahabuddeen 1983: ch. 15]. In this context, "the entire community outside of the planter class and the immigrants was mobilized by the argument that subsidies for immigration could be deployed to sponsor minor industries, build roads in the interior, provide teacher training and so on" [Rodney 1981a: 175]. "No Surrender", the motto of this 'reform movement', was to later provide the material for one of the colony's popular songs, an early calypso by Lord Caresser [Rohlehr 1990: 146]. The first African to be elected to the court, Mr Benjamin Brown, made his appearance at this point [Beatty 1970].

These pressures gave rise to constitutional changes in 1891, albeit mainly cosmetic. The agreement to institute the secret ballot from the year 1896, however, enabled these forces to break the political hegemony of the planters [Moore 1987], a process that was not always peaceful, as may be seen from the 1905 disturbances, for example.

Postslavery Land and Labour Markets

The first major fracture in the planter/metropolitan capital articulation came with the abolition of slavery. Abolition paved the way for a nominally free market in wage labour. A second and quite as fatal fracture was the move to freer trade and, more specifically, the termination of imperial preferences in order to secure for English consumers adequate quantities of sugar at reasonable prices [Shahabuddeen 1983: ch. 5]. Coupled with the loss of protection in the English market, abolition gave rise to severe problems in the colony's sugar industry. By 1847 the industry, which had in the previous half-century displaced the main agricultural activities such as tobacco, cotton and coffee, was in crisis. As a consequence, so was the entire economy.

Many sugar plantations[9] collapsed, giving rise, inter alia, to precipitate declines in the demand for rural wage labour. Small and medium-sized plantations were hardest hit and the number of plantations declined dramatically from 308 to 173 between 1848 and 1851, reflecting the exit of these smaller enterprises.[10] They were, for the most part, acquired by larger, frequently foreign, operators and merged with existing plantations.[11] Geographically, the hardest hit area appears to have been the county of Essequibo, where the number of sugar plantations declined from 37 in 1834 to 11 in 1883. Some evidence that this decline in numbers was primarily attributable to amalgamation may be deduced from the fact that in the latter year only seven of the original plantations had been abandoned [*Daily Argosy* 1883; Moore 1987].

Over the period from the 1840s to the 1850s, therefore, both the average size of the plantations and the extent of absentee ownership increased significantly. The succeeding decades, the 1860s to the early 1880s, were periods of rapid growth in the industry, unparalleled since the 1790s. The industry consolidated and expanded and at the same time, large producers began to exercise an inordinate degree of control over the revamped industry's output and the disposal of that output.[12]

Following this period of expansion and prosperity the industry, again hit by recession, consolidated and further shed smaller operators. During this depression of the 1880s and the 1890s, the country experienced the demise of plantations such as those owned by Quintin Hogg and the Colonial Company which had dominated the colony during the previous quarter century. The number of sugar plantations fell from 173 in 1851 to 95 in 1890 to 29 by the turn of the century. There was also a transformation in the nature of ownership namely from individual to corporate entities and a further shift in the locus of owners to the metropole [Shahabuddeen 1983: 91–92]. By the latter period a single enterprise, Bookers Bros, McConnell and Co. Ltd, in one way or another, controlled the disposal of 80 percent of the sugar output of these enterprises [Adamson 1972; British Guiana 1932]. By that time the public had already popularized an alternative interpretation of the abbreviation, 'BG' – Bookers' Guiana [Smith 1962: 59; Colonial Office 1942]!

The abolition of slavery was to have a profound impact on both the land and labour markets. In anticipation of its consequences the planters employed a wide range of 'protective' measures. In the face of these, the reaction of African labour was remarkably ingenious and initially successful.

In the labour market, African labour found various means of coping with the transition from slavery to wage labour. These included itinerant task gangs and the reapportioning of their labour between work on plantations and private provision grounds which effectively enabled them to maintain a certain scarcity in the market, adherence to minimum rates for certain tasks and to undermine the efficacy of nonmarket methods employed by the planters to depress wages [Rodney 1981a, 1981b; Shahabuddeen 1983: ch. 10; Schuler 1988]. During the latter half of the century, however, labour experienced a reversal of fortune [Adamson 1972: 136–38; Schuler 1988].

The causes of this change of fortune are to be found in the modernization of sugar manufacturing and the establishment of a labour (and complementary land) market which functioned to ensure a continuous supply of abundant and cheap labour to the sugar industry.

We turn now to the factors contributing to the unfree labour market. It needs to be emphasized, first of all, that most of the country's labour force remained physically under the direct control of the plantations long after the abolition of slavery. It is often erroneously asserted that the former slaves fled the plantations en masse after 1838 [Hanley 1975; Reno 1964; Sukdeo 1978; Klein et al. 1985: 261]. However, initially the only significant 'voluntary' withdrawal of labour from the plantations was that of women and children [Schuler 1988]. Whilst some male labour had managed to flee up-river as far as the North West District [Adamson 1972: 100–103; Smith 1962: 38–40], most remained within the confines of the plantation economy [Beatty 1970].[13] Doubtless the supply of labour fell as a consequence [Adamson 1972; Shahabuddeen 1983: 143–51]. However, a greater loss was probably attributable to high levels of mortality. There may have been a deterioration in the regularity of that supply also [Moore 1987] although the statistical basis for that contention has yet to be established. The available data reveal that in 1850 some 20,000 Africans were still resident on sugar plantations. In addition to these full-time labourers, another 21,500, that is half the village population, supplied labour on a part-time basis to the plantations. Such was the import of an off-farm source of income to farmers that one author observed that "when labourers could not find estate employment in their own districts they moved. For most of those men (Canal Number One Polder) and for a third of the women, an estate work week of two days became the rule" [Schuler 1988: 105]. By 1871 the number of Africans resident on plantations stood at 17,800, representing an 11 percent decline in two decades. Over this very period it appears that the proportion of village labourers providing part-time labour fell from 50 to 29 percent [Moore 1987: 121]. This, it appears, is the area on which immigration made its greatest initial impact.

2.3 Group of East Indians, 1909. *Source*: Bayley 1909.

The labour that remained on the plantations as well as that which sought to operate from the villages[14] was coerced via a plethora of devices, into maximizing the supply of labour of one kind or the other to the plantations.[15] This "time-honoured" [Moore 1987] coercion took various forms and its consequence was to confront labour with limited opportunities for profitable employment outside of the plantation. In this regard, the ability of the planters to mobilize the instruments of the state, such as the police and military as well as fiscal powers, to serve their ends are too well-documented to warrant repetition here.[16] Suffice it to say that these restraints all served to depress the returns to labour and to limit its options.[17]

There had been some semblance of administrative wage rate setting at the commencement of the period of apprenticeship in 1834 [Adamson 1972: 165–66; Shahabuddeen 1983: 171–75]. In addition, other instruments were employed, including the Master and Servants Act of 1846,[18] anticombination legislation and the infamous tenancy-at-will system under which rents and wages were manipulated to maximize labour supply to the plantations.

Notwithstanding these circumstances which favoured continued access by the sugar industry to cheap and abundant labour supplies, the administration embarked on the extensive importation of labour solely to satisfy the needs of the sugar industry.[19] Unindentured labour was recruited from Barbados. But it appears that the planters were not terribly keen on imported African labour in

2.4 East Indian immigrants at depot in Georgetown. *Source*: Bayley 1909.

any form – perhaps it attracted too much unwelcome attention from the local churches, such as the London Missionary Society. Additionally, they were still wary of the activities of the antislavery lobby. Thus, although in 1895 the Sir James Hays Commission recommended colonization by way of Barbadians, the planters were only prepared to recruit them on a short-term basis [British Guiana 1919d, 1932 (particularly the appendices), 1933, 1939a].

They preferred instead indentured non-African labour and after trying Portuguese, Chinese and Indians, settled for the latter. Chinese labour attracted unwanted attention from the British public [Ramphal 1983] and the Chinese government. The Portuguese suffered no such disability but like the Chinese encountered difficulties with the climatic and health environment which conspired to decimate the stock of early immigrants and discourage significant inflows. The special advantages of East Indians have been explored elsewhere [see note 19].

Attempts by other plantation sectors to join this bandwagon of village-subsidized, imported labour failed. Their efforts to import labour for non-sugar plantations were successfully opposed by the sugar planters. In 1872, for example, the Combined Court refused to permit the use of the Immigration Fund to finance immigration from Barbados for employment in the hinterland [British Guiana 1939a: 31]. The demand for full- and part-time African labour was the point at which these policies had their greatest impact.

Land policy complemented this labour policy. Abolition paved the way for a market in land. "When dependence on plantation-supplied housing and provision grounds made bargaining difficult after emancipation, some labourers began to acquire land and houses" [Schuler 1988]. This reaction gave rise to the 'village movement' in 1839 [Adamson 1972].

It was recognized however, that the development of peasant agriculture posed a threat to the plantations' labour supply. Since good arable land was necessary for the development of peasant agriculture, throughout the postslavery Caribbean obstacles were erected to the acquisition of land for such purposes [Beckford 1972; Post 1978].

Acquisition of land could be effected either by way of private purchase, purchase of Crown or colony lands or by (five-year) licences of occupancy. African labour utilized the first of these as the main device for acquiring land because that method was unencumbered by government controls and in addition the land was usually already cleared and drained. In so doing, however, they frequently paid prices as much as one hundred times that at which Crown/colony lands were sold. Most lands it seems, were acquired at prices ranging from $240 to $1,180/ha compared with $11.80/ha for Crown lands.[20] These high prices were paid for individual plots in proprietary villages as well as for group purchases such as that of Plantation Brook in 1839 [Adamson 1972] by eighty-four ex-slaves.[21]

There were other barriers to the acquisition of those Crown and colony lands. In the view of one author, "planter policy on Crown lands was applied with special virulence to throttle the growth of peasant proprietorship" [Shahabuddeen 1983: 233]. The parcel that could be purchased was set at a minimum of 40 ha for a price of £2.47/ha, giving rise to a prohibitive 'upset price' of $1,000 for a minimum purchase of Crown land [Shahabuddeen 1983: 229–33]. This 'upset price', implemented on the instructions of the secretary of state for war and colonies in 1836 [Adamson 1972], needs to be juxtaposed against a statutory minimum daily wage for agricultural labourers of 24 cents per day and actual wages of 4 to 8 cents per day in the 1880s. At the latter levels of remuneration it would take the average labourer 35 to 69 years to accumulate $1,000 if he saved all of his earnings. Among the most serious of the other barriers were ordinances numbers four and one of 1851 and 1852, respectively, which limited the number of collective purchasers of land to twenty. In addition, there were onerous regulations.[22]

Moore has argued convincingly that the local administration's intent was to prohibit acquisition (purchase) of Crown lands by Africans whilst making licences of occupancy (leases) relatively attractive. The issue of licences was, of course, discretionary and could be revoked when convenient. The fee could also

2.5 The sea wall esplanade, Georgetown. *Source*: Browne *c*. 1910.

be manipulated. Indeed, the upset prices were increased by the legislature in anticipation of emancipation and their enthusiasm for further increases had to be tempered by the Colonial Office. The inequity of the system was evident to the point of being ludicrous. In 1887, land within ten miles of a public road cost $12.33/ha whereas abandoned estates were selling for $2.47/ha and virgin land in the interior for $24.71/ha [Moore 1987: 112].

After the failure of the 1848 strikes, many Africans fled upriver particularly to the Pomeroon (see Maps 1 and 3) and Suriname [Moore 1987: 121]. In keeping with Caribbean-wide policy, in 1854 the local administration therefore issued instructions that the titles of plantations along the banks of rivers should be investigated and repossessed where appropriate [Caribbean Commission 1947: 365]. In Jamaica similar efforts at suppressing squatting led to its total elimination by 1900 [Satchell 1990]. Although the result was not quite so spectacular in Guyana, it did serve its purpose.

Related to restrictive land policy was the state's influence over, and regulation of, praedial organizational forms. The appropriateness of any organizational form is dependent on the specific circumstances in which it is set. Development of the hinterland was dependent on the establishment of a specific form of social relations or organization. It can be argued that Guyana's share of the "island of the Guianas"[23] is peculiar. We realize, of course, that this assertion risks raising the ire of those who accuse Caribbean social science of fostering a "cult of uniqueness" [Brookfield 1975: 161]. However, the nature and influence of the

15

2.6 A 'koker' or sluice – a key part of Guyana's drainage infrastructure.
Source: Bayley 1909

peculiarities of the coast in particular have been extensively documented [Rodney 1981a: 2, ch. 3; Lewis 1968; Thomas 1979; IBRD 1953: 193–206; Richardson 1975; Kirby 1973; Adamson 1972; Sattaur 1990].[24]

Among the most notable features are the 'public' nature of coastal and riverine drainage and irrigation (D&I). The persuasive case for systemic relationships between environment and technological conditions and social responses to them cannot be ignored [Young 1958: 190, ch. 9; Harriss 1982; Boserup 1965; Williams 1985]. In this context it is arguable that effective exploration and utilization of resources in areas requiring D&I and in sparsely settled hinterland regions were crucially dependent on large-scale organizational or management units – the state,[25] the plantation or a canton-type cooperative. In the absence of any of these organizational forms, the management of the communal villages in particular started to break down after 1845 as voluntary labour and collection of revenue and the like succumbed to the Prisoners' Dilemma. In the words of Adamson [1972], "thus fragmentation began and the communal villages added themselves to the proprietary villages in the formation of a new peasantry".

The planters' determination of the rules of the game served to inhibit the enactment of regulations which would have permitted the establishment and effective operation of such decision-making units in the villages [Young 1958:

155; Rodney 1981a, 1981b]. The law, for example, forbade gatherings of more than five persons in villages. This, one might add, applied in villages purchased collectively by more than one hundred persons. Meetings for the purposes of decision making were therefore impossible. In addition, the rules were often manipulated to the detriment of the villagers. Those who controlled the administration of D&I, for instance, did so in a manner far from helpful to the villagers. Thus, where villages were adjacent to operational sugar plantations, the former would be extensively and mysteriously flooded with excess water from the neighbouring plantation precisely when that plantation was in need of labour for harvesting! Because the administration of the D&I system lay in the hands of planter-dominated authorities the village communities were unable to secure remedies of such wrongs [Mullin 1929; Hubbard 1969; Adamson 1972; Daly 1975]. The consequential destruction of crops no doubt helped to frustrate the emergence of a vibrant peasantry. It might be added that the immediate postemancipation period was also marked by direct destruction of fruit trees and provision grounds by planters.

The African 'Peasantry' and the 'Village Movement'

African villages emerged between 1838 and 1852 against this background of a planter-constrained or "sugar-coated land and labour markets". The village movement, to which reference has already been made, is estimated to have resulted in the acquisition of some $2.5 million worth of property between 1838 and 1850 by Africans [Beatty 1970; Moore 1987]. It promised a great deal in terms of the growth of a peasantry [Farley 1954, 1964]. These purchases and the village movement have been deemed a "breach of the White power structure" [Moore 1987]. However, unfavourable signals about the longevity of this movement were evident quite early in the movement's life. The Herculean effort involved in raising the capital with which to purchase the lands, not surprisingly, came close to exhausting the financial capacity of the villagers and rendered them unable to raise funds with which to undertake necessary investment in stream drainage or working capital [Adamson 1972; Moore 1987]. Additionally, whereas the decade commencing with indentureship was characterized by a relatively buoyant labour market and rising wage rates, the period 1850 to the 1900s was notable for a secular decline in those rates. By the 1870s agricultural wage rates were as low as one-quarter to one-sixth of the statutory minimum [Rodney 1981b]. Thus the Africans' major means of accumulating capital had been removed.

This phenomenon would have been problematic by itself. It was, however, wedded to an equally pernicious fiscal policy.[26] The burden of taxation was to be carried by the working class. The pursuit of this fiscal objective was unswerving and single-minded [Shahabuddeen 1983: 121–22; Moore 1987; Adamson 1984]. This was effected first via a shift from direct to indirect taxation and by earmarking tax revenues for the benefit of the sugar industry. Put another way, when there was an insistence that the sugar industry meet directly some (half) of the cost of immigration, the former through their control of the legislature, successfully managed to offset their existing tax payments against those obligations [Shahabuddeen 1983: 166–70].

As early as 1833 the abolitionist Viscount Howich had proposed a tax on land not used to produce crops for export, as a means of discouraging the drift of slaves to provision grounds. Immediately after emancipation, indirect taxes on consumer durables, food, clothing and some luxuries were increased by percentages ranging from 40 to 200. Tobacco attracted a tax of 245 percent, flour a tax of 42 percent and codfish one of 20–25 percent. Most luxury items and those consumed or produced by the sugar industry were exempted, such as diamonds, ice, fresh fish, fruit and vegetables and machinery. Essentials alone contributed some 67 percent to government revenues compared with plantation produce which yielded a mere 7 percent. The taxes on basic wage goods, namely flour, rice, dried fish and salt pork, alone contributed 50 percent of current revenues [Adamson 1984]. A poll tax of $2 per annum, equivalent to 24 cents per week or two months' wages of a male labourer, was imposed in 1856 [Moore 1987]. In 1867 consumption taxes accounted for 94.5 percent of revenues. It is hardly surprising to find then that the per capita level of taxation borne by Guyana ($9.81) was the highest in the Caribbean.

Furthermore, the proceeds from these imposts were not directed to enhancing the welfare of the villagers. A considerable proportion was devoted to the immigration exercise. Between 1832 and 1928, one-third of the cost of repatriating immigrants was met by the villagers and their urban counterparts [Bourne 1975]. Between 1847 and 1873, 22 to 34 percent of public expenditure was devoted to meeting immigration costs [Adamson 1984]. Tax revenues were also being used to fund medical facilities and health care exclusively for immigrants. As Rodney so dramatically explained, "Creole taxpayers were subsidizing their own retrenchment" [Rodney 1981a: 175]. Every effort by the governors and Colonial Office to reduce these taxes or to attenuate their incidence on the low-income group was met by offsetting measures in the legislature. Thus in 1851, 1872–77 and 1884–88 when the taxes were reduced, some other impost, such as income taxes or levies on plantation produce, was either removed or considerably lightened. It may be further argued that the fiscal system was doubly pernicious, for the transfers it effected also served to reduce the investable surpluses of the villages.

By the 1860s it had already become more profitable for villagers to rent drained plantation land at $59.31/ha than to cultivate village lands. "This signified the final demise of the independent village economy as the creole peasantry themselves became dependent on the plantations for survival" [Moore 1987: 119; Adamson 1972: 84].

As if to make assurance doubly sure, the legislature moved to take these lands out of the legal control of the villagers. Ordinances numbers one and four of 1866 and 1883, respectively, put the villages under the absolute control of the government and the colonial executive itself. This move by Governor Hincks, which brought 160 villages under central control by March 1866, did not go unchallenged. Even the Colonial Office demurred. But it was implemented nonetheless and subordinated the villages to the state which was now symbolized by the forced payment of burdensome rates. The 1883 ordinance, in the words of one author, "was tantamount to expropriation of village lands without compensation" [Moore 1987: 104].

The transfer of the lands was effected under the watchful, 'nonpartisan' and depoliticized aegis of the judiciary,

Parate execution sales facilitated the concentration of rural property in fewer hands. Simultaneously, it sparked off a transfer from Creole Africans as a group into the hands of Indians, Portuguese and Chinese. This process was particularly noticeable on the Corentyne – affecting the villages numbered 57, 58, 64, 69, 70 and 71 in the 1880s and transforming Rose Hall from a predominantly African into a predominantly Indian village by the early years of this century . . . Reports of changes in and ownership also came from the East Bank Demerara in the 1890s . . . some of these lands were lost to Creoles after many years of frustrating experiences with respect to roads and drainage . . . When African rights to the land were overlooked and preference seemingly given to Indians, this automatically increased racial tension. The estates were expanding to take in the third and extra depths of pegasse backlands which had been previously used for plantains and provisions (as in the Canals Polder), while they were fleeing exhausted front lands from cane and renting to rice farmers. Translated into racial categories this meant displacing African small farmers with Indian small farmers. [Rodney 1981a: 182–83]

Rodney has argued that these experiences could give rise to conflict between the two ethnic groups. He has also pointed to the potential for collaboration, notwithstanding the bifurcated struggle against the dominant capital [Rodney 1982: ch. 7]. Moore, however, has observed persuasively that Rodney significantly underplayed the racial conflicts that resulted as well as the attitudes and perceptions that developed.

Perhaps it needs to be said that the potential for conflict was greater because this policy of labour market segmentation was active, not incidental. The policy was applied equally effectively against all immigrants, including Africans, but it was tempered by colour and external factors such as home country policies [Shahabuddeen 1983: 152–53] and the antislavery lobby. It is reasonable to assume that the external countervailing influences in favour of Africans were far more specific and temporary than those that affected the Chinese, for example. Hence, the Chinese and Portuguese, although segmented for purposes of manipulation and exploitation, came to enjoy relatively privileged positions vis-à-vis the East Indians and Africans. The factor that gave the Portuguese this advantage was ethnic affinity. It was not only that the sugar industry needed additional cheap labour but the white community, being extremely small, felt that additional recruitment to their ranks, however socially inferior, was necessary to ensure their survival. In their pursuit of this shared goal, the planters and the middle class whites found support from the Colonial Office. A number of devices were employed to enable the Portuguese to realize this preferment. First, the authorities declined to enforce the requirement for these immigrants to serve out their indenture, notwithstanding the fact that they were financed in the same manner and terms as non-European immigrants. Second, the system of licensing of economic activities enabled the authorities to indulge their preference for this group through the exercise of discretion. So important was this instrument that when in 1848–49 fees were suspended as a result of the dispute over the Civil List, they agitated for it to be restored [Moore 1975]. Other privileges enjoyed by the Portuguese also included either fewer restrictions against capitalist activities, and therefore the possibility of exploitative relations with the Africans, or help in achieving certain types of positions, for example, petty commodity trade. It is clear that their role in a socioeconomic context was intended to be essentially that of a buffer. They were denied representation in the legislative institutions even when they chose to take British citizenship. Nonetheless, the group was committed to supporting the system. The pivotal role they played in the events leading to the wages collapse of 1848 is well documented and attests to this [Moore 1975]. The violence directed against Portuguese shopkeepers in the latter part of the century needs to be seen against this background of their privileged and early exploitative relations. Therein lay the answer to the issue. Access to land was also of relevance in this regard which explains why squatting in the Essequibo (for example, Wakenaam) and Corentyne, in particular, sometimes gave rise to intercommunal violence.

Another set of constraining measures was directed at non-sugar economic activities. The planters used their political clout to stymie, either by omission or commission, economic activities which were seen as potential rivals for rural labour [Shahabuddeen 1983: ch. 13].

Action by the state, and the Colonial Office in particular, which would have been necessary to provide an appropriate framework for investment in the mineral sector, was not forthcoming. One area that this policy affected adversely was hinterland development. Imperialist rivalries created serious diseconomies. Ease of access to outlying border areas and control of lawlessness would have had to be facilitated by close political cooperation with Guyana's neighbours. One reason for inaction in this regard probably lay in the threat that this development might have posed to the yield of competing investments elsewhere in the British Empire [Spackman 1975; Smith 1962: 73]. There was, in this regard, some conflict of interest between domestic and metropolitan capital. As a result, lawlessness on the borders contributed, in the case of the gold and diamond industries, to the low level of development of the forces of production. The industries therefore remained largely undercapitalized and as a consequence were both labour intensive and weather dependent. The seasonality of their operations was such that far from competing with the sugar plantations for labour, their demand was complementary [Smith 1969; Spackman 1975].

Other nonagricultural activities showed some promise but never secured enough support to realize their potential. Thus, although in the 1860s and 1880s forestry and, later, cattle ranching in the Rupununi emerged as viable economic activities, none of these activities expanded significantly enough to challenge the dominance of sugar during the years of buoyant sugar prices.

In any case, opportunities to enter these fields were severely restricted by prohibitive and discriminatory licensing requirements [Shahabuddeen 1983: 246]. In forestry, balata bleeding, and gold and diamond prospecting, low-income entrants were "constrained to become hired employees of grant-holders who were invariably white, including Portuguese" [Moore 1987: 121]. Many hinterland settlers therefore found themselves still closely linked to the plantation economy from which they had attempted to flee. In a sense, this reluctant marriage of quite different economic activities also provides an example of the articulation of modes of production [Taylor 1979].

Contract labour of the kind employed by the planters was, in the words of one author, "typified by unmistakable, if concealed, doses of coercion" [Cross and Herman 1988: xiv; Bolland 1981]. As was the case elsewhere in the region, this labour often served to make life even more difficult for the freedmen. "Indentured labour had the intended effect of limiting the bargaining power of the ex-slaves to keep wages above subsistence" [Mintz 1985: 2, 5]. The 1848 strike, for example, was broken with the assistance of immigrant labour.

Recapitulation and Conclusions

In this chapter we have sketched the mosaic of smallholder policies against which LSSs were established in Guyana. An important aspect of Guyana's political economy was the strong identity of interest between the planters and colonizers, the local colonial state and the metropole, a plantation 'mode' and the capitalist metropole. The fractures in these links that occurred from time to time offered varying opportunities for the development of labour.

In the aftermath of the historic fracture leading to the abolition of slavery and the loss of a preferential market for sugar, the planters and their allies set about mediating the operation of the free market in wage labour. Land policy supplemented the regulative and physical policies as well as the labour policies. We have argued that the former slaves were not permitted to flee the plantations. Instead, they were tied to the sugar industry, if not to the plantation physically, via a variety of devices fashioned and managed by the state in the interest of the planters, in the first instance. The effect of these devices was to render African labour abundant and cheap by reducing or capping the level of returns from alternative (non-sugar) economic activities.

Although these direct policies weakened the efforts of the labourers who had moved to communal villages, it is also obvious that the forms of organization in these villages and the system of land tenure may not have been entirely appropriate given the physical features characteristic of agricultural activities on the coast, the fiscal powers of these villages and the financial resources available to the individual villagers. As a consequence, small-scale own-account farming was regarded as an activity of last resort.

In spite of this, the planters found it necessary to import both unindentured and indentured labour. These latter immigrants did not 'save' the industry as is often alleged but rather enabled the planters to extend the longevity of the 'mode' of production based on unfree labour. In the process, the labour/capital tension which characterizes radical advances in technology and relations of production was considerably relieved. In the words of one author,

indenture allowed Trinidad and Tobago planters to manipulate all forms of available labour, whether bound or free, in order to depress wages and retard the development of an independent peasantry . . . By employing this strategy in British Guiana and Mauritius the plantocracy was able to ensure the pre-eminence of the plantation as a mode of production. [Saunders 1984, intro.]

The segmentation of the labour market cast a shadow over technological advances in Guyana well into the twentieth century. Needless to say it also meant "impoverishment and privation for the Indians themselves over this period" [Satchell 1990].

The continuing ruptures of planter-Colonial Office-local administration links also determined the importance attached to the peasantry as a source of labour as opposed to commodities. As a result of the depressions, the planters became increasingly preoccupied with preventing the permanent loss of labour to the economy (read sugar). One of the instruments of the early success of labour policy was the pernicious division of labour by race [Rodney 1981a; Moore 1987]. This was also true of Suriname. We see the active utilization of land policy to attract and retain African labour. On the other hand, subsequent to the abolition of slavery, in addition to the other measures the legislature sought to engross all abandoned land in order to prevent either its legal or illegitimate occupation by free labour [Young 1958: 102–4]. In reality there was a zero-sum game of replacing African occupants of land by East Indians as a matter of general form. This gave rise to racial tensions which, whilst for most of the time was counterbalanced by a bifurcated struggle against a common foe, sometimes gave rise to violence [Rodney 1981a: 184; Cummings 1973; Shahabuddeen 1983: 384–85]. The LSSs to which we now turn should be seen as part and parcel of this mosaic.

CHAPTER 3

THE ETHNIC APPROACH, 1865–1905

The estate was not interested in Pheasant because it no longer drew
labour from it. The bush was claiming Pheasant. Pheasant was at
its own ease.

Janice Shinebourne, *Timepiece*

In this chapter the factors linking LSSs with indentureship are outlined together with
the implications for the nonindentured labour and African villagers in particular. In
order to ascertain the intention of the schemes, the terms under which land was
acquired by the state and transferred to settlers is examined. The varied influences on
the quantum and type of support and administration of the LSSs are also set out. The
impact of the schemes on the establishment of a peasantry, the nature of that peasantry
and the consequences for output, land and labour markets are explored.

The Political Framework

The planter preoccupation with controlling the colony's labour supplies
spawned a number of changes. One of these was the further import of labour
which served to widen the mélange of ethnicities in Guyana. In so doing, the
planters created a number of new points of tension in the politics of the colony.
In the rather jaundiced but prescient prose of one author, "the serious evil of
stocking the country too rapidly with ignorant and degraded barbarians of all
nations, may at some future day be developed to the misfortune of the colony"
[Dalton 1855: 479].

A major factor contributing to these tensions was the rigid social stratification of the society. As was observed earlier, the objective of the colonial powers
was to maintain that structure in a manner consistent with its own ideology. It
should not, however, be assumed that nothing changed. Appearances certainly
did change. In addition to early immigrants who had somehow managed to lift
themselves from the ranks of labourers by way of petty trade, there emerged
what Dalton euphemistically termed "young men and women of colour" born

of African/European unions. These progeny had the benefit of formal education and training, frequently in Europe. These qualifications were not those required to gain them acceptance by the 'First Society' however [Beatty 1970].

The exclusion of these Creoles, coloured or mixtures from positions in the society, notwithstanding their education and other achievements, was a source of some tension in the country. Although there is more than a hint that such exclusion from the 'First Society' "disappointed and mortified" them, what was perhaps even worse was their exclusion from all but the most junior forms of employment [see, for example, Webber 1988: 8–52].

That there was a class as well as a racial dimension to this is irrefutable. A fascinating glimpse into the divisions and discrimination within the society is provided by Webber, Guyana's (or is it Trinidad's?) first novelist [Webber 1988]. *Those That Be in Bondage* exposes the comprehensiveness of the reach and the extent of plantation power. We are provided in the context of the novel with an outline of the stratification of the white society of planters, attorneys/managers, overseers, soldiers and so on in the early 1900s. The novel, largely set in Guyana's plantation society, also affords an insight into "the tyranny of the social system and the reactionary nature of the church in the society" [Webber 1988: chs. 5–6].

Frequently, the church itself practised racism. Of course, its role changed over the years, as did most other things on the social front. But even in its progressive mode, the propensity of the church leaders for proselytizing from among, and therefore of 'protecting' one ethnicity to the exclusion of others, served to reinforce racial stratification. The work of Beatty [1970] on the activities of the Lutherans in Guyana since 1743 provides a brief and readable testimony to this phenomenon.

That situation was found half a century after the worst excesses of the slave plantation had been abolished. The reaction to these changed circumstances were observed by contemporaries. Speaking of the 1850s, Dalton stated that

in the early social state men were necessarily divided, as they are now, by their avocations and pursuits. It is no matter of surprise that at first, they should be startled to see members from the lower order, raised either by connection or wealth, to a level with themselves; and the earlier the period at which this elevation took place, the greater the surprise and the more bitter the resistance. At length however, it became apparent that the circumstances of society were undergoing an organic alteration, that whilst one class was sinking, the other was rising and that the time would come when they would meet. [Dalton 1855: 312]

3.1 Assembly of a local church's superstructure and its associated ethnic mix.
Source: Crookal 1898.

Objectives

When the planters were faced with the prospect of having to hire 'free labour' to produce sugar for sale in a market without imperial preference, they sought to reduce the cost of that labour by whatever means they could, including immigration-cum-indentureship. These changes enabled them to extend the period for which the labour was to be tied to sugar and the cost thereof. Among the terms included in the contracts of the indentured labourers was the right to be repatriated to their place of recruitment on completion of their 'renewable' five-year contracts. Initially, little advantage was taken of this repatriation clause since death, desertion and local settlement restricted the number of 'time-expired' (eligible) Portuguese and Chinese settlers. However, by 1894 some 6,000 Chinese labourers were eligible. Lower mortality rates among the larger number of East Indians[27] led to a steep rise in the number of eligible East Indian labourers during the early 1860s. By 1868 there were around 30,000 such persons in Guyana. By 1880 the number had doubled and the cost of their repatriation was roughly equivalent to 26 percent of current revenues [British Guiana 1882; Young 1958]. In order to avoid the heavy drain on financial resources which repatriation of all of these labourers would have involved, the local administration undertook to provide settlers with land in lieu of their return passages.[28]

From their very inception, the objective of these LSSs was to protect the sugar industry's labour supply. The ostensible objective of the first settlement in 1865 was solely the 'salvation of souls'. It was, however, linked to a proposal, accepted by the administration, for the further importation of 250 to 300 Chinese labourers monthly for general agriculture [Young 1958: 150]. With respect to the ethnic group it served, the LSS at Hopetown was unique but it heralded the commencement of a policy of ethnically exclusive settlements.

Subsequent settlements were planned for Plantation Best then Nooten Zuil in 1871.[29] However, the second scheme actually implemented was Huis t'Dieren in 1880. The stated objective of those subsequent schemes was to retain labour in Guyana. The immediate factor giving rise to this effort was the wish to reduce expenditure devoted to return passages. It has been observed that the law (Ordinance 21 of 1850, and 21 of 1851) had provided for grants of Crown land in commutation of return passages since 1850 but had not been utilized [Shahabuddeen 1983: 235, 393]. Presumably this was the case because it was not seen as being of any special benefit to sugar. Other objectives can be inferred, however, even at that early date, and as the events unfolded the importance attached to retaining a pool of immigrant labour became quite evident and possibly paramount.

Initially, the lobbying for the schemes was undertaken by the local administration. More specifically, the Office of the Immigration Agent General recommended a scheme in 1863 [Nath 1950: 24] and in 1888 the Alexander Committee was appointed by the legislature to draw up a "scheme for discouraging people from exercising their return passage rights" [Nath 1950: 97]. Shahabuddeen [1983: 237] has suggested that in this regard, the local administration was reacting to pressure from the Colonial Office "to reduce its accumulating return passage bill".

3.2 Chinese wood carrier, 1898. *Source*: Crookall 1898.

The planters, for their part, were initially ambivalent about the schemes, probably because it was felt that they might serve either as havens for runaways or would discourage reindenture. In the words of Shahabuddeen, "land settlement came to be grudgingly allowed for . . . and diffidently promoted" [1983: 235].

This partial change in land policy was self-serving. It was accepted because by the 1860s the mechanisms were in place to coerce immigrant labour and render it captive. It has been observed that, "in its [LSSs'] financial aspect, it reduced the cost to the planter and to the country of supporting continuing immigration of cheap indentured labour . . . [In] its residential aspect, it ensured that the services of the settlers would still be available to the estates . . . but . . . there would be limitations ensuring that [they] could not become economically self-sufficient" [Shahabuddeen 1983: 235]. By the 1870s the concerns and lingering doubts were dispelled. With the onset of the depression, planters sought to cut their losses by reducing variable costs and most important among such costs was that of unindentured village-based labour [Rodney 1981a]. Eventually, the planters even unable to pay the wages due to the indentured labourers, agreed to provide irrigated land in lieu of wages to the latter [Adamson 1972; Rodney 1981a, 1981b].

Later, lands were rented to labourers on condition that they guaranteed to supply a given minimum quantity of labour to the plantations [British Guiana 1931a]. The Hays Commission recommended that immigrant families be given land in close proximity to plantations to which they would be bound to supply labour for a stipulated period. The labourers were also desirous of securing land on which to settle. The earliest initiative in this regard came from the Chinese 'adventurer', O Tye Kim (Wu Tai Kim), who successfully petitioned the Court of Policy for the establishment of the scheme at Hopetown, Camoenie Creek on the Demerara River [Young 1958: 149–60]. In 1877 and 1879 the governor was petitioned by groups of East Indians also desirous of securing land. Thus, a coincidence of interests between the administration, potential settlers and planters emerged after the initial controversy and there was little resistance to the establishment of the schemes, save for the grumblings of those who were eventually called upon to provide the finance and to vacate the lands, points to which we shall return.

One rare instance of resistance took place in 1880 when the Colonial Office vetoed the proposed scheme at L'Amitie on the Mahaica Creek because of objectionable tenure terms. Undaunted, in 1881 the Combined Court established a fund of $100,000 for purchasing, draining and improving land for settlement [Moore 1987: 77].

The Framework of Settlement Administration

It can be shown that changes in the mode of administering these schemes were triggered by both external and internal factors. Initially, the administration of the schemes was, in the words of one commentator, "simple and direct" [Young 1958: 153]. A zamindar, or superintendent, was appointed to run each scheme. A number of modifications were made to the regime before 1905. In keeping with the office's close link to East Indians and to the sugar industry, the Immigration Agent General (IAG) continued to play a central role in the administration of the LSS after 1894. This agency was already responsible for managing the supply of immigrant East Indian labour to the plantations and it is fitting, given the 'real' role of the scheme, for this expertise to have been called up in the service of the plantation.[30] Later, sub-immigration agents were assigned the task of administering the settlements under the supervision of the IAG. Given this key role in executing policy it is hardly surprising that appointees were carefully selected and specially rewarded [Nath 1950: 99–100].

In that selection we are able to see the links between the civil service and the other elements that help to make up the state. In the case of Hopetown, the Anglican church had dispensation to appoint the superintendent. Mr O's embrace of Christianity seemed to be a major consideration in explaining his appointment to a post that would normally have been reserved for whites. After Mr O's departure from his £300/pa post,[31] a Mr Knight replaced him in 1871 as missionary. Although the new incumbent's responsibilities may not have been as extensive as those of his predecessor, who also served as banker, they included the provision of medical services and mediation between settlers and the state. The church was well established in this latter role as an agent of the state. Beatty [1970] observed that from 1824 until 1921 those of them favoured by the planters received financial support from the authorities.

As the number of settlements increased, a range of problems, such as the lack of adequate preparation and coordination of agencies, came to the fore. Finance had to be secured. The Immigration Fund was resorted to initially. The impotence of a regime without the powers to levy compulsory labour or rates was very evident and in this sense the LSSs experienced the same difficulties as the villages [Young 1958: 155].

Consequently, in 1896 a departmental committee, styled the "Commutation of Return Passages" Committee, was entrusted with the responsibility for planning and establishing the settlements. The committee was comprised of the senior immigration agent and one assistant surveyor. Three years later, a superintendent of settlements was appointed. Responsibility for the upkeep of infrastructure on the schemes was assigned to the superintendent who was answerable to the governor through the IAG. This appears to have been a full-time post. The superintendent was vested with powers, including fiscal powers, akin to those enjoyed by the local authorities.[32] This upgrading of the reporting line was probably attributable to the severity of the global economic crisis and the need to hold labour during this temporary phase as well as to the influence of the Colonial Office as reflected in the 1897 commission's support for the promotion of peasant agriculture.

These changes were contemporaneous with the reduction in the upset price of Crown land. The cause was also external. In 1896, in reaction to the popular disquiet about dependence on an industry clearly unable to carry the country through the severe crisis, the governor, in the face of sugar industry opposition, forced through the legislature a statute reducing the upset price (minimum value of purchases) of Crown land from a near prohibitive $1,000 to $3.75 [Will 1968]. Partly as a result of this dramatic reduction and the removal of restrictions against the acquisition of Crown lands by immigrants, many East Indians were able to acquire land for the first time [Young 1958: ch. 8].

It should be added that on this point the governor had the support of the Colonial Office, which had been pressing for the promotion of peasant farming as a means of ameliorating the impact of the depression [Shahabuddeen 1983: 237]. In a sense, this change in policy reflected a fracture in the close link between planters and the metropole. It was to be a source of future problems for the former. The matter was not, and probably could not be, actively, let alone effectively, pursued in the face of opposition by the local planters who dominated the legislature. It appears that the Colonial Office lost interest in this objective as soon as the immediate crisis passed.

The interdependence and mutual support between Guyana's domestic agrarian capital and the metropolitan administration was a critical factor in the evolution of sugar in Guyana. In neighbouring Suriname, in the absence of such a mutuality of interests, this recession heralded the last throes of plantation sugar, provided opportunities for the proto-peasantry and incentives for new economic activities.

In pursuit of the intention to keep the state's administration of the schemes temporary, an ordinance was enacted in 1905 repealing the legislation that had conferred special status on the LSSs. All existing schemes were converted to village or sanitary districts, self-governing and liable to pay rates and taxes and falling under the responsibility of a village council or local authority [Laws 1905].[33] Thereby they were put on the same footing as the African villages. These statutory bodies employed overseers, rangers and watchmen to check on the infrastructure and to collect rates. By this time the depression was over and the schemes were showing signs of some internal vibrancy based on rice production. We shall return to the consequences of these changes (chapter 4).

This development may also constitute a clue as to the reason for the change in land pricing policy. After 1882, free grants of land were terminated in favour of sales, ostensibly on the grounds of allowing the settlers greater freedom of choice with respect to location [Young 1958]. An alternative explanation may have been the government's concern to keep the cost of settlement below the expenditure foregone to meet return passages of East Indian immigrants. There is ample evidence in the literature of the unsatisfied demand for land [Young 1958: 155–59]. Consequently, it was feasible to sell it. Some of the settlers at Huis t'Dieren and all those at the subsequent schemes (except Helena), such as Cotton Tree, were therefore required and were prepared to purchase their plots (see Table 3). The asking prices for these plots have been described as "staggering", not only because the planters had acquired state lands at lower prices but also because in some cases nearby land could be bought for far less. The purchase price for comparable land was alleged to be around $12/ha [Nath 1950: 86]. In the case of Windsor Forest, settlers secured land at $2.47/ha for the first year and $14.83/ha per annum, subsequently. The purchase price for land outside was $24.71. At Hague, rent was $7.41/ha during the first year and $12.35/ha per annum, subsequently [Young 1958]. At Huis t'Dieren and Middlesex the price of $59.31/ha compares with $12.35/ha and $9.88/ha for 'similar' private land in the Essequibo Islands and Mahaicony, respectively [Moore 1987]. In a sense this debate is largely theoretical for, as may be seen later, many of the settlers received titles to land without much more than the deposit, if that.

It is possible that this pricing policy may have been a reflection of the planters flexing their fiscal muscles in a bid to avoid the degeneration of the schemes into purely subsistence own-account farms. With more than nominal rents, each settler's family would have either to produce for sale or (preferably) sell labour services to earn part or all of the income needed for rent. In keeping with this objective, no training or technical guidance was provided to settlers. Facilities were rudimentary and most depended on the neighbouring sugar estates for a plethora of paternalistic handouts, including services and marketplaces.

Underlying Issues and Paradoxes

It is commonly assumed that the LSSs were intended to facilitate the establishment of a peasantry or at least to expand substantially the base of smallholder farmers already extant in the villages [Hanley 1987; Lobdell 1988].[34] There are two reasons for not attaching too much credence to the contention that such a motive was consistently pursued in Guyana during the period under review. First, the existing peasants, the (African) villagers, were excluded from these arrangements altogether. In 1906, a proposal to support rice growing settlements for Africans was rejected by the legislature [Shahabuddeen 1983: 400]. Indeed, as has already been noted, Africans were ejected from some lands that were to be used for LSSs [Rodney 1981a: ch. 7]. Second, the immigrants were neither the sole nor the main beneficiaries of land grants during the latter decades of the century. In the 1870s and 1885, before the immigrants were given access to plots of land, the planters, through the legislature, had granted themselves nearly 20,000 hectares of land gratis or at nominal (12–37¢/ha) prices [Adamson 1972; Gyanchand 1963].

It is common knowledge that much of this land was acquired by planters for speculation and to deny access to the peasants [Beckford 1972]. In the last two decades of the century, less than 60 percent of the total acreage of the prime land held by the plantations was utilized. The acreage sown to sugar amounted to about 49 percent of the total cultivated acreage in the country; the volume of unutilized land was therefore far from insignificant.

The type of land granted to settlers provides some indication of the intent of official policy. Lewis asserted that LSSs were regarded as, "the step to be taken when the estate had gone bankrupt, and is in danger of abandonment" [Lewis 1951: 80]. It can be contended that the choice of land reflected the fact that the interests or well-being of the settlers themselves were only marginal considerations in the decision.

During the mid century crisis referred to earlier, the plantations encountering difficulties were simply abandoned or sold to private buyers. It is significant that in the crisis of the 1880s and 1890s, the very much larger businesses were, apparently, not required to take this route. The state acquired their lands. We have already noted the influence of these planters at home and abroad, and it is this influence that explains the land acquisition by the state.

Nationalization in Guyana first took place at the behest and in the interest of plantation owners. Furthermore, land was not the only asset so acquired. The railway company, for example, was nationalized when its precarious financial status jeopardized the movement of sugar to the ports [Odle 1975: 67; Reno 1964]. The nationalization of former sugar lands was, therefore, not an isolated or purely fortuitous occurrence.[35] It is quite likely that in the circumstances the state's purchases, in effect, assisted planters to liquidate their insolvent enterprises, to retrieve and to repatriate some of their capital.[36] In other words, the state played an influential role in the restructuring of the industry by mediating in the process of valorization. Cases in point were Hopetown and L'Amitie in the Mahaica Creek. This phenomenon is testimony to the nature and strength of the links between the metropole and the periphery, and it may even be considered as another example of the articulation of different modes of production across national boundaries. Lewis, in the comment referred to earlier, was therefore only touching on one half of the issue.

Settlement sites and quality of land

There is strong evidence that some of the lands provided for settlement were inappropriate. Shahabuddeen, for example, rather graphically describes the first site proposed, Plantation Best, as "gelatinous territory" [1983: 235]. It is important, however, to dispel the impression that, as a rule, the lands of these former plantations were qualitatively bad. Soil exhaustion on some estates, or parts thereof, may have given rise to sale or abandonment, but this was by no means true of the bulk, or even a significant proportion, of the plantations. We have, after all, been arguing that most of the properly drained and irrigated land lay on the plantations.

The available contemporary commentaries, far from citing poor land or yields, indicate that some of the plantations in question, such as Helena and Cotton Tree, were model plantations prior to their demise. In many cases factors other than agronomics occasioned abandonment or sale. "Huis t'Dieren came to an end more abruptly than most. Its boiler exploded with fatal results" [Rodney 1981a: 184]. A very instructive comment can be found hidden away in the remarks concerning four plantations purchased for settlement. These plantations were said to have been abandoned, "simply for want of labour at such a price as would admit of making common process sugar at a profit". [*Daily Argosy* 1883: 1]. The same author contended that many of the plantations "never lacked anything except good management . . . or cheap labour" (p. 3). In other words, the change in market preference or demand had occasioned a switch from muscuvado to yellow crystal sugar. Associated with this shift in taste was one in technology, from 'common process' to vacuum pans and centrifugals. Those who would or could not adapt would only be able to survive by procuring very cheap labour. This was not always possible.

The problem cannot therefore be defensibly portrayed primarily as a result of the allocation of the inferior lands to LSSs. Such land represented a significant qualitative improvement in D&I terms, over that available to villagers. In this regard, the following comment on the Island of Wakenaam lend support to our contention: "in general, the lands which supported the sugar industry at the end of its reign were the choicest areas of the island, both in terms of land quality, and in accessibility and infrastructure" [Kirby 1973: 50]. In fact, the peasant farms lying between the Boerasirie and Bonasika Rivers provided a very good test of the assertion and of the impunity with which the plantations damaged peasant interest. Prior to the departure of the Dutch, these areas, amounting to around sixty-eight square miles on the east bank of the Essequibo River, supported the intensive cultivation of sugar, coffee, cocoa and cotton. In 1929, subject to flooding, they were being considered for LSSs. The cause of the flooding is instructive. There were leaks from a conservancy established in 1889 and enhanced by way of a canal. Since the latter flowed backwards, the tributaries of the Bonasika had to be dammed. Unlike earlier cases mentioned, this was not apparently deliberate flooding of peasant lands, but the Boerasirie-Warima conservancy, which raised the water levels in the first place, had been constructed to bring water to the sugar plantations as had the malfunctioning canal. The water conservancy commissioners refused to accept any responsibility for the consequences of their actions, and as late as 1929 the investigators sent by the governor to look into the matter could report that, in spite of $80,000 being made available ten years earlier to remedy the problem, there had been "no serious attempt to ascertain what works are required to protect from flooding this large area of Crown land and private property and to drain it and make it productive once more" [Mullins 1929].

As already indicated, the D&I requirements of coastal plantations were such as to put them in the realm of 'public goods'. In this context, atomistic peasant management and decision making often proved to be either inefficient or inappropriate. The administration refused or failed to select and organize the schemes with an eye to the needs of smallholders with defined farming systems and therefore specific constraints. Alternative and suitable freehold land already empoldered, often with some degree of assistance from the state, for example, was not considered for settlement [British Guiana 1931a]. This option served sugar's interests ever so well. The problem therefore appears to have been attributable not so much to the intrinsic quality of the soil as to the incompatibility of the farming system (and associated overheads) with smallholder management.

Determinants of LSS sites

In a sense, the problem could also be portrayed as one of location. In areas requiring extensive D&I resources, appropriate institutional support and arrangements were necessary, as has been argued earlier. But they were not the only areas that could have been considered for settlement. The location of schemes in the hinterland was pre-empted by the availability of the 'cheap' and 'appropriate' estates on the coast. The choice of area was mainly dictated by the needs of the plantations. Thus the Commission on Return Passages recommended in 1895 that land grants should in future be located near the plantations and markets [Adamson 1972: 99].[37] In keeping with this, Whim,[38] established in 1897, was sited close to plantations Port Mourant and Albion. In establishing the LSSs in the vicinity of the plantations, the state was, deliberately or not, providing settlers with the wherewithal to undertake some production of food with which to help meet part or all of their subsistence needs. This could serve to minimize the plantation's wage bill by reducing pressure on the wage rates. Indeed, the schemes also externalized the wage and social overhead burden of the sugar industry by sparing the plantations part of the wage cost as well as the cost of housing and of full provision of social services for these workers.

It also served the planters' interests to ensure that the schemes provided no more than part-time employment. In a sense, they intended 'no settlement beyond subsistence'.[39] This objective was reflected in the provision of inadequate-sized plots to settlers. It may be seen from Table 1 that the land allotments were fairly small; too small, it might be argued, to sustain peasant production given the current state of husbandry.

Adequacy of plot size and facilities

Initially, settlers over ten years of age received 0.2 ha for a houselot and 0.8 ha per person, freehold.[40] But subsequently at Helena, Whim, Bush Lot and Maria's Pleasure the allotments were reduced to 0.5 ha. Tenure arrangements compounded the problem of inadequate size, for leases contained no reference to beneficial occupation, subletting or sale of allotments. Evidently, the paramount concern of the state was to have been freed of the obligation to finance the repatriation of the indentured labourers [McCormack 1979: 36].

It should be further noted that state support for the schemes was kept at a level that was not sufficient to facilitate economic operations by settlers. As early as 1888 the range of provision was deemed quite inadequate by the Alexander Committee. Although the committee recommended the provision of better facilities on easy terms, little more actually materialized. Only the initial cost of land acquisition, some site development and the maintenance of public roads were met by the state. The D&I facilities provided at Helena and Hopetown, the artesian well at Whim, and the 3.5-mile fresh water canal at Bush Lot were notable precisely because they represented exceptional infrastructural facilities on pre-1905 schemes.

Vining, in his identification of reasons for the 'failure' of the schemes, has singled out "isolated, poor and deteriorating hydrologic facilities", as well as inadequate roads at Huis t'Dieren, Bush Lot, Whim, Maria's Pleasure and Helena [1976]. There can be no doubt that the state of these facilities placed serious limitations on the use that settlers could make of the opportunities offered by the access to land. In fact, it has been argued that some of the schemes actually settled were largely responsible for immiserizing settlers. It was claimed, for example, that poor irrigation facilities resulted in the ruin of many farmers at Whim and Bush Lot in 1889 [Nath 1950: 100–101].[41]

Financial support of LSS

As was the case with African villages initially, no regulation existed either for the collection of rates or the compulsory provision of labour to maintain infrastructure for irrigation and transport. In order to avoid a consequential collapse of the schemes however, the government was prepared to subsidize the services provided to settlers through the Immigration Fund until 1902 or 1903. Some forty years after Governor Hincks levied similar imposts on African villages and thirty-seven years after the first LSS was established, regulations for the management of East Indian schemes were passed and a rate of 20¢/lot was levied on each occupier [Young 1958: 155–59].

Although resources could not have been made available to adequately upgrade D&I and important infrastructural facilities, some were found to pay settlers' arrears of rates and to hold the facilities together when resumption threatened to give rise to abandonment or the degeneration of the schemes.

In the cases of Helena and Whim, assistance to the tune of $2,500 and $1,000, respectively, was provided in 1890. Similarly, many of the early settlers on schemes such as Huis t'Dieren were given titles to land irrespective of whether they had made more than the $10 downpayment required and notwithstanding the resumption of some plots (for nonoccupation) in 1887. It does appear that part of the reason for the 1886 and 1890 amendments and the subsequent revamping of local government legislation lay with the experience in this area.

It is worth dwelling on this issue of facilities for just a while longer because it could not be said that the state was unwilling to put funds into LSSs per se. As was observed earlier, in Guyana as in the rest of the Caribbean, funds were more than generously provided to procure land and in the process provide liquidity to landlords in financial difficulties. In addition, the state held some of the plantations idle for several years before assigning them to LSSs. Unity/ Lancaster, for example, was established as an LSS some ten years or so after its acquisition.

Results

Establishment and survival of LSSs

It may be seen from Table 1 that some seven schemes were established in the three counties of Guyana during this first phase. Plantations Best and L'Aimitie were also considered. There can be no doubt that the schemes encountered many difficulties. Indeed, most of the literature on the subject is devoted to such 'problems' and, judging from this literature [Brown 1954; Adamson 1972; Vining 1976; Sukdeo 1978; Shahabuddeen 1983], most of the schemes were failures.[42] The perception that they were on the verge of collapse prompted a series of changes in their administration in 1899. Mandle has opined that "four estates were purchased by the government in the 1890s . . . within a very short time, however, the settlements proved to be failures and were disbanded" [1973: 37]. A 1917 report concluded that schemes on virgin land had not been a success (GSO 3891/17). The fate of the first scheme was so inextricably linked to that of its promoter that when in 1867 the latter "fled the country . . . to evade charges of immorality . . .", it also declined [Young 1958: 151].[43] Although this may have been an exaggeration, that scheme, which at its height prior to 1881 consisted of several hundred settlers, was by 1906 so insignificant that it lost its status as a Country Sanitary District [Young 1958: 151].

There is not always unanimity as to the causes. One author, for example, argues that Nooten Zuil, planned in 1871, attracted no settlers at all because the steam power needed for drainage was never provided [Adamson 1972: 96]. Moore on the other hand, attributes the noninterest to the "vexatious village laws", inter alia [1987]. Poor irrigation facilities are alleged to have ruined many settlers at Bush Lot and Whim, as already mentioned. In spite of three expensive kokers (sluices) installed between 1882 and 1885, Huis t'Dieren was liable to encroachments from the sea and to floods from the bush water of the interior [Nath 1950: 95–97]. Absenteeism was the norm on this scheme, as was the case at Helena also. Land sales aimed at establishing schemes at plantations Cotton Tree, Brighton, Letter Kenny, Dead Tree, Farm, Massiah and Maria's Lodge attracted only sixty-one takers [Moore 1987]. By 1900, only Whim had attracted a significant number of settlers and, even so, many of those settlers had already had recourse to the Poor Law authorities for assistance.

It is difficult not to concur with Lewis' contention that, "small farming must be handicapped if it is to be confined to the least productive lands" [1951]. It is arguable, however, that one would have to look beyond "soil exhaustion and the scarcity of women" [Young 1958: 151] to fully understand the dynamics of LSSs and their problems. The immigrants were, for example, prepared to acquire private land. Given their exposure, settlers were more familiar with cane farming than any other. However, the cultivation of sugar cane on LSSs was prohibited so their output would not be bought by the factories [Shahabuddeen 1983: 44]. At the same time, no training, technical support or guidance of any kind was provided prior to 1918. The value of the subsequent visits by the initial agricultural instructor to the LSSs has been described as of "doubtful" value by one commentator [Kennard, letter to author, 1988].

Forces of production

Contemporary evidence attests to the consequential limited development of the productive forces on those schemes with settlers (see Table 2). No fertilizer or manure was utilized and soil exhaustion was commonplace [Young 1958; Rodney 1979: 22]. Mixed farming was rare. Where it was practised, livestock husbandry complemented rice farming and provided the motive power for many farm operations and transportation. It could also provide manure. In the absence of any assistance from the administration, livestock husbandry was hardly developed, however, and selective breeding unknown [Miller n.d.]. Up to the late 1930s, technical inputs into the development of the livestock industry were fairly rudimentary and confined to the importation of exotic stock for cross-breeding [Fraser 1935: 143]. There was, in addition, poor nutrition and excess water on grazing lands. In any case, absentee farming and part-time cultivation precluded the keeping of livestock on the majority of peasant farms as did the continuous extension of rice cultivation and the cyclical movement of the areas under sugar [British Guiana 1948: 179, Vol. 2].

In the case of rice farming, paddy was still cut by sickle and broadcast exclusively by hand. In 1907–8 sun-curing, threshing via bull-mashing and winnowing were common. Edible grain was extracted by mortar and pestle. Peak demand for labour was often met by the use of communal labour, including that of women and children, but there was little specialization by task [Greenidge et al. 1978]. But even in rice farming, there were few improved or nontraditional techniques of production or harvesting (see Table 2). In the light of these factors, it is safe to argue that LSS agriculture was, in a technological sense, no different from that of the villages and, like the latter, stood in stark

3.3 Sugar cane handling, from punt to factory with machine and animal power.
Source: Leechman 1913.

3.4 Peasant rice threshing – entirely manual. *Source*: Leechman 1913.

contrast with the plantations until after 1900, however, when technological advances were evident. The latter were the result of investment undertaken in areas such as rice milling – the introduction of single-stage huller – transplanting and parboiling (see Table 6).

Impact on repatriation

It may be argued that an appropriate test of the efficacy of the schemes would be their impact on repatriation (and repatriation-related costs) since these were the stated objectives of the LSSs. A total of some 75,547 East Indians were repatriated between 1843 and 1949 [Smith 1962: 49], but whereas over the years 1872–76 an average of 3,000 persons availed themselves of this facility, by 1885–1905 the numbers had fallen to 1,738. This 'success' should not necessarily be attributed entirely to the LSSs. LSSs affected less than 3,000 households by 1900. Indeed, in 1938 only 6,000 out of some 30,000 East Indians entitled to land in lieu of return passages had claimed their right [Sukdeo et al. 1978: 52]. Furthermore, after the effective termination of East Indian immigration in 1917 and indenture in 1920, the numbers seeking repatriation fell even more dramatically [Adamson 1972: 94–99]. The main economic reasons for this lack of interest could have been the depressed socioeconomic conditions in India and the post-1900 requirement that returnees pay part of their return fare.

Sociological factors such as the development of family ties in Guyana may have also been contributory causes. These were probably more important influences on the rate of repatriation than the establishment of the LSSs.

The LSSs therefore failed in the sense that, by themselves, they may not have significantly halted the repatriation of East Indian labour. If, however, the efficacy of the LSSs is examined from the standpoint of the attempt to create a pool of abundant and cheap labour for the sugar industry, quite a different conclusion might be formed.

Impact on wages

By 1879 a large pool of labour on which the industry could draw was evident and downward pressure on wages was an endemic feature of the labour market [Adamson 1972: 136–38]. Money wage rates are estimated to have taken eighty years to reattain the levels achieved in the mid 1840s [Landis 1971]. It has been estimated that over the years 1884 to 1904, real earnings of sugar workers fell by just under 50 percent [Adamson 1984].

Establishment of peasantry

Many of the assertions about the failure of the LSSs are based on the assumption that the schemes were supposed to and could nurture a peasantry in the same manner as the village movement. However, this never appears to have been a serious objective pursued by the administration. It is also questionable whether such an outcome could have been spontaneously realized, given all the circumstances [Stavenhagen 1973: 91–93]. In this sense, some authors have been guilty of embracing what may be regarded as a 'populist' position [see, for example, Kitchin 1982; Gellner 1969; Thorner et al. 1966]. More specifically, they assume that the existence of an idealized, undifferentiated peasantry in a somewhat static form is both possible and desirable. For this reason, some of the traditional and recent Marxist theories on the 'articulation of modes of production' and empirical studies attempt to avoid such a pitfall by investigating peasantries in the theoretical context of transitional precapitalist modes of production [Boesen 1979: 154–61; Harriss 1982]. Many factors militated against the establishment and promotion of a stable peasantry.[44] The social relations governing production were such that the lot of the smallholder was distinctly precarious. Share tenancy and disadvantageous marketing arrangements were devices by which they lost control of their own labour.

It has been said of the farmers who survived the drought at Whim, on the lower Corentyne river, a "great many of them fell into the hands of money lenders who charged exorbitant rates of interest and on account of this they took a long time to pay off their indebtedness" [Nath 1950: 101]. Many settlers on schemes were faced with indebtedness, resumption, abandonment and sale of land. One consequence of the schemes, therefore, was the enlargement of the market in land and increasing differentiation among smallholders, landlords and agrarian capitalists. Support from the state aimed at alleviating the adverse consequences of these developments was actively and successfully opposed by plantation and metropolitan interests.

Some support did evade this opposition, however, as was pointed out in an earlier section. In the case of Hopetown, for example, the government and businessman John Ho-A-Shoo jointly funded the construction of a dam to empolder approximately 212 ha in 1902. They thereby removed a major restriction on agricultural activities. In the following year the settlers were provided with a free grant of 370 ha in trust to the administration of the scheme [Crawford 1989: 45; Kirkpatrick 1993: 50, 51].

Hoarding of land, speculation and landlordism were also the counterparts to the above. These were the main devices through which the more fortunate or better endowed settlers entered the arena of capitalist farming, retail trade and the so-called informal sector [Jagan 1966; Young 1958; Burrowes 1984].

Judging from the available information on Hopetown, the range of economic activities – charcoal, shingles, ground provisions, coffee, rice and retailing – afforded settlers reasonable incomes. However, when stands of accessible trees had been depleted, charcoal could no longer underpin the other activities to the extent that it had done formerly. Migration to Georgetown then increased.

Apparently, in the wake of the lowering of barriers to retailing, in response to Portuguese pressure [Laurence 1965], individual Chinese settlers followed the opening of the communal shop in Georgetown with shops of their own. Many of these erstwhile settlers "opened groceries and rum shops . . . and it is a well-known fact that every other Chinese was either a grocer, gold or silversmith. Others took to tailoring whilst others . . . were not content with a shop to sell to miners which could and did make many Chinese rich. Instead, a group formed the Truimph Co. and set off to search for gold and diamonds themselves" [Kirkpatrick 1993: 51–52; Crawford 1989: ch. 3]. The Portuguese retail monopoly was thus broken in many areas.

Some of the consequences for economic concentration are graphically highlighted in the following passage on Wakenaam: "in fact, the most important millers on the island, those with the greatest through-put of grain, also tend to own relatively extensive areas of land, operate the local transport services, and some of the coastal shipping, carry out cultivation and harvesting on a contract basis, and act as merchants and money lenders" [Kirby 1973: 56]. There were less obvious implications for the flexibility of supply, for tenants could not alter land use without the permission of the landlord. Since many of the latter were millers, it became difficult, if not impossible, for tenants to move out of rice.

Case study on land distribution

Maria's Pleasure and Maria Johanna, on the Island of Wakenaam in the estuary of the Essequibo River provide an interesting illustration of the contrasting evolution of LSSs and African villages during this period.

There are basically two differences between the villages. Maria Johanna was purchased and populated by former African slaves and their descendants, while Maria's Pleasure was a Commutation of Return Passages scheme. The second difference was related to the system of tenure. In the case of Maria Johanna, the land was communally owned and there was no provision for individual inheritance. The successors of the original purchasers "hold the land in trust for the future" [Kirby 1973: 35]. In Maria's Pleasure individual inheritance prevails.

Following their establishment, the villages undertook similar economic activities. Initially, they experienced similar economic and social disruptions, fortunes and misfortunes – absenteeism, emigration and abandonment of land. Coconut cultivation appeared to be unviable under the systems employed.

Maria's Pleasure received a new lease on life when alternative employment opportunities materialized in the form of the conversion of a neighbouring estate, Meerzorg, to rice. This estate proved to be the main source of employment and income for Maria's Pleasure. Farming activities did not decline. Indeed, quite the opposite was the case. But share tenancy/cropping and inability to market took its toll on settlers. The impact of these factors on landholding and on concentration of land ownership was such that by 1971 Maria's Pleasure, which had commenced with just over 0.5 ha per family, had 39 percent of its land owned by 10 percent of the landowners. Less than one half of the cultivated area was rented by those who farmed it and 38 percent of the farmers were tenants [Cummings 1973: 22, 89].

The subsequent experience of the two settlements has been quite divergent. In the case of Maria Johanna, the cycle of obstacles to progressive land development – underutilization, absenteeism, emigration and abandonment – is too well documented in the literature on communal ownership and the traditional institution known as "Children's Property" to warrant repetition here [Momsen 1987; Kirby 1973: 34–35, ch. 4]. The land had to be demarcated again in 1921. However, not surprisingly, the old problems re-emerged and were compounded by squatting and praedial larceny from neighbouring East Indian settlements such as Meerzorg [Kirby 1973: 45].

It appears, therefore, that under neither system of tenure could a stable peasantry be said to exist. They both eventually served as sources of labour for off-settlement destinations. In one case, however, viable and legal capitalist agriculture was left behind.

Ethnicity

As was mentioned earlier, indenture was intended to help hold down the wages and bargaining power of free labour. The plantation labour market had always been characterized by the social division of labour by race. With indenture, another layer was added to the social division of labour by ethnic groups.

East Indians opting not to return to India found three main outlets. Significant numbers migrated to Suriname where, as a consequence of the collapse of the sugar industry, the scope for peasant agriculture was now greater than it was in Guyana. Others moved to the urban areas and, in this regard, La Penitence appears to have been a major staging point. Many entered commerce and petty commodity production. Potter [1975] has noted increasing East Indian penetration of the Portuguese preserve of commerce after 1880.

With regard to their entry into African villages. Potter has employed the term 'invasion' [1975], but the problem that emerged centred not so much on their presence per se but from their hunger for land and the device of squatting which was widely employed to satisfy that hunger [Young 1958: 158; Cummings 1973; Kirby 1973; Moore 1987: 180; Shahabuddeen 1983: 384–85; Rodney 1981a: 184]. Even today, such squatting remains a major source of inter- and intravillage tensions. Much of the Africans' land was held collectively and the constraints that this implied for development by progressive individuals have already been mentioned. The impact of the 'African attitude' to land, if indeed such exists, as outlined, for example, by Besson [1987: ch. 1], would have reinforced this. As a consequence of the factors outlined in the preceding chapter (extra economic force, law, unfavourable conditions for own-account farming), there was undoubtedly considerable underutilization of (African) village lands.

It might be added that all of the above evolved in relation to an African population becoming obsessed about its inability to maintain itself without immigration [British Guiana 1919b; Dalton 1855: 412].

Recapitulation and Conclusions, 1865–1905

It has been argued that in the face of the development of a market in free labour, the increasingly monopolistic sugar industry, anticipating certain adverse consequences for profits and the mode of operation of the industry, set out to reassert control over the labour market. Whilst the abolition of slavery and the loss of the preferential market access represented a mortal blow for the articulated metropolitan/planter interests, it did not necessarily mean the death of 'unfree labour'. Various devices were employed to defer the establishment of a free market in wage labour. Immigration by indentured labour was one of those devices. The reasons for the avoidance of Africans in this exercise is not difficult to discern. They were excluded from consideration because the Colonial Office and antislavery lobby were still 'watching' and the local legislature was not prepared to take on the abolitionists again. But extra-economic forces were applied consistently and powerfully. There was the establishment of a paramilitary police force to keep the Africans in hand and rules to frustrate them from developing in directions deemed inimical to sugar.

The establishment of LSSs was an objective that commended itself to each of the other groups for different motives. Thus a strong coincidence of interests arose. The support extended to the elements of this articulated mode was asymmetrical. The assistance that came by the smallholders or village agriculture was usually self-serving or quite incidental. Clearly, this was not the consequence of a lack of resources or a lack of interest in the fate of the sector. This is evident from the ad hoc injections of cash and the periodic changes in 'rules'. The objective appears to have been to retain labour for the sugar industry and to do so at as low a cost as possible.

Technological and environmental factors reinforced the policies of the state as orchestrated by the planters, thereby ensuring that rural labour remained tied to the sugar plantations in one way or another. This was true of village (predominantly African) labour also. In this way, there may be said to have been the articulation of different modes of production. From time to time, exogenous factors such as depression shook some of the labour loose. For various reasons, this led to the early 'loss' of African (field) labour from the plantations. But own-account farming was unattractive for all groups until the 1890s and, as a consequence, labour tended to leave both the LSSs and villages when viable alternatives offered themselves.

There is little evidence to substantiate the assertion that the schemes were set up to establish a peasantry. Even if this was the case, however, objective factors, including market forces, militated against a stable peasantry and tended to work towards growing differentiation among smallholders. An associated development was a rise in the incidence of wage labour and dispossession.

The LSSs appear neither to have had much of an impact on the rate of repatriation of time-expired Chinese and East Indian labour nor on the creation of a peasantry. But there were other consequences both deliberate and unintended. The LSSs were a useful adjunct in that they helped to maintain downward pressure on the wages of unindentured labour. They do appear, therefore, to have been of service to the sugar industry and to have been relatively low cost. This analysis is by no means peculiar to Guyana [Miles 1987: 85–93; Fitzgerald 1989: 199–203], but it is no less valid for not being unique.

The efficacy of this nexus between sugar and East Indian labour has generally tended to be masked by analysis which starts from the assumption that in Guyana, East Indians 'saved' the sugar industry. In reality, their introduction slowed the emergence of capitalist farming and a labour market, and reinforced the position of the planters. What has been argued here is that when the planters were faced with the prospect of hiring 'free labour' to produce sugar for sale in a market without imperial preference, they sought to reduce the cost of that labour by whatever means they could, hence indentureship. When the excessive abuse of that system and the expiry of indentures started to pose problems, such as the loss of labour, they considered LSSs as a means of extending the period over which labour was to be tied to sugar and the cost thereof.

The East Indians also had an interest in acquiring land. The ethnic basis of the schemes, when set against the background of the destruction of the village movement, was to mar these programmes for their entire existence. Ethnically exclusive LSSs could not commend themselves to the African populace. It should be evident from the above that the rise of ethnic conflict in Guyana predates the immediate post-1955 era with which it is most commonly associated [Cross and Herman 1988].[45] The salience of ethnicity, though not a neglected factor in Guyanese history, is far from fully researched. Little attention has so far been paid explicitly to the rural origins of this phenomenon, except in very general terms.

CHAPTER 4

BITTERSWEET POLITICS, 1906–1947

*They could not be part of the white and coloured professional and
commercial middle class, although they themselves were coloured, but
they retained a sense of the exclusiveness they had learnt at St Stanislaus,
they mimicked it and transposed it to lower class situations, like the
newspaper office where they behaved like an elite.*

Janice Shinebourne, *Timepiece*

This chapter traces the reaction of the local administration and the Colonial Office to
the changing politics and the times and highlights the implications of those reactions for
the agricultural sector. In exploring the changes in the labour market consequential on
the termination of indentureship and the rise of bauxite mining and rice farming, the
chapter touches on the controversies over the ethnic bias of the schemes. The selection
of land, tenure arrangements, adequacy of plots and land prices are also examined, since
the exigencies of the First and Second World Wars made themselves felt on the structure of production and the division of labour vis-à-vis the metropole there were implications for support to the peasantry and developments in the forces of production. The
postwar attempt to restore old structures and to resolve the competing demands of the
rice and sugar industries for labour are also of importance in this era.

The Political Framework

Capital-labour relations were to undergo extensive qualitative changes during
this particular epoch, 1906 to 1947. These relations may be said to have been
modernized in large measure. The changes were partly presaged by events that
took place during the final decades of the nineteenth century and the early
twentieth century, in particular. We turn briefly to the factors which, inter alia,
were to force the industry to revisit its labour policies – that is, one aspect of the
modernization cited by Cross.

As was explained in the earlier section, the fracture between the forces allied against labour and peasants in Guyana occured with the abolition of slavery. The plantation sector reacted by securing the agreement of the Colonial Office and the local administration to import additional labour which was then employed in markets characterized by coercion and the use of nonmarket forces.

Traditionally, the activities and physical conditions in Guyana were such that the population could not maintain itself without immigration. Until the 1920s the natural rate of population growth had been negative. Thus, despite the additional 54,168 Africans introduced to Guyana between 1832 and 1917, the African population actually fell by 25 percent over those years. After seventy-nine years of immigration, the East Indian population was some 20 percent less than had been imported [British Guiana 1919b; Adamson 1972; Nath 1950; Mandle 1973]. It took the termination of immigration for the industry to begin to devote resources to the enhancement of the quality of its labour force.

Immigration of East Indian labour was terminated in 1917 and indentureship in 1920, a little over three-quarters of a century after the cessation of slavery. The sugar industry had failed to convince the Indian government that additional East Indian immigrants would receive fair and humane treatment on the plantations to which they were destined. The plantation owners were unwilling to bear the full cost of implementing the safeguards required by the Indian government [Singh 1987: 29, 50]. There was resistance to taxation of the non-sugar sector and the working class and public employees in particular, for the benefit of the sugar plantations. As a result of these factors, the hazards of wartime, sea transport which added to the risk and cost of the exercise, and competing demands by the Indian authorities for labour for the draft, indentured immigration was terminated. Another factor which may have been responsible for its termination was its apparent contribution to the rising tide of Indian nationalism [Nath 1950; Rodney 1966; Fraser 1981; Shahabuddeen 1983: 190; Singh 1987].

With the termination of indentureship the sugar plantation sector was, for the first time in its existence in Guyana, called upon to pay attention to the size and physical well-being of its labour force. That event in itself was the single most important reflection of the changed capital-labour relations. It heralded a move from the more crude exploitation of labour – primitive accumulation. In this sense, it is possible to challenge Cross who has argued, admittedly in the context of the Caribbean as a whole, that it was the depression of the 1890s that modernized capital-labour relations [1988: 9]. Whilst that may have been true

4.1 Labourers' dwellings on a sugar plantation, *c.* 1920. *Source*: Fenty 1984.

elsewhere, additional factors were to fuel the subsequent developments which occured in Guyana.

Earlier we explored the factors giving rise to the emergence of local agrarian capitalists, rentiers and landlords. Now the changes besetting the colony would serve to reinforce the emergence of a relatively free rural wage labour force with an urban proletariat.

In spite of the best efforts of the sugar planters, other industries rose to challenge their dominance and to erode their labour supply and political power. The first of these was the emergence of a rice industry which was the outcome of a fortuitous conjuncture by way of increased access of smallholders to land at the turn of the century and a shortage of imported rice from India and Burma. The resultant high local price of rice stimulated a terrific expansion in production among small, particularly East Indian farmers. Rice was a popular choice among these farmers because the aquatic habit of the crop made it suitable for the flat coastal plain with its heavy soils and susceptibility to flooding. Demand was also stable and buoyant, for, in addition to being the staple food, it was also employed in religious ceremonies.

During the 1920s a bauxite industry was established in spite of imperial opposition [Shahabuddeen 1981]. This success was attributable both to the guile and to the tenacity of the US-owned transnational corporation (TNC), Alcoa, and the intervention of the US government [Spackman 1975; Girvan 1967]. It remains the only major, modern industry to have avoided domination by sugar and to be located off the coastal strip (at Linden, Ituni and Kwakwani).

Having established itself in defiance of sugar, it adopted the plantation legacy with a vengeance.[46] As with sugar, production was monopolized, to all intents and purposes, by a single firm which engrossed vast tracts of land in order to deny access to competitors [Shahabuddeen 1981]. Its treatment of labour was not much different either.

In the hinterland, economic activities centring on forestry (including balata bleeding – tapping natural rubber), gold and diamond mining as well as cattle ranching remained semi-feudal. Gold mining, which at one stage threatened to join bauxite as a major industry, flattered to deceive and by the end of the period was essentially an artisanal activity with a labour demand profile complementary to that of rice and sugar.

The travelogue of Evelyn Waugh [1934] provides an eloquent insight into relations of production in some of these industries. Waugh, who found himself transported to Guyana as a result of a (alas, still too frequent) confusion of Guiana with New Guinea, is a surprising witness to European settlement and control of the hinterland and its occupants, Guyana's indigenes, European prejudices about other races [pp. 36, 71, 160] and monopoly in the diamond market [pp. 144–49].

Clearly the process of modernization of capital-labour relations was neither complete nor comprehensive at this point in time. But by the end of the period there were the makings of an industrial as well as a rural proletariat. Associated with the ruling class were capitalists who were not British. The nationality of the TNCs is not a neutral or unimportant factor in decision making. We shall return to this aspect later. In a sense, it meant that an additional source or influence became relevant in the country's politics. Furthermore, with the establishment of the rice industry came rural capitalists, millers and merchants. They were potential additions to the strata of rural landlords, rentiers and moneylenders as well as to the strata of compradors. Superimposed on all these developments was the racial dimension.

The labour force of the bauxite industry was overwhelmingly African and the industrial relations of the industry was significantly influenced by the ethnic division of labour.[47] The managements of sugar, bauxite and forestry were entirely in white hands. With the geographical and occupational shifts alluded to earlier, labour of the sugar and rice industries eventually came to be viewed primarily, though not exclusively, as East Indian preserves whilst non-plantation, non-rice agriculture and mining, were quickly dominated by African labour. This period was to witness some incorporation of the coloured, mixed or Creole elements into the higher echelons of the civil service and the private sector, such as the press. Smith has contended that this incorporation into the administration and the executive arm of the state was a function of colonial ideology. In other words, the myth of the fairness of imperialism and of its benefits required that there be evidence of this. It is surely true that this recruitment of the Creoles was not simply a reflection of the demand for and supply of labour. The crucial point to note is that the structure of decision making was made more complex to incorporate them without shifting the centre of power. In the words of Smith, this incorporation was "a struggle for power in which social practice was conditioned by ideology" [Graham et al. 1977: xiv].

The changes in voter eligibility would have had the impact of opening up the political space. It had implications for the privileged groups. The Creoles, Portuguese and Chinese utilized the space. From time to time, the jockeying for power among them was dramatic enough to capture the attention of the most critical of social commentators, the calypsonians. In this regard, Rohlehr reminds us of the significance of the Bill Rogers' song "Daddy Gone", a parody of the events leading to the electoral defeat of the Portuguese politician, Fernandes, at Cove and John on the east coast of the Demerara [1990: 141–42].

In contrast to Trinidad and Tobago, for example, union as well as political representation became strongly communal and, "labour organizations were widely seen as reflecting social interests" [Cross and Herman 1988: 301–3]. Various administrative and physical devices were employed to ensure that the labour movement did not constitute itself into a set of general rather than industrial unions [Shahabuddeen 1986a; Cross and Herman 1988: 301]. Industrial relations arrangements therefore reinforced the ethnic specialization, and industrial disputes, like political conflicts, often took on racial and violent overtones [Cross and Herman 1988].

If the depression of the 1890s helped to modernize the sugar industry, subsequent developments made life difficult for the labour leaders. Endemic depressions seemed to be the order of the day. Wage reductions, a feature of the late nineteenth century, continued in this period and workers were forced to accept them. Well into the century workers enjoyed no legal right to organize or to unionize and there was no machinery for the settlement of industrial disputes. Additionally, technical change and rationalization of facilities reduced the volume and regularity of wage employment.

The opening decades of the twentieth century witnessed, therefore, the recrudescence of the struggle between wage labour and the plantation owners. Once more, sugar was in the forefront of this struggle. But effective organization of this industry had to await the formation of the Manpower Citizens'

Association (MPCA) by Ayub Edun in 1936. The interim organization of labour for industrial action was focused primarily on the urban and municipal workers and the dockers.

In 1919, the first trade union in the West Indies, the British Guiana Labour Union (BGLU), was established after a number of failed attempts. This union and its leader, Hubert Nathaniel Critchlow, were to dominate the movement until well into the 1930s. Reference was made earlier to the obstacles that collusion between colonial officials and plantation interests placed in the path of labour and peasant agriculture [Rodney 1981a]. In the face of these obstacles, which included reprisals by employers and physical exclusion from premises, the movement was less effective than it could have otherwise been. Between 1924 and 1937 membership suffered a precipitate decline, as did contributions, in the face of a tighter labour market and falling wages.

It has been observed that during this era the movement probably exerted more political influence than it had on the movement of wages and workers' conditions [Marx 1964]. The labour movement was, in other words, gradually becoming a vehicle for achieving political as well as industrial relations objectives. In spite of this, the BGLU was unable to convert itself into a political party. It is widely accepted that the quality of leadership of the movement was one of its major weaknesses. It is difficult to deny this assertion. Leadership rivalries and financial problems were characteristic of the movement. One factor was the inability to attract skilled leaders from among the black middle class which provided some advice to the movement but little else. This less than enthusiastic support may well have been attributable to the fact that the workers did not have the franchise, at least until 1947.

Despite these barriers the movement managed some remarkable achievements. But it was not an easy exercise. Although the Trade Union Act passed in 1921 gave legal recognition to the unions, the movement was not able to secure the right to organize and unionize until 1943 – seventy-two years after similar rights were obtained by workers in Britain. By 1937, machinery for the settlement of industrial disputes had to be enacted, although it was only instituted after industrial action on the part of the workers. From time to time the movement managed also to collaborate across the racial divide. In 1872, African labourers refused to help suppress East Indian strikers at Devonshire Castle. The two acted together in 1905, 1924 and again in 1939.

The struggle between wage labour and the plantation owners that was involved in the latter cases was, of course, not new, but by the 1930s the struggle was no longer entirely one-sided. With the termination of indentureship, wage rates and the unionization of sugar, labour could no longer be restricted by the device of binding workers by statute. Workers now had recourse to a body of national and international expertise and experience in industrial dispute with which to inform their struggle [Hart 1987]. The effective organization of the sugar industry came with the formation of the MPCA in 1936 and the industrial confrontation over its recognition which culminated in the bayoneting and fatal shooting of four strikers at Leonora in 1939.

By the 1940s the absence of the middle class contribution to the movement had apparently been remedied. In addition to the MPCA, the Transport and General Workers' Union and the Guiana Industrial Workers' Union (GIWU) had been formed, and formed by solidly middle class leaders. Discussions of the Caribbean labour movement in the late 1940s are not only replete with references to its domination by middle class spokesmen, but also with references to the frequency with which they compromised their credentials as leaders [Lewis 1958: 39; Harris 1979; Post 1978; Shahabuddeen 1983: 197; Quamina 1987; Marx 1964].[48] The result, it has been said, was to leave the movement with a markedly spontaneous and ad hoc character which frequently manifested itself in unorganized violence [Hart 1988: 6, 59; Shahabuddeen 1983: 198]. Doubtless the routine enlistment of the state machinery to confront and physically coerce the movement played a part also.

The Colonial Office displayed increasing concern about this radicalization of the labour movement which they recognized was attributable in part to the local administration's confrontational stance. They sought to isolate the radical labour leaders and promote institutionalized collective bargaining in order to stifle labour militancy [Craig 1977: 63]. The new approach, spelt out in the Passfield Memo of 1930, required unions to be encouraged but closely scrutinized. In 1938 the first labour advisers to the colonies were appointed and peddled the British Trades Union Congress' (TUC) line of noninvolvement in politics. The special commissions that had been established to help diffuse the tensions at the time of the riots in the 1930s all reflected this philosophy [Johnson 1978] but, in addition, called for attention to be paid to non-sugar agriculture and the "establishment of a peasantry" [Post 1978].

The devices of the Colonial Office were not sufficient to entirely suppress the radicalization and politicization of the labour movement. In 1938, the Labour Congress of the West Indies and British Guiana, meeting in Guyana, called, inter alia, for the nationalization of sugar, universal suffrage to an elected legislature, a land ceiling of 20 ha, a national minimum wage and a forty-four-hour work week. In Williams' words, "the nationalist movement was on the march,

World War II strengthened the nationalist cause . . . the Atlantic Charter was announced and the Four Freedoms enunciated" [Williams 1970: 474]. Three years earlier it had elected a woman as president [Latin America Bureau 1984].

In the late nineteenth century, as already mentioned, a challenge to sugar's political hegemony had been mounted briefly. Fuelled by the depression of the 1930s, the challenge was again taken up by the emerging middle classes which saw monoculture as a threat to their livelihoods. When the economic diversification they advocated was not pursued, they attacked the privileges of the sugar interests and clerics in the legislature [Greene 1974; Smith 1962: 51–57; Lewis 1968: ch. 10].

Whilst the consequential changes in the constitution in 1891 had brought the propertied 'coloured' Africans and other elements of the middle class, such as professional East Indians into the constitutional area, neither the leadership nor the quantum of representation were sufficient to turn the tide of planter policy immediately. The non-planter influence grew, however, and by the 1920s it was strong enough to mount some challenges. These challenges were reinforced by a 'wave' (1917–30) of industrial and political unrest throughout the region [Hart 1988: 6, 49, 50, 59]. In Guyana, riots of various kinds in 1924, and 1928 were suppressed with bullets.

The local newspapers such as the *New Daily Chronicle* were prompted to help awaken public consciousness and to provide a forum for the debate. In 1926 the first political party was formed by A.R.F. Webber, a man of 'colour', and Nelson Cannon [Webber 1988: xi] and others such as J.D. Greenidge, the son of Barbadian migrants. The party's agenda, although not particularly radical in that it sought constitutional reform, did not find favour with the administration and it did not really achieve the modest goals its founders had set. The founding of the first radical political party eluded the colony until the end of the Second World War.

Within the legislature, conflict between the rising and increasingly vocal working and middle classes, on the one hand, and the local representatives of the sugar and bauxite industries on the other, erupted in 1928. The immediate cause was a dispute over export taxes, [Shahabuddeen 1983: 122–23]. The Colonial Office resolved the matter by again disenfranchising the 'non-plantation' sector. In 1928 the (1891) constitution was suspended and amended to enable the Crown to substitute the functions of the Court of Policy, the legislature. Elections were held under this 1928 (Wadsworth) constitution in 1930 and 1935. Henceforth, only fourteen of the thirty members of the legislature were to be elected. Within the legislature, the governor could substitute and decide on any matter for the body itself. At this point, the fault line in the legislature shifted from planters versus colonial officials to representatives of non-planter interests versus the Colonial Office and others, including the civil service.

Under constitutional changes in 1943, the number of ex-officio members of the legislature were reduced from nineteen to three. Then two prominent union representatives were appointed to the Executive Committee, the highest decision-making body. These appointments heralded the movement's acceptance into the political mainstream, endowed them with respectability and facilitated the introduction of an unprecedented number of labour bills [Chase 1964: 105]. It did not, however, arrest the conflict [Shahabuddeen 1978]. A second wave of political and industrial unrest swept the region in the late 1930s and in 1948 industrial disputes in the Guyana sugar industry were again violently suppressed. But the Enmore rally and its violent suppression marked a turning point in the influence of the sugar industry and its control of the colony's fortunes.

By 1953 the power of the sugar interests had been eroded sufficiently to be reflected in legislative arrangements which permitted displacement of the planter interests by a fully representative legislature under universal adult suffrage.

Settlement Objectives

The stated objectives associated with the establishment of the first schemes did not alter radically during this second phase. However, the intention of saving repatriation costs was rendered redundant by the lack of interest exhibited by the newly time-expired labourers.

The substantive objective of the LSSs continued to be the establishment and retention of labour for the sugar industry. This objective now assumed added urgency because of the emergence of an absolute scarcity of labour. The state was so concerned that in 1932 the sugar producers were invited to identify appropriate sites on their plantations for LSSs and forms of land settlement [British Guiana 1932]. Although most estates held unutilized lands, many declined the establishment of schemes on those lands. Indeed, it was said of Lusignan, Mon Repos, Good Hope and Annandale Plantations, where 27 percent of the total of 3,215 ha lay uncultivated, that "the estate authorities do not wish to lease these lands, as they fear it might interfere with their present labour supply" [British Guiana 1932: 106, Appendix 8]. Those prepared to entertain the proposal did so on the condition that settlers agreed to be 'tenants at will' (see chapter 2) supplying a guaranteed quantum of labour to the estates. Two of the main schemes established during this phase, Vergenoegen and Windsor Forest cum annexis, were located in, or close to, the heartland of cane-growing Demerara and were apparently intended to help retain labour for plantations in that locality (whilst impeding rural-urban drift) [Standing and Sukdeo 1977]. The 1947–56 Development Plan [British Guiana 1948] specifically mentioned that Vergenoegen settlers would be able to obtain part-time employment on the two nearby plantations whilst the LSSs would also draw off the surplus population.

A related objective, or rather a variation on the old objective, was to facilitate further recruitment of additional overseas labour. In 1917, for example, proposals were formulated for the automatic settlement of time-expired labour on prepared land. The intention was to persuade the (British) Indian government to rescind its ban on further emigration to Guyana. The sugar industry's representatives attempted, unsuccessfully, to impose on the legislature the bill embodying their proposal [British Guiana 1919a; Jagan 1968].

A few years later, in 1927, a parliamentary commission recommended, inter alia, *interior settlements* populated by means of massive Jewish immigration[49] [Odle 1976: 72]. This process of groping for a hinterland thrust was in keeping with the new policy articulated in 1925, and although this specific set of proposals eventually culminated in what has been termed "the astonishing Jewish fiasco of 1938" [Lewis 1968: 26], it eventually spawned the first serious effort to identify hinterland areas suitable for settlement – a point to which we shall return [British Guiana 1939b].

The seminal paper on land policy [British Guiana 1928: 7, 8] identified agricultural production as a prime and separate objective of LSSs from the recruitment of wage labour for the sugar industry. Even though this was not implemented, the very fact that it could have been adopted as explicit and publicly stated policy in a near classic plantation economy is an indication of the waning planter strength in the legislature and its influence on the Colonial Office. The decline in the availability of imported food that occurred in 1915–17 and much more acutely in 1939–45 [Greenidge 1982], as a result of the two world wars, provides a simple explanation of this particular change in official pronouncements on the objectives of the LSSs.

It is notable, however, that the first LSSs to be mentioned in this context were those in Essequibo (Governor's Memo no. 1) [ICJ 1965] where there were no surviving sugar plantations. The Essequibo schemes were initially earmarked for rice production, and it should be noted that LSSs throughout Guyana have remained, with few exceptions, firmly wedded to rice (see Table 1). The objective was, however, not easily accepted even where no conflict with the interests of the planters occurred.

As was implied in the foregoing, acceptance of LSSs as a device for increasing nonagricultural production coincided with the need to provide employment in the face of plantation closures. In 1907 the Settlement Committee examined the abandoned plantations of The Bell and Mon Desir as possible sites for settling unemployed labour. After the last sugar plantation on the Essequibo ceased operations in 1925, the need became more urgent.

So one new objective which emerged during the period of economic depression was the provision of employment for surplus rural labour. The views of the 1897 Royal Commission have already been cited. In the 1920s and 1930s these views were again aired by a royal commission [Shahabuddeen 1983]. It should be borne in mind, however, that these commissions were established to attenuate current problems and to head off crises, not to formulate fundamental solutions or restructure the mode or social relations of production [Johnson 1978].

What now confronted the Colonial Office and the local administration was exactly that which the Colonial Office and its directorate had feared. There existed a class of workers with little prospect of employment except through wage labour. The depression now ensured that there was little or no wage employment available. The local planters, whilst also concerned about actual or impending riots and distubances which could result from high unemployment levels, were more preoccupied with the need to preserve an accessible supply of labour for plantations in Demerara and Berbice. It was with some relief, therefore, that they conceded the need for a device such as the LSSs – in Demerara and Berbice only.

Consequently, the enthusiasm with which this objective was pursued by the local administration is a matter of controversy [Jagan 1966: 6–7, 112; Smith 1962: 88; Lewis 1968]. But what does emerge is that whatever local enthusiasm was manifested was the direct result of the work of governors such as Lethem, who together with his civil engineer may well have been recalled from their posts for overzealous pursuit of a policy of diversification [Shahabuddeen 1983: 251–52].

The Framework of the Settlement Administration

So evolved the development of alternative economic activities and therefore outlets for labour, particularly rice farming and mining. In addition, the dismantling of barriers to the acquisition of improved land and challenges to the political hegemony of the planters, in spite of the growing monopoly in the production and marketing of sugar, served to facilitate the growth of other economic activities. To these undercurrents might be added the impact of two wars, global in range, the rise of bauxite mining beyond the coast of Guyana and the termination of indentureship and sugar-sponsored immigration. The changes were reflected in the planters' loss of legislative power, the growing resistance of taxpayers and merchants to financing the needs of the sugar industry, the Depression, and the need to produce food for local and regional markets.

Prior to 1925, the identification and planning of the schemes remained the responsibility of the ad hoc and departmental committees to which reference was made earlier. Government involvement in the schemes up to that time remained minimal. The major changes in administration in 1925 were heralded by policy papers, the first of which was prepared by the governor in 1924. Fourteen principles were intended to govern the process of future settlement [British Guiana 1928: 7, 8, 1929a, 1929b]. As already mentioned, LSSs for agricultural production were to be a prime and separate objective from the recruitment of wage labour for the sugar industry. The principles included the following: LSSs were to be open to all the existing agricultural population and not merely East Indians; no increase in taxation was to be levied to finance the establishment of new schemes; in future, both coastal and hinterland settlements were to be considered; and at least one main agricultural activity was to be developed on each scheme and that was to be integrated with livestock farming.

In 1925 the legislature acceded to the governor's recommendation concerning the establishment of a board and secretariat on land settlement [British Guiana 1925]. The functions of the board were to be purely advisory and included the:

    i. coordination of existing information on and the results of LSSs

    ii. initiation and preparation of proposals for LSSs with the assistance of other departments

    iii. examination, and preparation of reports on questions referred to it by the government

Subsequently, in 1929, a colonization department was established and it absorbed the duties and staff of the Immigration Department, that is, the operation and running of the existing schemes. The chief colonization officer (the director of agriculture), his deputy, the commissioner of lands and mines and the conservator of forests were to be members of the department. Apart from a brief spell in 1932–33, the Department of Agriculture was, to all intents and purposes, the key agency in this arrangement; reflecting for the first time the intention that some seriousness was to be attached to the goal of production.

In 1929, on the basis of a memorandum (no. 2), an investigation into the suitability of the North West District was undertaken. A 'chemist-ecologist' was appointed to undertake research in those areas considered of likely importance for settlement. Furthermore, work was undertaken to prepare Henrietta, Essequibo as an agricultural station and ultimately an 'auxiliary' LSS, and land clearing commenced in 1929 for the establishment of an LSS at Bush Lot, Essequibo in accordance with the memorandum (no. 4) [Wilson 1929].

Other changes in policy which were to prove of significance for LSSs, were accepted by the Legislative Council in 1943, as a result of recommendations by a committee on land settlement. By then it was recognized that viable land settlements required more than the mere allocation of land to settlers (see also GSO 389/17). An agency was to be established and charged exclusively with the promotion and development of LSSs.

It should not be thought that these changes were implemented without resistance or that they were unidirectional. Thus, although it was agreed to establish a land Settlement department, this was not implemented until 1954. At some point in the interim the administration of the existing settlements, with the exception of Anna Regina, was transferred to the Department of Local Government. Planning and policy were to be the responsibility of an advisory committee, including the commissioner of lands and mines. This new administration was required to ensure the provision of facilities additional to those commonly furnished on the previous schemes.

Underlying Issues and Paradoxes

During the entire period 1906–47 some nine LSSs were established. There was a marked lull between 1924 and 1944, as may be seen from Table 1. The pattern of these settlements was in keeping with that of the previous phase, namely all schemes were sited on the coast (see Map 2) in spite of the policies promulgated in 1924–28.[50] Furthermore, all the schemes survived as smallholder farms in one form or another.

The practice of utilizing abandoned sugar lands for LSSs remained the norm during this phase. The inadequacies of this approach had, however, become so evident that the Olivier Sugar Commission (1930) felt obliged to recommend that "land given to small farmers for settlement should not be the worst land in the country and the question of its suitability for sugar should not be taken into consideration" [Williams 1970: 448].

Faced with a straight choice between protecting the interests of smallholders in general and one of the major spheres of interest – the metropole, emergent (nascent) rural capital, plantations – the local administration opted to submerge smallholder interests. This assertion can be substantiated with the help of examples in pricing policies, expenditure policy, tenure arrangements and D&I policies. These issues are explored below:

Tenure

The issue of land tenure affords an instructive illustration of the resolution of conflicting class/group interests by the state. Lewis had suggested that concern with improving the conditions of tenure may have prompted state interest in LSSs in the Caribbean [1951: 60, 64]. There is, however, no evidence to support this in the case of Guyana. Rather, not only had the establishment of LSSs benefited the sugar plantations, but the tenure changes which were implemented tended to reinforce this privileged position.

In the 1900s, as the economic climate improved, a debate was kindled over the basis on which state lands were to be alienated – lease or freehold. From a theoretical viewpoint, the two forms of tenure can be made to embody exactly the same safeguards about beneficial occupation – around which the debate raged. If Lewis was right in asserting "that the use of any land, must be subject to public controls, in the interest of maintaining the productivity of the land" [Lewis 1951: 88], the state had been palpably negligent. Most of the 1,572 sq km alienated by the Dutch colonial power (up to 1814) had been subsequently abandoned or neglected. Although existing legislation allowed resumption of such land by the state, "this right of the Crown had never been used directly" [IBRD 1953: 206]. The state was either unable or unwilling to enforce this legislation on the beneficial occupation of freehold land [British Guiana 1917a, 1917b, 1943; West Indies Royal Commission 1946; Crane 1938].

The reason for this inaction on the part of the state is not hard to find. Engrossment of land by the plantations was a well tried and accepted device for denying land to competitors, including smallholders. In 1948, for example, 44 percent of the country's empoldered land lay idle under the control of the plantations. Given that control, it is hardly surprising to find that the local administration was impotent on this score.

In 1905 legislation was passed ostensibly to enforce beneficial occupation of freehold land. The timing suggests that it may well have been formulated in reaction to the reduction in land prices and aimed at the smallholders who had recently acquired land. The concerns of the planters appear to have been heightened by competing demand for labour resulting from, inter alia, the increasing attractiveness of own-account rice farming. It was claimed, however, that this act empowering the government to repossess derelict land was too cumbersome and quite ineffective.

In spite of the well documented disadvantages of leases – discouragement of long-term investment, inadequacy as collateral, difficulty of transfer [British Guiana 1917b] – they were adopted in place of the outright sale of Crown lands in 1913. Leases, it was argued, would ensure that "disposal of land would go hand in hand with beneficial occupation" [British Guiana 1917b]. This was the line of argument that seemed to find favour with the planters.

There is no denying the continuing popularity of freehold property. Nath has asserted that most of the prospective settlers, former victims of capricious tenure arrangements on the plantations, were wary of, or hostile to, leasehold. The depth of this aversion, however, was probably overrated, as witnessed by the prevalence of squatting by rural East Indians to which we have already adverted. As it happens, analysis of the deliberations of, and submission to, the committee set up in 1917 to recommend appropriate tenure arrangements shows clearly that the fight for freehold was carried not so much by the peasants and smallholders as by a lobby comprised of wealthy members of the rural community especially and including East Indian landlords, moneylenders and merchants, who also favoured the sale of larger parcels of land and higher sale prices [British Guiana 1917].

Following the 1913 statute, ninety-nine-year leases or licences of occupancy were issued but in 1921 these were reduced to twenty-one years. Over the period 1919–38, conditional freehold grants were available for ten and later five years.[51] However, abuse of all the regulations rendered the distinction between leases, and freehold academic. In 1938, therefore, the issue of conditional grants was suspended [Gyanchand 1963].

In 1943 it was decided that settlers should be offered leases of twenty-one years duration, in the first instance, with the possibility of extension after ten years.[52] There were to be penalties for failure to develop land so leased. This manner of resolution of the problem no doubt owed a lot to the intervention of the Second World War and the efforts of the local administration to promote self-sufficiency in food production.

Having so resolved the issue, however, the state was still unable to enforce the beneficial occupation clauses after 1945. Extensive subdivision and fragmentation of ownership, land speculation by landlords, and inelasticity of holding size were characteristic of both forms of tenure, although fragmentation and subletting seemed particularly widespread under leasehold. One notable example of fragmentation was cited by Brown in Windsor Forest where a settler had 4.05 ha spread over four plots [see, for example, West Indies Royal Commission 1946].

Further insights into the nature of the relationship between the state and the settlers are afforded by another aspect of tenure, namely, the issue of land rents, D&I rates and purchase prices. The prices at which land on LSSs were sold appear to have been influenced by the need to recover the costs associated with the acquisition and rehabilitation of the plantations. To the extent that the latter costs were exorbitant, the settlers could be said to have been 'taxed' to finance the restructuring of the sugar plantations. There are conflicting views over the financial terms on which the lands should have been made available to settlers. Lewis argued that the terms of purchase/rental appear to have been much less generous than those of neighbouring countries. Repayment periods, for example, varied from five to twenty-five years on the Guyana schemes. On comparable schemes in Puerto Rico and Jamaica, the average repayment periods appear to have been twenty-five and forty years, respectively [Lewis 1951: 91].

Discussing the cost, Lewis, in the first comprehensive examination of Caribbean LSSs, contended that the annual cost of each lease should be almost zero. With relatively low interest rates prevailing at the time and given the long-term nature of the land settlement exercise, rent collection could easily become "a system by which the state enriches itself at the expense of the farmers" [Lewis 1951: 91], if prices were not carefully determined.

It is evident that LSS rents and leases varied widely – from as high as $49/ha on the older schemes to $0.77/ha in the case of some established towards the close of the period. Holdings at Windsor Forest were leased in 1915 for ninety-nine years at a fixed annual rental of $14.83/ha. Settlers at Bush Lot were able to purchase their holdings outright after three years rental. The rent amounted to $17.30/ha and the $1.21/ha plot cost $500 taking the rent into account. The families at Cane Grove, a post-1943 scheme, received land on the basis of a lease but at the end of that period the purchase price was $0.49/ha.

The variations may have been informed by estimated maintenance costs on the various schemes as well as market prices (see chapter 3). It has been argued that the rents appear to have been high relative to those charged for non-scheme land [Colonial Office 1942]. Nath asserted that in the case of Anna Regina, the twin problems of high rents ($14.83/ha in 1930) and small size forced most farmers into debt [Nath 1950: 106–10].[53] There certainly was a problem of growing arrears of rents and other charges. We have already observed that the legislature had provided planters with land at $12.37/ha. On the other hand, Lacey, in a 1952 study, contended that rental and irrigation charges on existing schemes were low relative to the cost of provision of the services provided. In this he was supported by Dumont [1963: 115]. But Young ventured an alternative explanation to the effect that "valuable time had already been lost, and the failure to impose a rate from the outset had given the settlers time to develop the characteristic aversion to the payment of a rate" [1958: 157].

Arrears

Some idea of the significance of current debts and arrears on the schemes in the 1930s may be gleaned from available data. Of the five schemes, including Bush Lot and Huis t'Dieren, for which such data are available, only two generated operational surpluses in either of the years 1933 and 1934. In Clonbrook, 1934 debts represented 260 percent of the deficit on the current account [British Guiana, Administrative Reports of Director of Agriculture 1933, 1934].

The question of the adequacy of plots allocated reared its head during the 1940s. It was decided that cultivation plots should range from 1.2 to 6.1 ha depending on "whether or not areas adjacent to the settlement provide the settlers with other avenues of employment" [British Guiana 1948]. This suggests that when other opportunities were available, the LSSs should not be providing sufficient land to assure full-time employment. If McCormack's claim that during this period schemes were being established to provide full-time employment to settlers [1979: 6] is correct, it could not be considered a geographically universal objective. Indeed, the reality seemed to have been that in the interests of protecting existing industries from competition for labour, underemployment on LSSs was fostered.

Domestic food economy and labour demand

Another important dimension, which in a systemic sense served to inhibit the development of the LSSs, was the structure of the economy. Dependence on imported supplies of food and its corollary, circumscribed local markets for domestically produced commodities particularly food, were basic characteristics of the plantation system [Beckford 1972; Pryor 1982]. Initially, no attention had been devoted to the crops to be produced on the schemes (see Table 1). Settlers produced ground provisions such as cassava and eddoes for their own consumption and, like their counterparts in the villages, they disposed of their surplus produce as best they could [Adamson 1972].

Without the hostilities in 1914–18 and 1939–45 those characteristics would have remained unchallenged. The significance of the two European wars lies in the impact they had on this market for foodstuff. The presence of British and US troops in the region added to the demand for food whilst the wars themselves reduced the inflow and increased the cost of imported foods. Given the neglect of the domestic food sector, urgent and sustained action had to be undertaken to cope with this new situation. Incentives were provided for expanded food production. Until the advent of that war, the state's involvement in regulating and promoting development of the non-plantation agricultural sector had been limited to the grading of rice (1930), the inspection of livestock and the licensing and certification of timber for export [Shahabuddeen 1983: 260]. Some idea of the impact that the demands of war brought on the economy and the domestic food sector may be had from the case of rice, the main crop in this regard.

Rice was first grown in Guyana in the eighteenth century by slaves. Apparently, efforts by plantations to develop the crop on a large scale on the basis of varieties imported from the US failed. Subsequently, 'dry land' varieties of rice continued to be cultivated in the villages, but these varieties were relatively low yielding. The first significant expansion in rice production occurred with the conjuncture of the wheat and rice shortages of 1901 and 1915–17 and the availability of reasonably well-irrigated land to which reference was made in the previous section. East Indians, like the Africans, were familiar with the cultivation of the crop but, unlike the latter, were prepared to cultivate it under 'aquatic' conditions.[54]

In face of the improved market situation, rice production expanded rapidly although somewhat unevenly. Self-sufficiency was achieved in 1918 [Hanley 1984] and a pre-1930 peak of 25,000 ha was attained in 1919. A constraint to increased production and exports was speculation and the low level of the forces of production. As was mentioned earlier, the administration paid little attention to these problems except for the grading of rice. Among the consequences of this neglect was the industry's inability to maintain the Caribbean market, established in the latter 1900s.

The factors influencing the local administration's approach were twofold. On the one hand, they were faced by the sugar industry which was concerned about the competition for labour. At the same time, extensive speculation on the part of Georgetown merchants who were, as it happens, well represented in the administration, could not be controlled. Speculation in 1910–15, for example, adversely affected production and availability. In fact, such was the strength of the merchants' influence in the administration that attempts by the governor to address the problem in 1914–18 almost cost him his job [Odle 1976]. The administration therefore remained wary of upsetting these powerful comprador, and mainly Portuguese, interests.

The first attempt to improve the quality of paddy varieties was organized in 1927[55] but the export market remained unattended until 1930. A rice marketing board was established in 1932 with this objective in mind. However, in 1938 the board was suspended for four months with disastrous consequences. A serious attempt to tackle the issue of marketing had to await more propitious circumstances.

Those circumstances took the form of the Second World War. Between 1940 and 1943, eastern supplies of rice to the British West Indies were cut off and the local availability of food declined. Under cover of the wartime emergency regulations and hostilities, measures were taken to curb destructive competition in the export market and to enforce price and quality control and licensing of rice exports. The Defence (Rice Control) Regulations of 1939 were notable in this regard. Under this provision, the board was to control, purchase, sell and distribute all rice. All production except the producers' domestic needs was to be delivered to the board [Caribbean Commission 1947].

Assistance was also extended to the farmers by the Colonial Department of Agriculture. That assistance included intensified research into varieties in a bid to increase yields and the hardiness of the crop, selection of appropriate agronomic techniques and the provision of technical advice through extension services. The area under rice expanded rapidly. By 1946 the acreage devoted to rice cultivation overtook that under sugar. The state was even in a position to sponsor an agreement for the export of rice to the British West Indies.[56]

Mandle has shown conclusively that after 1945, expanded rice cultivation was only supported when its demands on labour and land resources did not conflict with those of the sugar industry [Mandle 1973: ch. 9]. It is clear from the development plan that the dominance of sugar was to be re-established after 1945. After 1945, therefore, the wartime incentives were dismantled. In addition, restrictions were placed on double-cropping by the industry, and strenuous efforts were made to promote mechanization so that the labour demand profile of rice might be lowered and flattened [British Guiana 1948]. In this regard, Thomas has argued that the promotion of small cane cultivation in 1948 was a related ploy to further tie smallholders to the sugar industry [Ghai et al. 1979: 218].

The attempt to resolve the sugar and rice industries' competing demands for labour generated its own problems in that underemployment on small farms was aggravated, as was already mentioned. In the presence of bottlenecks elsewhere in the rice industry, for example in milling and marketing, increased mechanization probably reduced per hectare employment of labour at a time when annual increments to the rural population were far in excess of net rural job creation. Between 1939 and 1951, for example, the average number of days per week worked by sugar labour amounted to 3.5–3.7. In 1946, two-thirds of gainfully occupied farm labour had to find additional sources of employment or income.

Financial support and infrastructure

Facilities on the schemes remained poor, although an improvement over comparable peasant settlements, because of the inadequacy of investment. In 1938 a proposal from a local magistrate called for a target of at least $700 per settler on the schemes [Crane 1938]. The commission formulating proposals for the settlement of Jews in Guyana's hinterland recommended per caput expenditures of $1,500–$2,000 to cover, inter alia, the cost of land clearing and fencing, a house, a shed, tools and working capital and food until the first harvest. In addition, the state was expected to provide roads as well as infrastructural and commercial facilities [British Guiana 1948]. In Puerto Rico the farm homestead scheme provided assets of $3,000–$4,500 per family (12 ha farm) excluding housing and a total of $479/ha ($5,800 per family) excluding land purchase, clearing roads, schools and potable water supply [Lewis 1951].

The executive chose not to implement the recommendations of the 1943 committee which the legislature had adopted by resolution. Those recommendations included pre-settlement D&I, erection of houses by the government and the provision of living amenities [Development Plan 1947: 291–92]. A rough estimate of LSS investment costs suggests that the state spent considerably less than $700 per family (excluding land acquisition) on the most generously endowed scheme in Guyana [British Guiana 1925–34: 17].[57]

The relative miserliness with respect to LSS expenditure in Guyana was reflected in the range and quality of facilities on the schemes. One exception to this general picture of meagre facilities was to be found at Anna Regina where a rice factory acquired by the government with the estate was sold to the farmers' cooperative [British Guiana 1917b: 5]. Mechanical equipment for cultivation and harvesting was made available for hire to settlers at Vergenoegen. But, generally speaking, Lewis' strictures, about the need to make capital available for modern commercial cultivation as an integral part of settlement policy, went unheeded [1951: 77, 83].

The fiscal dilemma

The investment required to adequately furnish an LSS could constitute a significant burden on taxpayers, particularly in view of Guyana's narrow tax base and regressive tax structure [Adamson 1972]. On a per acre basis, fewer resources would have been required in the short run to support the existing sugar industry. In the long run, however, given the problem of markets, the sugar industry as such would lead the economy to a cul-de-sac. This longer-term problem was not given much of an airing, for the representatives of the planters, still wielding considerable influence in the legislature, were able to make the case against smallholders on the grounds of fiscal responsibility and cost effectiveness. Support for small farmers was sacrificed ostensibly in pursuit of a balanced budget.

This is ironic because the fiscal system rested heavily on the non-sugar, non-plantation low-income groups, including settlers. The sugar interests and the middle classes waged a long and largely effective battle to block efforts to distribute the burden more widely via the reintroduction of income taxes, for example. As late as 1947 there were only 2,951 persons and institutions paying income taxes [British Guiana 1947, 1961].

Income tax was reintroduced in 1929 but, on the basis of the other recommendations of the Small-Wilson Commission, the export tax which had been introduced in 1915 was abolished. Between 1932 and 1952 a number of miscellaneous and basically minor taxes – acreage and distillery – were introduced. The main impost of substance finding favour with the legislature was an excess profits tax, which obviously crept in under cover of the hostilities (1941) and was just as surreptitiously removed in 1945 [Shahabuddeen 1983: 121–23].

Indirect taxes therefore accounted for the bulk of central government revenues, undergoing a massive leap from 39 percent in 1947 to 54 percent in 1948 and attaining a peak of 57 percent in 1951 and 1952 [British Guiana 1947; 1961]. Customs duties on imported food, drink and oils accounted for the lion's share of revenues from indirect taxes. Subsidies, which had been provided on certain foods during the Second World War, were removed in 1949. Thus, the import duties, which had been previously remitted on flour, salted fish, condensed milk, split peas and cocoa powder, were discontinued in 1949. In their place, a stabilization fund was established for flour and bread. In addition, an advisory committee on the cost of living was established.

The effectiveness of these alternative measures has not been ascertained, but the available data on the cost of living of both Georgetown and "working class East Indian families on sugar plantations" suggest a significant deterioration in real incomes over the period 1938–51. In the case of sugar workers, the index moved from 100 to 299 [British Guiana Annual Reports 1935–52].

The smallholders' need for financial support was treated as a peculiar psychological weakness or aberration. Hence, in the 1947 development plan, which also included a framework for future LSSs, it was felt necessary to mention

that there is no intention of indefinitely sheltering settlers by affording them facilities not possessed by other areas; when once the land is beneficially occupied, it is considered that the settlers should form a local authority for the management of their affairs and so provide for maintenance of works in the settlement as in ordinary villages and country districts under the administration of the Local Government Board. [British Guiana 1948]

Earlier, the royal commission, in discussing the same issue, had argued that, "experience has shown that settlers may be spoiled and lose their self-reliance if they are led to believe that they can rely upon Government for financial support whenever they encounter difficulties" [West Indies Royal Commission 1946: 315].

Whilst the statement implicitly recognizes the concerns of non–East Indians about discriminatory treatment, the rationale masked the fact that in withholding significant support for non-plantation agriculture in general and the rice industry in particular, the state was protecting the interests of sugar. The Moyne Commission report, for example, referred to the propensity of West Indians in general and East Indians in particular to be deviant with respect to paying rents and rates. The commission had no doubt that this deviant behaviour was attributable to the peculiar makeup of West Indians [West Indies Royal Commission 1946: xvii]. This conclusion is not, however, very helpful. There may indeed be some noneconomic causes which, in any case, could not be deemed psychological. But if one were to treat the commission's observations charitably they could be pointing to the type of settler. It could be argued that poor settler selection contributed in some degree to nonpayment of rates [Nath 1950], but this factor is much overrated and these type of explanations are akin to the 'dummy variable' employed in statistical estimation. However, this perception informed not only the treatment of rent but of LSSs in general.

Both Moyne and the local administration, had information at their disposal clearly demonstrating that the parlous economic state of many settlers was attributable to specific and identifiable factors. In one report, for example, it was argued that,

in the light of experience, it seems improbable that settlements with rice as the main money crop, with inadequate market for food crops and stock and no access for tenants to additional sources of income from wage employment, can repay the capital cost of land and housing and also the provision and maintenance of irrigation and drainage. [Colonial Office 1942: 113]

In fact, the accumulation of arrears and difficulty in cost recovery are common problems on LSSs throughout the world even today. There are many complex reasons for these phenomenona.[58]

In Guyana, many of the settlers actually retained places on the sugar plantations where they were provided not only with a range of social and communal services but also the decisions about the management of such services. Plantation residents had never been called upon to pay rates, sit on local councils or assume responsibility for their own communal amenities [Young 1958: 159–61; Lewis 1968: 266–69]. Initially, therefore, the settlers saw these requirements of non-plantation life as unfair burdens. So there was great reluctance not only to pay rates but to participate in local government administration even when settlers were entirely divorced from the plantations. Additionally, more recent work elsewhere has pointed to the adverse consequences that poor operations and maintenance may have on arrears or cost recovery [IBRD 1985: 50].

A case study

Before leaving the issue of the administration's attitude to smallholders and settlers, it would be instructive to look briefly at the case of Anna Regina which affords a very interesting example of the moments of state involvement in LSSs. It was said of Anna Regina in 1883 that "the works on this plantation are the finest in the colony" [Daily Argosy 1883: 1]. The plantation, famed for its 'yellow crystal' sugar, was purchased by the state in 1923 and together with the adjacent, abandoned lands was transferred to the Essequibo Land Settlement Ltd, a large private concern, to produce and process cane.

The entire property was subsequently sold to private interests when the company failed. In 1930 a portion, consisting of Bush Lot and four other plantations, was repurchased by the state for a seventy-seven-family experimental LSS.[59] The settlers were intended to grow rice on the 1.21 ha plots which they rented at $6.04 each. In 1934 and again in 1937, however, the land, except for Bush Lot, was leased en bloc to a rice miller for subletting. This step was taken because of the "considerable difficulty . . . encountered, particularly in connection with the financing of tenants and the recovery of advances and rents" [Colonial Office 1942: 113]. According to the same source, this was the only arrangement that allowed the government to balance its books for this group of plantations.[60] It should not be thought that this was an isolated example, for Plantation Ruby was also bought, sold and reacquired in a similar fashion [British Guiana 1929a: 1].

It is difficult, in the circumstances, not to be persuaded that the state's involvement was aimed at facilitating private agrarian capitalists rather than enhancing or promoting production under the peasant mode, and the fact that these schemes fell outside of the sugar belt should not be missed. The restrictive tenure conditions prevailing on these private schemes [British Guiana 1929c] point convincingly to efforts to establish the schemes as pools of cheap labour. Only under the pressure of wartime food needs and the cover of the emergency regulations (1940) did the government take over the plantation in its entirety and establish a formal LSS [ICJ 1965; McCormack 1979: 9–10].

Nationalization and its terms

The government continued to acquire plantations and estates on which to settle East Indians. Some were purchased and others, such as Windsor Forest on the West Coast of the Demerara (WCD), were acquired at execution sale.

The bulk of the state's investment in the schemes was devoted to such land acquisition and its reconditioning. Some idea of the relative magnitude involved may be had from Table 5. In relation to the two post-1905 schemes, the proportion of total expenditures devoted to the purchase of the plantation was 16–18 percent. It has been estimated that successful LSSs in Puerto Rico involved a comparable figure of 12 percent. Post [1978] has suggested that in Jamaica the figure was well in excess of that.

What is distinctive about the cost structure of the schemes in Guyana is not so much the inordinate share devoted to land acquisition (to which we shall return) but the proportion devoted to reconditioning (including D&I) and layout. Both these services were often provided by British firms and it was no coincidence that after 1929 layout costs were met out of the Colonial Development and Welfare (CDW) funds. This was part of the British government's attempt to promote employment in the UK.

The incidence of state purchases of sugar lands appears to have been less prevalent after 1920. However, the prices paid for those assets that were acquired became a bitter bone of public contention. This politicization probably arose because the objectives became transparent. In many cases, the state found resources with which to purchase plantations without any clear objective in terms of intended use. This is further proof that the purchases were often undertaken to protect specific private interests. Two cases in point were the abandoned estates of Cane Grove and La Bonne Mere which were acquired because neighbouring plantation owners feared that they would have been acquired by 'undesirable landlords' [Government of Guyana 1974: 296].

There can be little doubt that the prices paid for purchases such as Cane Grove – $100,000 – could not have reflected the full value of the investment in the property. The planters had initially acquired the land from the state at zero or peppercorn prices. Furthermore, during the booms and periods of buoyant sugar prices, many planters were able to recoup their investments (often in a relatively short space of time) [Adamson 1972; Rodney 1979]. It was therefore argued that these acquisitions should have commanded nominal prices.

In any case, when the state in turn disposed of some of these assets, it received far less than the acquisition cost. Plantation Onverwagt bought by the Abary Cattle Ranch Company from the state in 1910 for $1.24/ha was reacquired by the state at $61.78/ha, when eventually a price was settled. When settlement failed, Nooten Zuil had to be sold for far less than the price at which it had been acquired by the government [Nath 1950: 34]. The costs of other purchases such as plantations Campbellville and La Penitence were also condemned. It was alleged that the particularly generous acquisition costs of some of these plantations was not unrelated to the fact that some senior civil servants were shareholders in the companies that either owned or controlled them [Jagan 1966: 105–15].

Resolving D&I plantation and smallholder needs

The case of D&I affords a good insight into the manner of the state's mediation between the peasantry and agrarian capital. It is clear that schemes established during this phase had the benefit of improved D&I facilities. It can be argued that this effort was a by-product of the drive to improve the D&I facilities on the plantations. The need for a more comprehensive approach to water control had been evident since the latter part of the nineteenth century. During the 1920s, a twenty-year sketch plan was formulated by the colony's consulting engineer, F.W. Hutchinson. Hutchinson argued that the then current system of irrigation, by diversion from rivers together with the continued empoldering of the flood plains of the rivers, would eventually lead to flooding, inter alia. In its stead Hutchinson proposed a comprehensive and less wasteful coastal irrigation system that involved the storage of flood waters in shallow reservoirs behind the old plantations [IBRD 1953: 193–206, 246–47]. However, rather than implement these proposals, the legislature approved piecemeal schemes primarily geared to the plantations' needs. It would be useful to look at a specific case.

The Bonasika Water Conservancy, for example, to which we referred earlier, apparently served both the needs of the nearby plantations and the Vergenoegen LSS. Its extension to the LSS, however, was an afterthought. The immediate stimulus for the conservancy was the 1938–39 drought which cost the West Coast and West Bank Demerara river plantations some 7,500 tons of sugar, worth G\$0.4 million [Development Plan 1947: 109]. This scheme, like the East Coast Conservancy and the Torani Canal, represented extensive modifications to the concepts informing the original proposals in the twenty-year sketch plan. It has been alleged that this partisan modification of his plans and inability to make headway in the face of planter opposition so dismayed the engineer that he eventually resigned in disgust [Jagan 1966: 111–13; Lewis 1968; Smith 1962: 88].

Results

In the preceding section we attempted to show that underlying many of the changes in policy taking place during this era was a desire to preserve, for the sugar producers, such numbers of labourers as they deemed necessary for profitable operations. The schemes failed as a device for stimulating a further inflow of East Indian immigrants. For reasons that were entirely external, namely hostilities in Europe, the proposed Jewish 'experiment' was also aborted.

Promotion of non-sugar agriculture

Attempts to acquire immigrant labour for hinterland settlement foundered in the face of the hostility of the sugar interests and ostensibly a shortage of funds. Prior to 1930 no serious effort had been made to assess the resources of the

4.2 A fairly typical camp of hinterland travellers, late nineteenth century.
Source: Crookall 1898.

hinterland, but it was widely felt that most of the soils were poor and there was little by way of commercial minerals apart from gold [British Guiana 1933, 1939b, 1943]. This conclusion was hardly surprising, for, in the words of one author, "a Commissioner of the Interior genuinely interested in the interior was a nine days wonder" [Lewis 1968: 267]. A separate Geological Surveys Department was only established after 1945. Livestock raised in the Rupununi had to be moved 250 miles on the hoof to market with no provision for fattening or resting.

A most striking insight into the consequences of this attitude might be gleaned from Waugh's little known travel book of 1934, mentioned earlier, of which one reviewer in the *Irish Times* said, "he debunks the romantic notions attached to rough travelling – his trip is difficult, dangerous and extremely uncomfortable . . . [his] travel books are eloquent warnings against travel". Waugh himself, having outlined the frustrations experienced and risks he encountered in 1932–33 and the absence of government representatives or shops for hundreds of square miles, explains that, "much of this chronicle, perhaps too much – has dealt with the difficulties of getting from place to place. But that seems to me unavoidable, for it is the preoccupation of two-thirds of the traveller's waking hours and the matters of all his nightmares" [1934: 151].

4.3 Warden's residence at Arakaka, North West District, 1909. *Source*: Bayley 1909.

Plantations and other agricultural ventures in the interior could not command assistance from the colonial administration. The excuse that lent itself to blocking such assistance was fiscal responsibility or the need for a balanced budget. In 1925 there had been a promise that the schemes would not be financed by additional fiscal impositions on the urban taxpayers. In addition, between the late 1920s and 1948 the local treasury laboured under severe constraints. The political crisis of the succeeding years would have made it somewhat problematic to overtly renege on the 1925 promise and the sugar planters were not prepared to finance, via increased taxes, schemes for their own development let alone those for non-sugar activities. It would hardly come as a surprise, therefore, to find that attempts to establish rubber, coffee and citrus ventures foundered on the rocks of fiscal ortho-doxy. This left the hinterland, particularly the north-west of the country, with a Cinderella image or, as the Jewish Settlement Committee put it, "a graveyard of lost expectations" [British Guiana 1933: 9].

With regard to the employment impact of the LSSs, it has been estimated that wage labour in agriculture declined by some 76 percent over the period 1891–1952, whereas the number of small holders increased from 3,100 to 21,000. LSSs at best accounted for less than half of the latter increase. Unemployment and underemployment were, however, characteristics of the economic life of the settlers.

Vergenoegen was not atypical and Dumont estimated that on that scheme only 40 percent of the settlers were 'real' (full-time) farmers [1963: 110]. In spite of the apparent need, no scheme of any kind was established in the Essequibo until 1930 and then it only took the form of an 'experiment'. In a sense, therefore, LSSs had merely served to mask the proletarianization of rural labour. The schemes continued to be reservoirs of labour for the plantations.

Ethnicity

One final aspect of the employment impact of the schemes relates to the category of persons recruited. By and large, those selected were redundant sugar workers and employees of the relevant estates. This was certainly the case with respect to Windsor Forest and Anna Regina. Former sugar workers were settled at Cane Grove. Sometimes occupants of adjacent villages were also incorporated, as occurred at Vergenoegen.

The schemes did, however, remain overwhelmingly East Indian settlements. They retained this character in spite of the 1905 legislation [Crane 1938], in spite of proposals for schemes to be established in areas with interested African settlers and notwithstanding the policy paper of 1925. Indeed, in the latter regard, as early as 1929 a proposal involving a pilot scheme was announced – for East Indians.

This exclusivity was also seen in the villages. There were predictable consequences. Reference was made earlier to observations by Potter and Rodney about the East Indian influx into African villages. The result of these two trends has been the rise of exclusively East Indian villages even as African villages are becoming more mixed.[61] This and problems of squatting, to which reference has already been made, have sometimes led to abortive attempts by African villages to restrict land sales to East Indians.[62] Silverman cites the reaction of the village council of Bush Lot to such an attempt by the landowners of Hopetown, West Coast Berbice, a neighbouring village. With that at the backs of their minds, they approached a boundary dispute with another African village, Golden Grove, so that "the racism was transferred to Golden Grove" [1980: 113].

The fact that places on schemes were available at nominal cost whilst villagers or Africans on the estates were still being actively excluded from the land market may have been overlooked in time. In many cases the settlers ended up with facilities little better than their (African) village counterparts. However, the few advantages that they enjoyed, such as land with varying degrees of irrigation and generally better drainage, meant that some were well placed to take advantage of opportunities in the marketplace for domestic grain, namely rice.

A.A. Thorne took up this very issue in his memorandum on behalf of the British Guiana Workers' League to the Moyne Commission. He specifically referred to racially exclusive LSSs as a device to promote East Indian over Africans [Cross and Herman 1988: 302–3]. As late as 1937, one observer could claim, in calling for equal access for all races to these settlements, that "such petty attempts at land settlement as have been made in the past have been restricted to the East Indian population" [Crane 1938: 9]. Referring to the refusal of the local administration to provide similar incentives for Africans to stay in close proximity to the plantations, Shahabuddeen observed,

Nor did it seem to matter that . . . as a result of the attitude of the planters, the situation of the Creoles had deteriorated so far that it was feared that this highly valuable section of the population was in the process of extermination. The traumatic consequence of that prospect on creole emotion was itself an important complicating factor in the socioeconomic problems of the time. [1983: 234]

The significance of this point should not be overlooked since that rural-urban migration which did take place resulted in a declining and ageing rural African population. As a consequence, when serious attempts were made to recruit Africans, criteria such as age and farming experience (would inevitably) discriminated against them. We shall have cause to turn to the problem of recruiting urban labour for agricultural settlement.

Product markets

Over the years 1899–1913 the total acreage of rice increased more than fivefold while production almost septupled. The greatest absolute increase took place after 1940 and was associated with the Mahaicony Abary Rice Development Scheme (MARDS) (1943) and mechanized production [IBRD 1953: Supplementary Tables]. There was also considerable expansion in the numbers of non-LSS farmers, including Africans, involved in rice production [British Guiana 1931a; Crane 1938: 12].

It is unlikely that production on all the schemes in existence in 1913 could have approached 3,500 tons even if all the land had been brought under cultivation. The 10,000 ha of land associated with the LSSs by 1952 was small (7 percent) relative to the total area under rice nationally. Furthermore, since yields on LSSs were only moderately better than the national average, their total contribution would probably have been quite small although not insignificant, a conclusion supported by the findings of some researchers [Mandle 1973: ch. 10; Berrill 1961].

Forces of production

Up to 1938, the forces of production could be described as fairly rudimentary and depended predominantly on labour power and a few tools. This can be gleaned from Table 2. The family continued to be the unit around which production was organized.

The rice crop was originally sown by hand and the edible grain extracted by mortar and pestle. With the East Indian participation in the industry, transplanting and parboiling were introduced. Oxen were employed in ploughing, land levelling and for threshing (bull-mashing). Some mechanization was introduced in land preparation, particularly after 1945. Associated with this was the introduction of the steam-driven, single-stage huller. In this case the excess steam was used to parboil rice – a process that increased the nutritional value of the milled grain and toughened it in order to reduce breakage during milling. Mills were relatively small, however, producing only about 188 tons of rice per annum. They were also alleged to have been inefficient with respect to the use of power, the volume of broken grains, the waste of by-products (such as rice meal, bran, polishings and husks) and produced an inferior grade of (parboiled) rice. In addition, limited storage capacity frequently resulted in irregular mill operations. These factors are estimated to have added some 25 percent to the cost of processing rice. The overall result was said by the Colonial Office to depress the price settlers received for their paddy [1942: 104].

The rice industry did not at any time, therefore, with the exception of 1939–45, become entirely divorced from sugar as has been suggested by some authors [New World Associates 1966: 246]. A seasonal labour demand profile, an inappropriately high degree of mechanization, low returns to labour, limited government assistance and plantation control of some rice lands, all served to shackle one leg of rice labour to the sugar industry (or vice versa) [Richardson 1975: 206–12; Kirby 1973; Dumont 1963].

The level of development of the forces of production was even lower in settlement agriculture. Dairy production was hamstrung by underdeveloped breeds, pasture and herbage. State assistance was extended to the livestock sector for the first time in 1927. This assistance was directed primarily to the dairy industry and to a lesser extent swine and poultry. Neither the state nor the industry devoted such attention to beef cattle. Consequently, poor husbandry resulted in extensive variability of supply and jeopardized in particular the small market in the export of meat to Trinidad. Some processing of meat was undertaken by the Demerara Meat Company which made little use of by-products such as bone-meal and fertilizers [Dash 1935; Fraser 1935].

Financial services and other facilities

Generally speaking, the facilities provided to the schemes were poor, although they represented some improvement over their predecessors. Cultivation was plagued by poor water control in spite of the requirement that drainage and irrigation facilities were to be installed on the new schemes prior to the commencement of settlement. Unity, Lancaster, Windsor Forest and Bush Lot were provided with such facilities. The other schemes had a variety of arrangements which, provided all the settlers were willing to pay the rates, could be upgraded by the state, at the farmers' request. An extreme example of poor water control was Anna Regina where drainage was such a health hazard that two committees were set up to look into the problem. The incidence of malaria infestation was found to have increased to 83 percent during the lease of the latter estate to the private lessee [British Guiana, Administrative Reports of Director of Agriculture 1932a, 1933]! In addition, the supposedly potable water was (frequently) found to be muddy.

On the institutional front there were many inadequacies. In some cases, such as Cane Grove, the distribution of fragmented holdings was undertaken in an effort to have an equitable distribution of different soil types among settlers. Apart from the obvious management problem that could be expected to result, this arrangement also facilitated praedial larceny [Sukdeo 1978: 43]. It is difficult to ascertain the extent to which settlements were provided with the 'living amenities' stipulated in the policy paper of 1924. But the recommendation that the state erect houses for the schemes on the 0.21 ha houselots gave rise, for the first time, to regular assistance (up to $1,500 for house construction). Settlers could either have these constructed privately, via the Housing Department with assistance from the Rural Housing Scheme programme (suspended in 1953) or by aided self-help [British Guiana 1957a].

It is widely known that commercial banks and insurance companies would not lend to peasants on the basis of the security that they are usually able to provide. Indeed, it appears that the foreign owners instructed their local branches to facilitate only planters and public officers [Shahabuddeen 1983: 353]. District Cooperative Credit Banks (DCCBs) established in 1911 did not make much of an impact on this situation which in the 1920s and 1930s was compounded by the depression [Huggins 1935: 88–99]. Silverman attributes part of the difficulty faced by the DCCBs to their requirement that borrowers provide collateral and invest in share capital. This limited access to organized credit had adverse consequences for the settlers who were inevitably forced into the unorganized markets for credit – landlords, merchants, pawnbrokers. In circumstances where millers and landlords exercised considerable political power, declining to make use of the miller's services was probably not always a feasible option, however cheaper the alternative credit sources. Even today the interest rates in that market remain well above that of the organized credit market [Lewars 1977]. What is more, it is now fairly widely accepted that there is a tendency for lenders in such markets to induce default on loans in order to realize a capital gain for themselves [Bhaduri 1977].

Unequal initial capital endowment combined with differential access to credit were quickly reflected in the uneven acquisition of tractors and combines in rural areas as well as dispossession and landlessness. The consequence, uneven development among smallholders, was quite predictable. There was no doubting the acceleration of this process of differentiation among the smallholders in general.

In reviewing this state of affairs, the Moyne Commission contended in 1945 that the government had failed to view LSSs as part of the overall development of peasant agriculture. Consequently, the fundamental problems connected with cropping, marketing and agricultural systems had been left unsolved [West Indies Royal Commission 1946: 332]. It might be added that the wider peasant sector was itself neglected as the exigencies of 1939–45 receded.

Recapitulation and Conclusions, 1906–1947

During this third phase of LSSs, the interplay between the state and the competing factions became even more complex. In addition to the Colonial Office, the local administration, sugar planters and settlers we need to add three new factions:

  i. nascent agrarian capitalists who by virtue of their economic power were commanding significant political influence in the areas where they enjoyed monopolies or near monopolies
  ii. the rise of organized, especially urban, labour
  iii. international actors such as the Government of India, TNCs with their governments in tow

The strength of common interests that linked the Colonial Office, the local administration and the planters survived into this period and now included the bauxite owners. Sometimes they gave rise to public confrontations, for example, over land acquisition and sales. Once more, however, from time to time there were fractures in these common bonds. The moves to free trade in sugar, the termination of immigration, the cycles of economic depression and the wars contributed to such fractures. As each of these events disrupted, temporarily or otherwise, the common bonds, the settlers found themselves confronted by a changed environment which might or might not be either helpful or permanent. The planters fought to keep that environment manageable. As labour became absolutely scarce and the possibilities of physical control of that labour diminished, additional means were to be employed to retain labour for the benefit of sugar. In spite of this, some industry and labour escaped from the control of the monopolized sugar industry.

We have seen that the treatment of East Indians and Africans, settlers in Essequibo and elsewhere, varied according to perceptions about their likely usefulness to the sugar industry. Hence, Essequibo, in the absence of sugar, was the location of some innovations for the benefit of nascent private agrarian capitalists.

The continued use of economic and extra-economic forces, even in the new industries, to maintain a market in cheap labour helped to radicalize the labour movement and to create serious industrial relations problems and stimulated political agitation. The Colonial Office intervention aimed to attenuate the consequences of the confrontational local administration. At the same time, other factors tended not only to give rise to fundamental changes in the attitudes to LSS, but also laid the basis for putting the schemes on a more sound economic footing. The availability of state lands, the demand for foodstuff, examination of interior locations as potential areas of settlement, tenure changes and improved administration were all pertinent in this context.

War and the Depression led to the first real opportunity for small holders in general and rice producers in particular. So well entrenched were the latter by 1945 that, even in the face of policy reversals aimed at re-establishing the dominance of sugar, the industry could not be suppressed or reduced to a mere complementary (labour) appendage to sugar. LSSs did, however, serve to help control labour and wages in the same manner that indentureship had also done. Here was a further step in the modernization of capital-labour relations.

The new and more systematic approach taken to LSSs could not and was not pursued consistently. The schemes retained their racially exclusive character during this phase (1906–47) in spite of the policy pronouncements and legisla-tion [Crane 1938] and in spite of proposals for schemes to be established in areas with interested African settlers and notwithstanding the policy paper of 1925. This continuing predilection in public policy, termed the "racial approach" by Young [1958], was to have unfortunate and predictable conse-quences during the succeeding phases.

Several reasons may be offered for the failure of these schemes to fulfil their production potential. Most of these reasons rest on the poor physical facilities, but inadequate institutional arrangements also contributed. We reviewed the evidence on both counts.

Outside of the exigencies of war, the administration of LSSs, though improved, was bent on ensuring that LSSs, whether producing rice or not, played second fiddle or nursemaid to sugar. Some of the greatest strides were made outside of the sugar belt. The impact of the conflicts between sugar and the rest of the economy and its impact on the forces of production kept down the viability of own-account farming, especially prior to 1942. On settlements, rice became the basis of LSS economy. But difficult conditions for independent production facilitated the development of a reserve army of labour which would have the same effect on the provision and conditions of labour as extra-economic compulsion [Miles 1987: 92–93].

The conversion of the early LSSs into self-governing village authorities in 1905 (see chapter 3) spawned political activity on LSSs and brought into a single framework East Indian agrarian politics.[63] The administration itself shifted from handpicked individuals to those who were on the village council or were able to seize control of the village and district councils in which adminis-trative powers and some executive functions were formally vested. Settlement politics thus merged with that of the remainder of rural East Indian Guyana [see Young 1958: 159]. In that regard we have been afforded, by the work of Silverman, an excellent insight into the workings of one of the most prominent post-LSS villages. This study of Bush Lot village,[64] West Coast, Berbice yields an astonishingly detailed picture of village politics with its web of intrigue, alliances and confrontations in pursuit of power. Silverman has characterized the events as factional politics based on an interminable struggle of a small elite group to control the elected village council. The latter was a focal point of polit-ical competition because it wielded both authority and financial power (through its fiscal powers) and was an employer.

The story of factionalism in this context was one that played itself out over extremely long cycles and involved a few families who had managed to secure a head start in terms of access to resources and wealth. The exercise of their power, and in some cases the attainment of their initial position, was attributable to:

  i. their privileged access to money and their control of credit (patron-client relationships)
  ii. their embrace of Christianity and/or some educational attainment which provided links to influential actors or decision makers in the civil or clerical establishment or to preferred jobs such as teaching
  iii. kinship and to a lesser extent a wide network of friendship

Limited water control and inadequate supplies of land reinforced the position of these elite families. The small farmers had to await the coming of mechanization for these constraints to be relieved. As it happened, for some farmers, both mechanization and political change were on the horizon in the 1940s.

CHAPTER 5

LSSs IN THE STRUGGLE FOR INDEPENDENCE, 1948–1964

Only on the sugar plantations was the old struggle still going on. The people there were still fighting British domination while Georgetown was renewing its relationship with the British, and entering into a new one with the government of the United States, both anxious to prevent Guiana becoming another Cuba. And in Pheasant the struggle between the union which had supported the old government and this new combination of enemies shook the foundations at home.

J. Shinebourne, *Timepiece*

This chapter examines the rapid acceleration of the political changes that occurred after 1947 and their implications. It outlines the crisis of 1953, the reaction of the sugar industry and the implications of those reactions for the planter–Colonial Office–local administration alliance on the one hand, and the rural-urban labour alliance on the other. The approaches to diversification and support for the peasantry are explored. The mechanization of the sugar industry's field operations meant that for the first time labour surplus characterized the sector.

The administration of LSSs underwent a qualitative change although the ethnic factor emerged again to haunt the endeavour. Abuses became noticeable and problematic factors with consequences for the relations of production.

The Political Framework – Losing a Birthright

The run-up to 1953

The 1950s and 1960s are probably the two best documented decades of Guyanese history.[65] Consequently, although an appreciation of the historical background is crucial to an understanding of land and labour policies, the discussion will be confined to the essentials. We have been examining the evolution of the LSSs with reference to the changing class alliances within the society and externally. In the 1948–64 era, the internal alliances began to become more complicated and heterogenous.

The impact of the changes in legislation affecting local government and the removal of the 'literacy' qualification for election to the village councils (1935)[66] was far-reaching for the LSSs. They accelerated the participation of East Indians in local government and sucked LSSs into local government politics.

In addition to the legislative change, increased economic opportunities and the war effort (the Grow More Food Campaign, for example) facilitated diversification in the agricultural sector. The latter provided access to additional acreages[67] and, for some farmers such as those of Bush Lot, improved water control. Additionally, there was the establishment of the Rice Marketing Board (RMB) in 1939 and the availability of agricultural machinery. These developments severely undermined the dominance of millers in village politics, bringing to an end "a period of factional politics . . . an integrated game intimately linked with the resource structure of the wider community" [Silverman 1980: 75]. The breaking of that pattern of local politics, combined with the other events examined earlier, fed nationalist sentiments and fostered something of an urban-rural labour alliance. This alliance and its leadership stood in relatively stark contrast with other classes or strata that were emerging.

In response to the exigencies of the Second World War, several training opportunities were created for prospective leaders. Under the auspices of the CDW schemes similar opportunities arose as the shackles of Crown Colony statehood were released. There was more open access to education, and coloured and African candidates were able to gain access to hitherto restricted education facilities as well as employment.

Other elements of what approximated a nascent middle class were linked to the growth of services in the urban areas and by the establishment and expansion of the professions. As would be expected, this class resented being excluded from the corridors of power and agitated for what might best be described as constrained 'meritocracy'; constrained, in the sense that many of them were also people of colour or 'high' colour who attracted privileges in the colonial society (although many felt these were too few).

As we saw from the preceding section, a body of merchants as well as a class of large-scale farmers had been emerging for some time; their political interests were not necessarily those of the two foregoing groups. After 1945 Britain was coming to grips with its weakened international position. The aggressive attempt by the sugar industry to restore its dominance over the economy and over the labour market was to periodically propel the colony onto the international stage. The fatal shooting of the five sugar workers at Enmore in the course of a relatively peaceful industrial protest in 1948 was one such occasion and it caused outrage nationally and fuelled the call for the colony's political independence.

The means of converting this call into reality was already in the process of being fashioned. The People's Progressive Party (PPP), established in 1951, had managed to build a movement that transcended the ethnic divisions fostered by the local administration and plantation interests. It was facilitated in this exercise by the labour movement. The enhanced and strategic political importance of the unions became apparent with the advent of universal adult suffrage. The unions were the only mass-based organization of consequence. The leadership of the PPP as well as the union leaders recognized this and, as political alignments shifted, trades unions became the scene of manoeuvres for gaining control of union executives [Marx 1964]. By 1953 the PPP had virtual control of the union movement. The colony obtained universal adult suffrage and, led by the PPP, the nationalist movement won power in the 1953 elections – at the height of the Cold War. Not surprisingly, sugar was prominent on the radical movement's (particularly the PPP's) agenda of critical political issues [Jagan 1966; Thomas 1984: 223–26]. With a working class and peasant base they now sought to confront the plantation sector very early in the life of their administration.

The concentration in the marketing of sugar that had been evident at the turn of the century was extended to a production monopoly by 1954, Bookers McConnell Co. Ltd being responsible for 80 percent of output (the Demerara Company and Houston Estates for the remainder) and sugar being the base of the British Guiana economy.

A major concern of that movement was asymmetrical – planter/non-sugar – access to the country's resources, particularly land. As was mentioned earlier, profitable cultivation on Guyana's coast was limited by the high cost of empoldering land. The bulk of such empoldered land was monopolized by the sugar industry and almost half (44 and 48 percent in 1952 and 1963, respectively) of the empoldered land held by the plantations was not under cane at all. The plantations held some 64 percent of this land on lease or permits from the state and, in order to forestall revocation, located almost all their activities on this land rather than on freehold land. It is difficult to see why the industry found it necessary to hold all this land if not to deny its use for economic activities that might make demands on a labour force that the sugar industry regarded as its own.

5.1 Gold mining at Kurupung in the 1950s. *Source*: Norwood 1956.

It was therefore argued by the radical movement that land reform should be given high priority (over the empoldering of additional land). Given its control of prime land, a prime target of such reform was to be the sugar industry [Jagan 1966: 111]. This focus was given added urgency by the sugar industry's declining contribution to the country's development. Relative to its share in the gross domestic product (GDP), the contribution of the industry to total investment was low. This contribution had remained low even in the face of uncommonly buoyant prices in the 1950s. Its fiscal contribution was similarly regarded as unacceptably low.

Another factor bringing the PPP government into confrontation with the plantation sector was labour relations. In spite of the barriers placed in the way, there was increasing unionization of the sugar workers. This unionization was a highly politicized process, politicization being hastened by the alacrity with which the precolonial state came to the sugar planters' assistance with force [Shahabuddeen 1986] and latterly the persistent refusal of the industry to recognize the Guyana Agricultural Workers' Union (GAWU) as the workers' representative for collective bargaining. They stuck to this position in spite of the fact that the union enjoyed the support of the overwhelming mass of the sugar workers. The producers preferred to deal with the MPCA whose leaders were discredited in the eyes of the workers following a history of allegedly compromising agreements with the planters. It should be pointed out that the fact that the GAWU was the 'PPP's union' did not help matters.

The popularly elected government attempted to deal with the producers' recalcitrance by way of a now (in)famous labour relations bill. This bill was laid together with two others aimed at:

i. empowering the state to improve land and charge landlords for this service
ii. repealing legislation concerning the confiscation of undesirable literature
iii. controlling the economic power of rural landlords

The interim administration

The legislative proposals and the associated strike by the GAWU provided the pretext for the suspension of the constitution in 1953 [Layne 1970; ch. 9; Jagan 1966; chs. 7, 8] and the imprisonment of some of the leaders of the elected government after 133 days in office [Burrowes 1984, chs. 3, 4].

Behind this suspension lay a number of interests in alliance. First and foremost, there was of course the sugar industry and the leadership of GAWU's rival, the MPCA. Close behind was the US government on its anticommunist crusade. Third, there were the rural capitalists and landlords for whom the bill had direct implications. Finally, there was the Christian church and its allies led by a Portuguese and white faction fearful of the prospect of the government wresting control of the schools away from them. Their victory was the suspension.

The Colonial Office followed up removal of the PPP from office with other measures to protect British imperial and corporate interests. The actions on the political front have been extensively documented [see, for example, Reno 1964; de Kadt 1972; Layne 1970: ch. 9]. They represented one of the last major sets of actions undertaken by the Colonial Office/planter axis. The duly elected representatives were replaced by sympathetic appointees under the aegis of an interim government. That interim administration (1953–57) consisted of members largely of the middle class and of the mixed and minority races of Guyana. The old bureaucracy and the comprador class were strongly represented.

During its tenure this administration sought to divide the local alliance of progressive/radical forces. The fragmentation of labour in particular was actively fostered by the administration and the sugar industry and was supported by economic measures. The intention appears to have been to discredit and outflank the most vocal and radical elements of the PPP. Thus, increased resources were devoted to agricultural and social infrastructure. For the first

5.2 Slum housing in 1950s Georgetown. *Source:* Norwood 1956.

time, some serious attention was devoted to the diversification of the economy and associated with this were measures to support smallholders. This new approach was reflected in the commissioning of various studies on the economy, particularly on agriculture and fisheries, which were intended to inform specific policy measures [IBRD 1953; Smith 1962: 82; Greenidge 1982]. It should be added that the thrust, even in agriculture, was directed to attracting metropolitan capital by means of a variety of investment incentives and was given added urgency by increasing unemployment and a deterioration in GDP growth relative to the rest of the Caribbean [Newman 1964].

On the advice of the IBRD and others, the implementation of the 1953–56 portion of the development programme was to be accelerated. In addition to agriculture, the pivot of the programme, housing was accorded high priority [Smith 1962: 81, Odle 1976].

In keeping with the intention of outflanking the radicals, in 1956 the Rice Farmers (Security of Tenure) Ordinance was passed defining the period and the conditions of tenancy, the privileges of tenants and the functions of the management committee which it established. The pursuit of the objectives was most visible in the rice sector, to which considerable attention and resources were devoted.

The aims of the interim administration may be considered to have been successfully achieved, initially, in that the PPP was kept out of office. During that time the radical/progressive alliance represented by the PPP split primarily along ethnic (and therefore rural/urban, industrial/agrarian) lines.

The restoration of the PPP administration

In spite of all that the interim administration sought to do, when elections were held in 1957, the PPP under Dr Jagan was again elected to office. The PPP alliance had in the intervening period undergone a sea change. Since its removal from office, the PPP had shed a faction, that associated with Forbes Burnham and consisting primarily of the African leadership and some of its less radical, middle class elements – eventually to be renamed – the People's National Congress (PNC). The PPP had reacted to the hostile forces ranged against it in a manner that now appears predictable. It sought to make peace with and to gather in various strata of the East Indian vote. The effort was enough to secure its re-election without the former allies. Problems were to soon follow this realignment with the East Indian middle class, the rural capitalists (rice, coconut and saw millers, for example) and the shopkeepers, however. During the same year a radical African element, which had remained with the PPP after the split with Burnham, was expelled. The expulsion had been triggered by their opposition to the decision of Dr Jagan not to join the West Indies Federation, apparently out of fear of being swamped by the Caribbean's African majority. A contributing factor, it has been argued by some observers, was the incorporation of the East Indian "middle class, farmers and shopkeepers" in the PPP which heightened discrimination against Africans in the party [Pierce 1984; Manley 1982].

During this era the phenomenon of overt appeals to the electorate on the basis of race came into its own, never to leave Guyana's politics. Apparently this phenomenon had first reared its head in 1953 and PPP candidates were accused of being the perpetrators, especially in 1957. Although the approach was subsequently disavowed by Dr Jagan, its impact left an indelible mark on the political and social psyche of Guyana's nationalist movement.[68]

A great deal of energy has tended to be devoted to the justification for those PPP positions and the part played by Burnham and Jagan themselves. We are not proposing to pursue that debate here, merely to flag its implications. The unambiguous effect of all the manoeuvrings was primarily to deny the country political independence until 1964[69] and to sow additional seeds of postindependence crisis.[70]

These developments, and doubtless others on the part of other actors, helped to make the period in the run-up to independence so highly charged politically that to all intents and purposes there was a public policy vacuum in relation to the sugar industry. The sugar producers and their associates utilized the breathing space offered by this ensuing political vacuum (1953–57) to implement two measures aimed at strengthening their bargaining position vis-à-vis labour. First, they intensified their programme of factory modernization and replacement, rationalization and varietal improvements. All but harvesting and planting operations were mechanized.[71] Seasonality of employment remained high with an average of 40.3 weeks employment per annum per worker. As a result, over the decade 1956–66, total employment in the industry fell by 27 percent. The success of this exercise marked a turning point for the industry in Guyana in that it represented the first time that the industry had been able to sufficiently increase labour productivity via technological innovations to change the nature of the labour market. True, the market had been a buyers' market on occasions prior to 1953 but on this occasion that characteristic was not primarily the product of extra-economic forces. Excess supply was now a permanent feature of the market for sugar labour. The role of LSSs would therefore be somewhat different in future, for sugar was no longer in search of labour.

Preoccupied with, and divided by, the political struggle, the labour movement had allowed the industry to earn and repatriate very generous profits. Rises in the average wages of the industry were less than increases in either the marginal physical or marginal revenue product [Brewster 1969]. Over the years 1956 to 1966, the ratio of issued share capital to profits in all activities of Bookers was in the region of 37 percent [Thomas 1969: 18–22].

The second response of the industry was to diversify both its output and its geographical location. It is no surprise, therefore, to find that between 1953 and 1957 some 65 percent of Bookers' global profits originated in Guyana [Smith 1962: 83]. On the basis of the Guyana earnings, the company transferred its operations across the Atlantic into a variety of new activities such as agri-services [Shahabuddeen 1983: ch. 8]. The former was welcome although belated but the latter step was to facilitate the disarticulation of Bookers from Guyana.

The industry also sought to effect a facelift of its social and public image. This effort has been well analysed by Shahabuddeen and includes the first significant improvements in hitherto scandalous sugar plantation housing [1983: 203] as well as a programme to employ Guyanese in senior positions – 'Guyanazation' [Pierce 1984].

The re-elected and re-composed PPP of 1957–61 maintained their policy pre-occupations but in changed circumstances. The labour situation in the sugar industry now meant that means had to be found to occupy hitherto scarce sugar labour in those very areas from which the PPP drew support. There existed the additional problem of mechanization of holdings, some 60 percent of which were less than 4.1 ha and therefore below the minimum optimum size for mechanized production. Radical change, presumably including land allocation, was therefore proposed. The PPP government decided that the new agriculture was to be organized around voluntary cooperatives and state farms. In the words of the planners, "voluntary cooperative agriculture had become an unavoidable practical necessity" [British Guiana 1957b: 65]. Policy was to be informed by the analysis of the data. There was therefore to be an emphasis on agriculture and particularly on rice. Between 1952 and 1967 there were no less than nineteen major studies and reports on this industry alone [Rhodes Checci 1967: vol 1].

According to the 1964–66 development plan (chapter 6), the peasant farmer was to be the object of special measures [British Guiana 1967]. The aim of agricultural policy would be to create and maintain a class of peasants on viable holdings of 4–8.1 ha [Ministry of Agriculture 1957].[72] Between 1954 and 1961 one-third of the total capital expenditure was devoted to sea defences and D&I. Some 90 percent of this expenditure was disbursed on three flood control projects only: Boerasirie, Black Bush Polder and Tapakuma.[73]

Action taken by the government in relation to the promotion of rice farming, predominantly an East Indian activity and an activity in PPP areas, was rein-forced by other measures. Control of the Guyana Rice Board, the statutory marketing agency, was vested in the Rice Producers' Association (RPA), an entirely PPP-controlled set of farmers' representatives. Following this coup in 1960, very favourable prices relative to (4.4 cents/kg above) those prevailing in the British West Indies were negotiated for the supply of rice to Cuba over the years 1961 to 1963 [Jagan 1966: 238; Henfrey 1972]. These changes marked the last phase of the mini 'golden age' of rice farming.

Outside of rice farming, the proposed changes and developments were not implemented to the same extent. Jagan explained the lacuna thus: "since we were generally obstructed in our industrialization programme we decided to concentrate on agriculture and the other productive sectors" [1966: 237]. The overall development programme, already short of funds, was further thrown off balance by the British government's blocking of access to funds from Eastern Europe and Swiss banks. The West, however, was not exactly forthcoming with substitute funds.

The PPP government then played into the hands of the opponents at home and abroad by compounding the differential and sectional impact of the devel-opment plan with the 1963 budget. The incidence of indirect taxes which had increased significantly after 1959 (from 47 to 50 percent of total revenues) now rose again [British Guiana Annual Reports 1959–61]. The budget increased domestic fiscal effort via pay as you earn (PAYE), compulsory savings, import duties, and the like, all of which were overwhelmingly urban in their incidence. As a result, and in accordance with predictions by several observers [Newman 1960; Boulding 1961], the PPP government "succeeded in alienating all the combined urban elements at the same time" [Layne 1970: 278]. The violent and traumatic aftermath is now history.

Settlement Objectives

As has been implied earlier, the interim administration sought to promote the consolidation of the peasantry and smallholders.[74] It saw this as a useful bulwark against its opponents. The British administration, like its surrogate, the PPP, had similarly come to see the virtue of a viable peasantry ostensibly independent of the sugar industry. Since a class of independent landlords or yeoman-type farmers was expected to be opposed to the socialist platform of the PPP, the administration sought to suborn this group. There was good reason to suppose that this ploy would be effective, for a great deal of the opposition to the ill-fated 1953 Rice Farmers (Security of Tenure) (Amendment) Bill, on which the 1953 PPP government floundered, came from landlords, large and small, many of whom were East Indians from the PPP's main strongholds.

The provision of gainful employment for the rural unemployed became an important objective of LSS policy during this period. The urgency of this objective was heightened by increasing mechanization of the sugar industry (field operations), which was contributing to falling employment levels, and increasing income disparities in the sector. Relatively slow growth overall also contributed to the problem. Although unemployment had been a matter of grave concern in the 1930s, that concern could not overcome the opposition of the sugar industry to the promotion of a peasantry. The new and compelling factor in the 1950s was mounting disaffection with the metropolitan power.

In dealing with this disaffection, the government could not rely solely on the draconian measures referred to earlier, so means were sought to ameliorate the problem of unemployment and placate the populace, including the rural element, in order to undermine support for the PPP [Burrowes 1984: 123]. The LSSs were seen as one of a range of measures aimed at achieving the type of programme outlined in the report of the Moyne Commission.

The PPP administration, on the other hand, initially suspicious of the class/position of landlords, by 1957 seemed satisfied about their radical potential [New World Associates 1966; Layne 1970: ch. 10, 243]. An examination of the debates on plan strategy reveals that for the first time the contribution of the peasantry to output and therefore GDP growth was being viewed seriously as a desirable long-term objective. In this context, LSSs were expected to make a significant contribution to increased national output of rice. An indication of the expected magnitude of the contribution of these schemes (established between 1955 and 1964) may be had from the fact that the average size of the schemes, including one hinterland scheme, was in excess of 3,000 ha. As may be seen from Table 1, attention was also being devoted to livestock production and tree crops. By the late 1950s, when the displaced PPP regained office, the level of rural unemployment was still rising and there was no hiding the growing concern about this phenomenon, the incidence of which was most evident in the densely populated coastal areas. For the PPP, the attraction of the LSSs was twofold: they could address the unemployment problem and also provide a means of rewarding their supporters. Thus, the largest and most important of the post-1945 schemes, the Black Bush Polder, established in the vicinity of the lower Corentyne soon after the closure of the Plantation Port Mourant sugar estate, was heavily promoted by the PPP. The closure had aggravated an already high incidence of unemployment on the Corentyne, Berbice and the scheme, actually constructed prior to the PPP's assumption of office, was seen by the interim administration as a means of attenuating the impact of the closure.

It needs to be said that not all the schemes lent themselves to such neatly classified objectives. Some schemes were undoubtedly prompted by specific factors. Wauna-Yarakita seems to have been one such scheme. It was established to enable the relocation of farmers from the Wauna River, where flooding and falling yields from permanent crops threatened the continued existence of the community.

The Framework of Settlement Administration

Until the commencement of this period, the state's input to the administration of the schemes was directed primarily at the establishment phase. Between 1953 and 1967 administration was greatly enhanced and extended, reflecting the concern of the Colonial Office to make this a viable political option. Statutory provision was made to protect the rights of settlers, notably in relation to unfair rents and eviction.

In 1954 the Land Development Division (LDD) was established and there was some rationalization of the reporting mechanism which enabled the head of the LDD to report directly to the minister of agriculture, forestry and lands. Subsequently, in 1961 the LDD was integrated into the Department of Lands and Mines. The reasons for this move are not altogether clear. It does appear that for some schemes this meant that the Drainage and Irrigation Department took over the administration of D&I. This was the case in Vergenoegen and Garden of Eden, for example, in 1960 [Sukdeo 1978]. In December 1964, however, the Ministry of Agriculture was separated from that of Lands and Mines. The LDD was then relocated within the Ministry of Agriculture.

The LDD was charged with the identification of locations, the planning and coordination of proposals for, and the implementation of, settlement schemes. In executing these tasks it was required to pay attention to farming systems, farmers' incomes and the promotion of the cooperative movement. In some cases, such as the Wauna-Yarakita scheme, the Ministry of Agriculture prepared the settlers' farm plans with outside assistance, including that of the

Food and Agriculture Organization (FAO). In 1964 the services of a resettlement coordinator were obtained under a UN programme of expanded technical assistance.

Day-to-day administration of each scheme was the responsibility of a land development officer and assistant. The state provided management assistance together with extension services, such as demonstration and seed production plots, to settlers. These schemes were still intended to stand on their own as quickly as possible. But in order to facilitate the administration as well as the transfer to self-government, a settlement advisory committee, consisting of members of the scheme, was appointed. In 1960 almost all the remaining schemes established prior to 1956 were converted into local authorities.

Arrangements for the selection of settlers were also modified. After 1955, the availability of places on schemes was advertised publicly and selection of settlers was entrusted to a panel of seven to eight persons which sometimes included the minister of agriculture, forestry and lands. In this process, the panel was supposed to be guided by criteria including farming experience, education, personality, age and size of family.[75] Another notable change, relative to the preceding era, relates to the selection of the sites for the LSSs. The propensity for acquiring former sugar plantations became a thing of the past. The new schemes were a mix of colonization, improvement of existing farming systems and the fragmentation of former plantations, not necessarily sugar. Settlers received their land on the basis of leases, except for Mara[76] where land was sold outright at $124/ha and Onverwagt where it was initially rented at $25/ha per annum. In the case of the BBP, the leases were of 25 years' duration.

Attempts to come to grips with the tenure problems were also contained in a 1955 ordinance which set out terms governing acquisition, compensation, distribution and repossession of land in connection with LSSs. Rents on the LSSs were also prescribed in this legislation. The ordinance stipulated that annual rents on the LSSs should not exceed 6 percent of the price for which the land was acquired in 1955 or the annual income derived from its use in agriculture. The rent on BBP was set at $25/ha per annum and the lease, initially twenty-five years, was renewable. These leases, prohibited subletting, voluntary transfers, interest in other land and the disposal of rice other than at a specified mill. Settlers were also required to take up residence within a year of allocation of the land. Finally, a land title could be revoked only if the settler violated the terms of the lease or if it was necessary to secure debts owed to the state.

One interesting feature of this statute was a formula that limited compensation to landowners of land purchased compulsorily to either the price paid for the land on 1 July 1955 or the capitalized value of the important net annual agricultural income of the land (net of necessary capital investment to restore it to a reasonable condition). This was intended to reduce the incidence of exorbitant payments by the state for land, the appreciation in value of which had been solely attributable to state investment in sea defences and drainage and the like.

On the subsequent schemes holding sizes do not appear to have been tied to family sizes as was the case with the earliest schemes. The range of approved holdings varied from just over 3 ha at Garden of Eden (10 ha that included just over 2 ha for citrus – the balance was for livestock farms) to 20 ha at Wauna Yarakita (Table 1). Concern with viability seems to have been the main determinant of holding size. On BBP the typical acreage of 6.9 ha was estimated to be sufficient to provide the settlers with an income no less than that of an average urban manual worker. No longer would the settler need to rely on securing part-time employment on a sugar plantation. Furthermore, the homestead was situated in close proximity to the rice plots.

The quality and quantity of facilities on these schemes, particularly BBP, represented a considerable improvement on what had previously passed for support on earlier schemes. The infrastructural facilities provided included an airstrip, sound roads, as well as D&I. Three large central rice mills and a machinery pool of tractors and combine harvesters were established. In addition, there was provision of credit, transport of produce to markets and some social services, such as dispensaries, police outposts and primary schools. Land was also set aside for playing fields and churches. Settlers at Vergenoegen also benefited from this new approach and the rice mill formerly operated by the Land Development Society was handed over to a farmer's cooperative in 1959 [Sukdeo 1978]. Many loans were extended to settlers by the credit cooperative.

There was for the first time material support to settlers during the critical settling-in period. Farmers at Mara were employed on the developmental works of the scheme prior to the availability of land for distribution. Similarly, in 1964, the government concluded an agreement with the World Food Programme under which 1,679 tons of food were supplied over a two-year period to 800 families at Brandwagt-Sari and Wauna, inter alia [British Guiana 1964c: 117]. In addition, presettlement training was extended to the prospective settlers. Those at Brandwagt-Sari were the first beneficiaries. Housing continued to be provided to settlers via the cooperative societies and the Guyana Credit Agency. For the first time, a relatively systematic attempt was made to rehabilitate facilities for the delivery of potable water on some of the schemes [Vining 1976].

It is noticeable that in the case of the only truly noncoastal scheme, Wauna-Yarakita, adequate provision appears not to have been made to cope with the heavy infrastructural requirements. Indeed, over 70 percent of the £200,000 CDW grant earmarked for the scheme in the development plan was utilized for a twenty-five-mile access road to Port Kaituma. As it happens, technical difficulties beset this exercise and settlers were left to operate an inaccessible scheme. As a consequence, severe difficulties were encountered in securing supplies of inputs such as breeding stock and planting material. When drought struck in 1965, the settlers had to travel some five miles to obtain supplies of potable water [British Guiana 1965a: 92]. Two pilot schemes, Brandwagt-Sari and Garden of Eden [ICJ 1965] were established for the purpose of examining LSSs and their needs.

Underlying Issues and Paradoxes

Two issues emerged and dominated this phase of LSSs. First, the state attempted to establish, in a meaningful way smallholder settlement based on rice production. Second, allegations of racial bias in the administration of the schemes rekindled the embers of the old debate.

Cooperatives

Three innovations or new directions were pursued in the bid to strengthen the position of the smallholders or peasants: settlers' cooperatives, mechanization and marketing. The first thrust related to devising an appropriate unit of management and ownership. On this front, it may be argued that the PPP government seemed to be aware of the types of handicaps under which the smallholders laboured and was prepared, in principle, if not materially, to address the problems. As mentioned earlier, some of the objectives set out in the 1964–66 development plan specifically addressed the smallholder problem. One point mentioned in that document was a proposal to establish an institutional framework to protect the economic independence of the smallholder.

In this regard, cooperatives or cooperative societies were seen as an appropriate device for overcoming the evident weaknesses of smallholder farming in a situation characterized by a high degree of 'publicness' in many goods and services. There had been a tradition of cooperation and collective provision of labour and finances among smallholders for many years and this tradition was to provide in part, a historical rationale for the active promotion by the state of cooperative societies on the LSSs [Hope 1975; Huggins 1935; Greenidge et al.

1978]. In some instances the material assistance provided by the state to the cooperatives was direct and considerable. As previously mentioned, major facilities were handed over to cooperatives on some schemes. The state's efforts met with considerable success initially, even in the face of entrenched suspicion on the part of many potential settlers. Many societies were established on schemes, as is evident from Table 9.

Forces of production and employment

The government's commitment to the consolidation of the peasantry was also reflected in considerable improvements in facilities to which reference has been made. A great deal of attention was devoted to the dissemination and diffusion of information on improved and mechanized techniques of farming. With the aid of generous loans from the Guyana Credit Corporation (GCC), the importation of tractors and combines expanded rapidly (Table 2) to a point where the industry was regarded as overmechanized. On small farms, farmers sold their cattle to purchase tractors and combines.

The choice of mechanical equipment was apparently inappropriate (in terms of size and traction) for Guyana's conditions. There were adverse consequences on operating efficiency. Increased mechanization of harvesting was also closely related to a deterioration in the quality of rice [Hanley 1975; IBRD 1953].

Dumont contended that if the objective of policy was to fully mechanize rice production, farms of at least 41 ha in size would be an imperative. Mechanization would not be viable on the 6.1 ha farms that characterized the existing schemes. On such farms, machinery services might best be profitably employed if land preparation were undertaken en bloc and the other tasks carried out by family labour [Dumont 1963]. It would be more appropriate, given the small farm sizes, to utilize animal traction and/or small rotovators. But it was hard to turn back the clock, and the government's preoccupation with wooing landlords militated against the full implementation of Dumont's recommendations on consolidation of holdings. Rather than opting for more appropriately sized machinery, the PPP government undertook to provide machinery services which, as it transpired, were not adequate relative to demand on the LSSs.[77]

Traditionally, allocative or communal labour was the main means of dealing with peaks in on-farm labour demand. With the uneven availability of machinery such forms of mutual assistance broke down. Those unable to raise the necessary working capital to hire machinery paid for it in kind. In extreme cases the entire set of husbandry activities was contracted out to the machine owner who was often the landlord. Underemployment therefore became the norm on rice farms. On the most successful of the LSSs, for example, settlers only managed forty days of work/employment per annum on rice [Dumont 1963; Kirby 1973]. In many places, however, the adoption of rice spelt death for mixed farming.

Furthermore, many machine owners engaged in the business of renting out their machinery would at the last moment withhold the services to small farmers, or extend them in such a manner that the smallholder would be financially jeopardized. The economics of hiring thereby gave rise to de facto dispossesion. These relations of exploitation were associated with and often compounded traditional means of exploitation based on race or religion.[78] They remain a permanent feature of Guyana agriculture to this day.

In a similar manner, the introduction of new varieties of paddy, for example, placed a premium on large-scale production and management of resources such as water. Two major and very visible consequences of these changes were, therefore, the increasing scale of operations and the alienation of lands allocated to settlers [Payne 1977; Kirby 1973].

There was significant progress as a result of the state's efforts in marketing and rice milling. By the end of the 1960s the state, which had taken upon itself the task of promoting and sponsoring the industry, secured relatively favourable prices and guaranteed markets under the West Indies Rice Agreements, acted as a stimulus to production. In this context it has been estimated that between 1958 and 1964 production increased by some 100 percent. In fact, almost all of the increase in GDP that took place during the period was based on rice.

With regard to milling, many farmers found themselves at the mercy of landlords-cum-moneylenders because with the low levels of efficiency of private rice mills most millers, who enjoyed a geographical monopoly, charged excessive fees and produced very high levels of broken grain, as was mentioned earlier. Numerous reports attest to the fact that the millers were commonly indebted to merchants, who in turn were blenders and exporters [IBRD 1953: 200–201].[79] For those farmers who could, it had become customary to retain ownership of the crop and merely pay for the service of milling and perhaps drying.

During the 1950s the government therefore embarked on a policy of breaking the geographical monopoly enjoyed by these landlord-miller-moneylenders. The number of government-owned mills was dramatically increased and relief was brought to many of the exploited by way of an alternative buyer with predictable grading criteria. This state involvement also provided some degree of protection for the smaller farmers and those who would find themselves a disadvantaged minority.

In addition to increasing the number of mills, the government also sought to introduce the larger and more efficient mills in a bid to modernize the industry and reduce the costs and wastage associated with the small single-stage private mills. Over the years 1957 to 1961 alone, for example, the total number of mills fell by 8 percent (Table 6) along with a significant increase in the average size and throughput. In the process of this rationalization many small millers were forced out of business.

These developments brought in their wake other problems for peasants in general and settlers on LSSs in particular. Improved private milling-drying-storage facilities reduced the uncertainty associated with post-harvest activities. Consequently, an increasing number of millers were prepared to purchase paddy outright at the farm gate. In such cases direct contact of the RMB with farmers was eliminated. The board was therefore not in a position to extend crop advances to farmers on the basis of the anticipated output. The way was once again clear for the customary agents, such as millers and landlords, to dominate the market in the provision of credit to farmers. In a study of the succeeding period, Lewars has provided some insights into the incidence and terms under which such loans were provided [Lewars 1977; Greenidge 1978].

The facilities provided to the LSSs varied extensively. LSSs in PPP strongholds devoted to rice seem to have attracted the most funds and facilities. Thus BBP and Tapakuma were the most generously endowed. Other schemes were relatively poorly served. Land clearing, the main D&I facilities, as well as access roads and housing sites were provided on all the rice growing schemes [British Guiana 1964c: 100–101]. On these schemes the land was handed over to settlers in a condition that they could proceed to immediate cultivation with tractor or plough. On most other schemes settlers were responsible (and paid) for land clearing and internal drainage at least.

On a few schemes where the government's input was very limited the lands were distributed to cooperative societies. On the first noncoastal settlement which was neither a rice nor an East Indian–populated scheme, potable water and access were notable inadequacies.

Ethnicity

Political patronage in the appointment of LSS staff rendered the administrative problems of LSSs doubly difficult [Hanley 1975: 141].[80] Closely associated with this question of patronage was the apparent bias towards East Indians in the selection of both LSS staff and settlers [Burrowes 1984].

The selection criteria for settlers was itself a problem. Of the five criteria that were supposed to have guided the panel in selecting settlers, experience and personality could account for as much as 60 percent of a possible maximum twenty-three points [ICJ 1965: 103]. Both of these were of course subjective. Of the other criteria, size of family could be expected to favour rural families and East Indians in particular.

The rural population of Africans was ageing relatively rapidly as a result of the high rural-urban drift of the young. Recruitment of Africans in proportions commensurate with their share of the total population would have required the attracting of urban Africans, a problem to which we shall return. But few rural Africans were either approached or selected.

African representation on six of the seven schemes established during this period was 11 percent, which was low relative to some of those established prior to the latter part of the 1906–48 era and in relation to the Africans resident in the nearby agricultural areas such as the Berbice River. Perhaps it should also be noted in passing that during this phase most of the lands utilized for the schemes were formerly unoccupied and the problem of intercommunity land transfers, which had reared its head in the 1890s and early 1900s in particular, did not arise. The backlands from Whim and No. 51 Village which constituted the Polder were formerly unoccupied swamp lands used as 'reservoirs', and the Brandwagt-Sari/Mara lands were former state lands, also largely unoccupied.[81]

The point of note here, then, is not whether or not the criticism of racial bias was entirely justified but that the apparent bias contributed significantly to the alienation of non-East Indians from these schemes. And as was intimated at the end of the preceding section, this was an alienation with a long gestation period [see, for example, Crane 1938: 9; Danns and Matthews 1989: 6, 87]. A concrete consequence of the perception of racial bias was the insistence of the PNC (post-1964) government on including LSSs in the terms of reference of the International Commission of Jurists (ICJ) which had been set up to enquire into racial discrimination in Guyana's public service [ICJ 1965].

Results

Although this period is frequently viewed as a unique success as far as LSSs are concerned, on many counts the 1948–64 schemes fared little better than their predecessors.[82] At least three of the schemes collapsed within two years of their establishment.

Size of LSSs

However, there were some positive aspects to the new schemes. For the first time, policy was directed to satisfying domestic food needs. This was reflected in the plans and acreages involved. The eight schemes established between 1948 and 1964 included one hinterland scheme and had an average size in excess of 3,000 ha. This represented a considerable increase in size relative to the predecessors, as may be gauged from Table 1.

Almost all the GDP increase over this period was attributable to increased rice production by smallholders. The bulk of the increase was the result of 37,000 ha of newly drained and irrigated land rather than improved yields. In this sense, LSSs had started to impact positively and significantly on production and incomes [Brewster 1969; Odle 1976: 146].

Administrative problems

The administration of the schemes left a lot to be desired. There were the usual deficiencies, such as inadequate provision of resources, poor staff training and poor coordination among a plethora of state agencies [Gyanchand 1963: 87; Brotherson c. 1969: 5]. It had been said of the LDD that it had "not achieved a large measure of success and the task of achieving the objects for which it was constituted has still to be defined" [Gyanchand 1963: 87]. There were also, partly as a consequence, a festering and extensive backlog of administrative problems associated with more than a century of LSSs. Among these problems was the failure to convert the remaining post-1905 LSSs into local authorities or self-governing entities.

Recommendations to this end had been submitted in the Marshall Report of 1955. The intention of the author of the 'practicable' reform of local government system was to, inter alia, incorporate the LSSs along with all other unorganized areas into a single local authority system. All residents would then be liable to rates and would in turn be provided with the normal set of local authority services ranging from maintenance to 'social welfare' [Marshall 1955: 26–27]. The proposals were not implemented until 1969.

On schemes such as Garden of Eden, Cane Grove, Vergenoegen and Windsor Forest, the LDD had moved out of the settlement prior to the issue of titles to settlers and prior to the completion of infrastructural works.[83] In the absence of infrastructure, the local authority was not legally empowered to levy local government rates, taxes or D&I rates. Withdrawal then, rather than helping the situation, actually added to the administrative chaos [British Guiana Development Plan 1964a: 87]. In addition, there was considerable deterioration in the country's D&I systems. The maintenance of land records, the issue and policing of leases became neglected in this situation and there was declining ability to collect arrears of rents as well as D&I rates [Gyanchand 1963: 39–40, Table 4]. As a consequence of these failures, the reorganization of the Department of Lands and Mines was recommended. In addition to being understaffed, staff training had been neglected [Gyanchand 1963: 39–40].

There were one-time problems such as the disturbances of 1963–64, which both discouraged the utilization of settlement places (Brandwagt-Sari) and disrupted the progress of construction (Wauna/Yarakita). It took some ten years for Onverwagt to come on stream. The major bottleneck appears to have been the inability of the state to secure title to the lands. Settlers could not therefore receive transport (titles) to their allotments. Incidentally, in view of the unsatisfactory nature of the D&I facilities inherited by the settlers – a contributory factor to the surrender of the area by the Rice Development Co. Ltd – the final sum agreed appears to have been generous ($600,000).

The administration failed to deal with the abuses in the operation of these schemes. On the BBP in particular, rice lands were gradually taken over by large landowners and machinery operators who were not settlers. The settlers retained formal titles to the land in order to avoid cancellation of the lease and reallocation. Related to this was the failure of the administration to evict negligent and absentee tenants/settlers. Rent collection was also inadequately enforced.

The provision of credit by the state was not fully utilized by the settlers, or rather loans were not easily recovered. Indeed, it has been frequently argued that many farmers, including those in the cooperatives, regarded the loans as a reward for supporting the PPP government or for helping them attain office. They therefore had no intention of repaying and did not expect to be asked to repay [Silverman 1980]. Since the government mills were in a position to deduct debts as a first claim on the proceeds of the sales of farmers' rice, farmers regarded them to some extent as enforcement agencies. As a consequence, on the LSSs there eventually developed among debtors the widespread practice of milling paddy at non-LSS mills.

Inadequate provision of social infrastructure has also been cited as a problem. The absence of a primary school at the Garden of Eden and of access roads at Brandwagt-Sari are examples of such omissions. But it is difficult to be too categorical about their impact, for while settlers at the Garden of Eden contended that they were discouraged from settling by the lack of a primary school, at BBP, where the pupil places/population was very generous, extensive truancy – over one-third of those eligible – was the norm. The apparent contradiction may have been attributable to the phasing in of these facilities or they may have been merely excuses of settlers who were landlords or secure tenants elsewhere.

Forces of production

Generally speaking, the forces of production on the LSSs still remained, compared with the sugar industry, relatively backward [Dumont 1963; David 1969]. Production levels were loosely and casually linked to natural factors and changes in the weather. Thus, Mara appears never to have recovered from the twin plagues of poor weather and rice blast disease that was visited upon it during its establishment.

A contemporary survey of the D&I systems on the coast, particularly at Cane Grove and BBP, concluded that the uneven height of fields, lack of sequential supply of water and lack of drainage constituted the major problems of the system. The result was frequent flooding, poor yields and high mortality of young livestock [Brotherson c. 1969]. Poor administration and maintenance of D&I facilities led to the deterioration of the infrastructure. On many of the schemes the quality of the infrastructure provided left a lot to be desired. This was largely attributable to poor workmanship by consultants and the prospective settlers themselves. And this took place in spite of the earlier adverse experiences with Brandwagt-Sari, for example [McCormack 1979: 28]. At Onverwagt, as was the case with the Torani Canal, the quality of the engineering of the D&I system left a great deal to be desired [IBRD 1953: 155].

The new schemes, it should be said, made a significant impact on rice production. The exact quantum of their contribution in the area of so-called nontraditional agricultural activities, however – green and leafy vegetables, fruits, ground provisions and so on – cannot be accurately estimated. But it has been argued, that with know-how and hard work a settler could earn a few times more than his urban counterpart and be self-sufficient in basic foods.

Once more the problem of dispossession reared its head. Landlords increased efforts to dispossess tenants via various tactics including subterfuge. These efforts were tempered somewhat by the operation of the Rice Farmers (Security of Tenure) Act, which was intended to protect tenants from arbitrary eviction and dispossession. A court settled all disputes arising under the act.

Recapitulation and Conclusions 1948–1964

It may be said that during the 1948–64 era the foundations were laid for the LSSs to be uncoupled from the sugar industry. Indeed, by the end of the era that uncoupling had been so effective that the LSSs were encountering problems as a consequence of their new importance in national politics. They have yet to recover from that association.

After 1945 the sugar industry attempted to reinstate its former dominance in terms of access to resources, control of the labour market and influence of the legislature, but too much had taken place on the political and constitutional fronts to permit that restitution. The economic base on which many of the changes had been launched held firm and the industry was not altogether successful in its attempt to turn the tide. The shooting of the Enmore five in 1948 lost them some allies, and the suspension of the constitution in 1953 served to bring to an end the industry's unchallenged access to the coercive machinery of the state to solve its problems. The attempt to separate sugar labour from the political leadership can be said to have succeeded temporarily. It resulted in splitting the urban and rural proletariat. The political leadership was similarly split.

The tenure of the interim administration afforded the sugar industry time to pursue a number of options which created some asymmetry between the dependence of Bookers and Guyana on each other. It also served to undermine the prospects for a common approach by the labour movement and the major races to independence. The re-election of the PPP administration in 1961 without most of its former African allies allowed the two traditional foes, labour and the sugar industry, to resume their old battle, including that of union recognition. But more ominously, it marked the heightening of a new struggle: that between the two major political parties for control of the labour movement and the rural, non-sugar vote. Events in the labour movement signalled what was to follow. The MPCA leadership, with its middle class and essentially Muslim background, was part of the anti-PPP alliance. Its contribution to that alliance was to mobilize its workers to join the general strike against the PPP government. The PPP retaliated. In the words of one observer, "in return, the PPP naturally attacked their opponents at their weakest point – by renewing the campaign to convert in a de jure trades union relationship their political control of the sugar workers" [Marx 1964: 232].

The urban proletariat, in a wide-ranging alliance with other urban-based middle class and capitalist forces, refused to support the sugar workers when they (with the PPP government) sought by way of strike action to force the sugar producers to recognize the GAWU. Part of the justification was that the latter had failed to show solidarity with them in their earlier strike for higher civil service wages. The recruitment of African strike-breakers and the retaliation by GAWU sympathizers set a now familiar and ominous pattern. "The politization of the trades union was complete" [Marx 1964: 232].

These developments were mirrored, to a greater or lesser extent, elsewhere in the country. In the rural areas, as in urban constituencies, political control was also an issue. The developments in LSS administration outlined above gave rise to a bifurcated system of local government and of LSS administration. We have been afforded a very useful insight into the impact of all of these on the factional politics of the rural community. A meticulous chronicle of alliances on a former LSS charted the struggle between the village council on the one hand, under PPP, and the district commissioner and/or local government board on the other, representing the central government. It has been argued that the former won the struggle.

The intensity of the political struggle between the two domestic factions culminated in extensive violence which was to have a lasting impact on the manner of political behaviour in the colony. Though prodded on by its US ally, the UK government was unwilling to resolve the conflict by force. The events of 1953 were still fresh in the minds of the international community and the decolonization movement was in full cry. Instead, the UK dealt with it politically, levering the representatives of the rural proletariat out of office.

The general mayhem of the period provided the US with a pretext for encouraging Venezuela's aggressive pursuit of its border claim against an arbitration decision which the US had not only helped to broker but which crisis it had precipitated in the first instance [Latin American Bureau 1994; Bertram 1992; Joseph 1998]. This action was to prove costly for Guyana since Britain was unwilling to provide any military protection similar to that later extended to Belize. The militarization of land settlements as well as of the society followed.

Peasant agricultural development, welfare services and housing in the urban areas, had benefited from the attempt of the Colonial Office to support its local allies. The PPP administration, which was eventually restored to office, continued the agricultural programme, focusing almost exclusively on rice. The non-coastal schemes attracted considerably less support and Wauna-Yarakita, Mara and Brandwagt-Sari were abandoned within a few years of their establishment.

Considerable changes and some progress were experienced in the administration of the schemes, although many problems remained, and for those schemes devoted to rice, a dramatic increase in the level and quality of infrastructural facilities was evident. As these schemes were breaking their ties to the sugar plantations they were linked in a somewhat different manner to them. Now the objective of LSSs was to cope with the growing rural unemployment attributable to the mechanization of the sugar industry. Of course, this was not the first occasion on which the sugar industry was shedding labour. It had done so in the 1880s and 1890s. On this occasion, however, the planters' control over the legislature was not strong enough to prevent substantial allocations of resources to the schemes. They were no longer simply temporary holding operations or custodial allies of sugar but production centres in their own right. This was evident from the facilities provided on the BBP project, for example, and holding size. However, it may also be argued that the industry for the first time saw a situation of labour surplus emerging from the relatively unfettered operation of the labour market. It did not therefore resist the loss. With regard to their impact on the level of output of rice in particular, the schemes were clearly a success. In many ways, however, little else was new.

In spite of efforts to strengthen their economic base and improve the framework within which the schemes operated, the process of uneven development of smallholders continued. This finding lends some credence to the conclusion that, in some areas, attempts to establish petty capitalist smallholdings with modern technology on unencumbered land has simply transferred dependency from "patrons in land" to "patrons in capital" [Pearse 1972; Jiggins 1981].

In terms of the numbers nationally employed, the contribution of the schemes was clearly insignificant. The coastal schemes that remained operative may well have contributed to slowing the rate of rural-urban population drift [Danns and Matthews 1989: 184, 187]. But the racial factor came to the fore as a political issue and there can be little doubt that the administration of LSSs was a contributory element to this controversy. Some part of the problem and the apparent discrimination in this area may have been the consequence of poor administration. Few doubted that these were the byproducts of political patronage. The inherent dangers of treating such a politically charged subject as state and communal land as a reward to supporters for voting the party in office ought to have been obvious to the PPP leadership. If it was, they either ignored or dismissed it. Thus what should have been an opportunity to reconstruct the radical alliance turned out to be a political albatross – a lasting monument to divisive politics.

CHAPTER 6

HINTERLAND DEVELOPMENT UNDER COOPERATIVE SOCIALISM, 1965–1980

The break from the old establishment to the new establishment was testing out the group. The previous government, Jagan's government as they called it, was too preoccupied with the old world, the past, with destroying the plantations and the poverty there, so Georgetown had overthrown it.

At high school in New Amsterdam she found a different world, where the idea of lacking education was unthinkable, the alternative barbaric. Only the future mattered, a future where the lawyers, doctors, dentists and wealthy commercial class lived in large houses, with American cars and holidays in Europe and North America.

Janice Shinebourne, *Timepiece*

This period witnessed changes in the political landscape stemming from the new and still changing alliances. The 'final phase' of the struggle between foreign plantation sugar and the local administration that centred on the efforts of the former to stave off nationalization is touched on here. External factors again emerge to influence the role of LSSs. In this period, however, internal alliances emerge as the most important influence on LSS change. This was reflected in the government's attitude to rice and the drive to hinterland development. LSSs seem to have become a panacea, employed to remedy a variety of ills. As a consequence, many different types of schemes were established to serve many ends. The administration of the schemes reflected this diffuse focus and the issue of settlement financing, viability of schemes and diversification are also explored.

Political Framework – Cooperative Socialism

The post-1964 era is undoubtedly the most controversial period in Guyana's political history. The main reason for the controversy has been the absence of consensus over the nature (the political economy) of the regime that succeeded the PPP in government. That difficulty arises from the internal political and social changes that took place after 1980 as well as the interrelationship between those external forces.

Once again the PPP government demitted office after the strike it called against the sugar industry backfired. By 1964 the labour movement on which the political parties had travelled was split largely along sectoral lines that coincided with the racial divide. The PPP had been displaced from government by an alliance of miscellaneous forces, whose future would be problematic because its was so heterogenous.

It is useful to look briefly at the question of occupational distribution and mobility and the impact that education and changing economic structures would have on the formation of socioeconomic strata and on political alliances.

As late as the 1960s, occupational status in Guyana remained primarily a function of colour and race. In response to the political changes of the late 1950s and 1960s as well as the policies of Bookers, in particular, some new opportunities for vertical mobility arose. The extent of the latter was limited, however, and in this regard Smith [1962] has argued that over the period 1881–1960 horizontal mobility was of far more significance than vertical mobility. At the same time, rising expectations and political pressures meant that the struggle for jobs and positions became acute. In response,

privileged individuals ensured that they and their children would maintain their positions and they did this partly by marshalling the support of those similar to themselves and with whom they felt they shared the same interests. Patronage thus flourished and bonds of kinship, religion and ethnicity became strongly articulated and assumed great importance in both the maintenance and achievement of status through the occupational sphere [Graham and Gordon 1977: 84–85].

The persistence of this problem of race and of the contradictions of the middle class in this milieu are attested to in the writings of many Guyanese authors such as Carew [1994]. It is somewhat uncanny in comparing the novels of two authors writing of the 1930s and early 1960s, respectively, to note the extent to which time seems to have stood still in this sphere as far as the colony's second largest town, New Amsterdam, and its hinterland were concerned [Mittelholzer 1955: 2; Shinebourne 1986: 69–74]. By the 1960s the Portuguese community was to be found mainly in commerce primarily as owners or managers of large foreign businesses. They were also found in own-account or family businesses. Their control of the local press was especially noticeable and had been used to great effect in the events of 1962–64. Among these Portuguese and other groups of light colour, dominance in commerce was assured by occupational inheritance in relation to which education was relatively unimportant. Personal contacts and influence were the main determinants of mobility.

The Chinese, prominent in the profession, also had a very strong presence in commerce. A study conducted in 1965 observed that there was also marked intergenerational mobility among the Chinese [Graham and Gordon 1977: 65]. Presumably this was a reflection of the additional impact that educational attainment could have on reinforcing the advantages of colour. The study highlighted that some 50 percent of these respondents, largely offspring of parents in commerce, were senior civil servants.

For East Indian and Africans the barriers to highly valued occupations remained strong. A disproportionately large share of (upper echelon) posts in the civil service and in the formal private sector remained open only to foreigners. "Recruitment to the public service was based on birth status and further career mobility occurred independently of educational qualifications" [Graham and Gordon 1977: 81].

East Indians formed the bulk of the agricultural labour force both as wage earners and owner occupiers. Few of them were employed in the management of the industry but over time they were taking advantage of growing opportunities in the sugar factories. Other than this, they tended to gravitate to commerce, in part because they were still excluded from urban occupations and teaching due, inter alia, to religious discrimination. Given the basis on which the commercial sector operated, the situation heightened for East Indians the importance of family connections and socioeconomic origins rather than education. In a sense, therefore, East Indians were able to move like the Portuguese and Chinese.

In the case of the Africans, who turned primarily to the civil service and teaching, occupational status depended on education and the occupational status of their parents (and therefore their influence) in the civil service. Their presence in teaching was attributable in large measure to their embrace of Christianity. They were less prevalent in the sugar industry than they were in the agricultural sector as a whole where they were largely small-scale farmers frequently renting land. Increasingly, they were leaving the sugar factories in the late 1950s but they, with the benefit of the Bookers 'Guyanazation' programme, were moving into some managerial and senior technical posts in the sugar industry. They constituted the bulk of the urban labour force, including the bauxite industry, utilities and related services.

The government which won the elections in 1964 consisted of the original African faction of the pre-1955 PPP as well as the United Force (UF), a conservative party. The core following of the PNC consisted of bauxite workers, urban labour in transport, utilities and related sectors and, rural Africans in towns and workers and farmers in the hinterland and the overwhelming mass of junior and middle level civil servants, teachers, nurses and the uniformed services. Its main allies in the labour movement were the MPCA, the Guyana Labour Union (GLU) and the Guyana Mine Workers' Union (GMWU). It had been able to attract some of the white- and blue-collar workers and professionals, including some East Indians and Creoles through its merger with other small parties, including the United Democratic Party representing some middle class elements and a spectrum of those of light colour. Middle class East Indian elements and some rural landlords and millers were brought on board by the instrumentality of some East Indian leaders who had defected from the PPP – Jai Narine Singh and J.P. Latchmansingh, for example.

The UF, whose membership and leadership included the owners of a signifi-cant portion of the media, primarily represented wealthy and privileged inter-ests. It carried the Portuguese vote, a significant proportion of the Amerindian vote and a mélange of the more conservative elements in the society. The PNC itself had been built around the African element of the labour movement – some of the small middle class parties represented and led by people of colour and an amalgam of Portuguese, Chinese and mixed rural groups [see Manley 1982: ch. 7; Pierce 1984].

The formal PNC/UF coalition was in office for the granting of independence by the UK in 1966. During its tenure from 1964 to 1968, the PNC felt con-strained by its conservative ally.[84] In 1968 a sequence of events including the resignation of the leader of the UF from the coalition, culminated in the elec-tion of the PNC to office without its former ally. Following quickly on the heels of those 1968 general elections, the official results of which had been disputed, was an attempted secession by white ranchers resident in the Rupununi, the area (southwest) bordering Venezuela and Brazil. This attempt was linked by the government to the UF's disaffection over the election result and its exclusion from government. [For some background on this debate see Latin American Bureau 1984; Manley 1982; Bertram 1992; Ferguson 1995: 28; and Joseph 1998.]

The nature of the PNC has been a matter of great controversy in the litera-ture on political economy. This is largely because it has always been a coalition consisting of an unusually wide spectrum of interests. It has been variously cate-gorized as a noncapitalist, state capitalist and an intermediate regime [Mandle 1977; Odle 1975; Jameson 1980; Thomas 1983; Pierce 1984]. The point of import in the current context is the evolving government alliance or constituency, with consequential kaleidoscopic interests. Discerning the influence which the various elements of the constituency exert in the context of politics marked by ethnic conflict is not an easy task, especially if the sole objective is to fit the regime and its policies into a simple taxonomy.

Given the complex (and arguably plastic) PNC constituency, it is not conceivable that the governement can be classified as pursuing simply pro-African (in the sense of being pro-managerial) policies or capitalist agendas.[85] Obviously a prime objective would have been to hold on to the core of its supporters. The government was therefore generous towards its supporters, a policy over which it was to come to grief from time to time because of the difficulty of distinguishing between the interests of functionaries and those of the masses they coordinated or were supposed to serve. This was especially true in the unions [see Quamina 1987 and Manley 1982]. But even as the government was often indulgent towards its supporters, the leadership was intolerant of internal dissent in its ranks since they were not in a position to fight the Opposition and supporters at the same time. When the fight with the Opposition was on the cards the leadership was likely to demand absolute sacrifice and support from its constituents and constituencies. (For a fuller discussion with a slightly different emphasis of this point and the issue of the authoritarian tendency of the PNC government, see Ferguson [1995: 46 and ch. 1].)

The extensive racial segmentation of the society (or at least the occupational specialization), which was still a fact of life, posed a threat to any government that challenged too many entrenched interests. Apart from meeting the needs of its predominantly urban supporters, the PNC would have to avoid falling into the same trap that ensnared the PPP in 1953 and again in 1964 – alienating all its opponents at the same time. The government was obviously sensitive to this dilemma.

Additionally, therefore, it sought to broaden its base. In order to do this the government would obviously need to pursue policies of interest to potential allies. Free education, investment in rice, as well as rural and farm-to-market roads could be expected to attract some East Indian interests. It has been persuasively argued that the PNC successfully sought to attract East Indians into the party to this end and, just as crucially, in order to prevent further African–East Indian violence. Initially, under the supervision of Mohammed Kassim, a Muslim wing was established by the PNC. In the words of one commentator, "the wing began building local parties in as many villages as it was possible to infiltrate" [Silverman 1980: 160]. It was to have a major influence on PNC policies and to provide several senior ministers for the government.

One commentator had argued that the approach of the PNC to the "ticklish racial situation" was to avoid allowing the balance of economic and political power to move too far in favour of one or other of the major racial groups [Jeffrey 1997: ch. 3]. It may be argued that the problem was more complicated and that, at least during our period of study, the PNC realized that staying in office required policies that would win support from the bulk of the key forces at any point in time. [For a more extensive exploration of this thesis see Hintzen 1989.] Rather than the passive approach that the balancing of access to benefits would imply, it would have been more effective to seek to actively manage the various interests or forces ranged against it.

So, in addition to incorporating the Muslim community, which for a number of reasons had long felt itself threatened by the Hindu dominance in the PPP, the PNC often sought to outflank the Opposition, if they could not be otherwise pressured into cooperation. They did this by adopting some PPP policies or suborning their supporters using the resources in the government's gift. Many sweeteners were offered, including posts, priorities in policies such as rural electrification, sugar bonuses and out-of-crop work for sugar workers.[86] It is in this context that the periodic efforts such as the Peace Plan of the early 1970s (eventually reneged on by the PPP) and the PPP's policy of 'critical support' should be judged. This is the sense in which the term 'intermediate' is relevant to the regime. Clearly, given the racial arithmetic of Guyana,[87] depending as it did on a minority (African) and declining share of the population, the PNC was constrained to adopt policies that would appeal across the racial divide. In that sense, it was necessary to avoid the fundamental reforms that carried risks of alienating a majority of the community at the same time. Some of these reforms, as we shall see, were to be found in agriculture.

But it is probably true that the core PNC support was interested in radical measures such as nationalization and the removal of ascribed status. In some of these goals they obviously shared the same objectives as the sugar workers. However, as some of the 1964 events showed, they had very strong views on the manner of sharing opportunities, particularly as regards the role of educational qualifications.

In 1970 the government declared its intention of pursuing a path of 'cooperative socialism' and in 1970 it opted to become a republic, the first English-speaking Caribbean state to do so. In the Declaration of Sophia, the PNC leader spelled out some of the pillars on which the new republic was to be built. It has been argued elsewhere that these policies, external developments and the strategy of outflanking the Opposition, mentioned earlier, helped to ensure that "there was an absence at this historical juncture of moderating voices and tendencies of sufficient credibility and standing that could have served to circumscribe the frenetic pace of the imposition of radical solutions across the spectrum of political, economic and social contexts of the society" [Ferguson 1995].

Four aspects of this policy are of interest of us in relation to LSSs: the expansion of public ownership of the critical industries; the pursuit of cooperative ownership and management; hinterland development linked to what amounted to a basic needs programme (to feed, clothe and house the nation [FCH]); and regional (Caribbean) integration. Each of these policies, important during our period, had special implications for the development of LSSs in Guyana. We start with regional integration and public ownership before looking at these and other aspects in the context of land policy.

There are factors of a historical and cultural nature that pull Guyana towards political ties with the English-speaking Caribbean. These are fully explored in the literature, as is the reason for the collapse of the West Indies Federation. Additional to those factors were special external forces that served to push Guyana towards a tighter political embrace with the region following that Federation debacle. The radical political stance taken by the government on the international front after 1971 and 1974, combined with the nationalization of TNC assets, put it on a collision path with the US, in particular, and other metropolitan powers constantly. It sought protection from retaliation largely by trying to wrap a regional movement around itself. Reinforcing the urgency of this approach was the fact that during this period Guyana encountered difficulties with two of its neighbours with regard to borders and territory [Burrowes 1984: ch. 9].[88] Given its population size (relative to Venezuela) and the pattern of settlement in Guyana, it was clear, at least in the Venezuela case, that a military solution would not favour Guyana.[89] Regional integration was seen as a very important means of combatting this threat to the country's 'territorial integrity' [see Manley 1982: ch. 3]. The efforts to promote regional integration culminated in the establishment of Carifta and the Caribbean Economic Community (CARICOM) in 1968 and 1973, respectively. Guyana's leading role as a founding member of the regional integration movement is widely acknowledged and can be more fully understood from this political perspective.[90]

The importance of the sugar industry was to further decline during this era. Except for a brief period in the mid 1970s, bauxite mining and processing gradually displaced sugar from its position of dominance in the economy.

6.1 New Amsterdam to Rosignol ferry, 1976.

Sugar's share of GDP fell steadily and its contribution to the central government's current revenues was a mere 5 percent over the years 1966–75. The sugar industry did, however, remain the largest single employer of labour. In 1975 it accounted for a total of 25,000 jobs and as a result of post-1978 expansion this had increased to 32,000 by 1980 [Greenidge 1980]. The overwhelming majority of these employees were East Indian. The occupational structure was not therefore radically altered by the 'socialist policies' and this rural wage labour/small farmer alliance remained outside the control of the PNC.

Although by 1980 the total cultivation under rice was still in excess of that under sugar, the latter still accounted for some 52,000 ha of developed land. The process of diversification of the industry mentioned in the preceding section came to a halt during the 1970s. Raw sugar, molasses and rum remained the centrepieces of the industry's output. Diversification of land use for other crops was given priority over by-product diversification [Greenidge 1982].

The final stage of our story of LSSs witnessed the recrudescence of the struggle with plantation sugar. Bookers and the Demerara Company had, during this period of uncertainty, attempted to insure against nationalization via a number of devices. These attempts at insurance included local share issues, the sale or donation of some 14,750 ha of unutilized lands to the state and private individuals [Litvak and Maule 1979; Shahabuddeen 1983: 237–38]. In addition, villages, cooperatives and independent farmers were permitted to grow sugar cane to be processed by the plantations' factories. The Cane Farming Development Corporation, funded by the industry, the Commonwealth Development Corporation and the Government of Guyana, was established specifically to facilitate this effort by way of loans and technical assistance. Incidentally, the price fixing formula for such cane, although now revised, guaranteed the processor a profit and exposed the farmer to all the risks. The acreage the company devoted to sugar was also contracted. More importantly, the lands adjacent to the main roads and highways, 'front lands', were sold in substantial quantities. Rather than investing their own funds in sugar development, the companies raided the Sugar Industry Rehabilitation Fund so extensively that by 1976 it had been exhausted. As mentioned earlier, the withdrawals were repatriated for other investments and, in a similar vein, the substantial sums realized from the sale of the front lands were promptly repatriated or invested elsewhere. Finally, there was also a localization programme under which Guyanese were recruited or promoted to local management positions.

Apparently, these devices were initially successful in staying the hand of the government, for by 1975 only the financial sector and sugar remained under TNC ownership. But as has been argued elsewhere, the government's tardiness in nationalizing sugar was really attributable to its position vis-à-vis the Opposition-controlled labour force of the industry [Greenidge 1976a]. If plantation sugar was to be successfully confronted, all the labour force had to be mobilized by the state. Nationalization of sugar was only undertaken when the two political adversaries – the PPP and PNC – came to an 'understanding' following nearly two years of civil resistance and noncooperation on the part of the PPP. This understanding took the form in August 1975 of "critical support" of the PNC government in return for implementation of progressive state policies [Jeffrey 1977; Jagan 1977] such as nationalization.

With the imposition of a variable levy on windfall profits in 1974, Bookers McConnell, the sugar enterprise, began to run down its assets, as did other TNC enterprises in anticipation of nationalization [Greenidge 1980]. This occurred before mechanization of field operations – planting and harvesting – had taken place. Mechanization of these operations would have required a change in the layout of the fields, flood fallowing and the development of alternative varieties of cane. The large commitment of funds that would have been required to carry out these changes was not forthcoming because of the uncertainty about the future of the private sector and government regulation of profits.

In 1971 the state embarked on a process of nationalization with the acquisition of the Demerara Company. This culminated in the takeover of Bookers' assets in 1976. As a consequence of these efforts, between 1970 and 1980 the state's share of total employment rose from less than 5 percent to over 45 percent. By the latter year, some 65 percent of productive resources were owned by the state [Greenidge 1982; Boodhoo 1971: 141]. The policy of nationalization had two implications worthy of mention. First, the nationalization of external trade destroyed the economic base of the old white and Portuguese compradors. Second, the takeover of the schools by the state did much the same initially for the established churches in general and the Catholics in particular, in the process turning the major churches against the PNC government.

In tandem with the nationalization of productive assets and trading was a programme to promote indigenous art, local culture, the writing and publishing of local textbooks and educational material, and including the Carifesta initiative [Manley 1982: ch. 7]. This programme further undermined the position of those who saw themselves as the guardians of local European culture. A good deal of Portuguese and other middle class emigration followed. But the programme also helped to launch a number of artists. A case in point is Mahadai Das, an East Indian and now an internationally recognized poet who published her first collection of poems, entitled *I Want to Be a Poetess of My People*, during this period (1977). And, interestingly enough, those poems, described on the sleeve notes as a record of her experiences, pertained to her 1975 stint in the Guyana National Service (GNS).

The change in ownership of the productive resources should have facilitated a thoroughgoing reform of the relations of production. But this did not materialize. A national insurance scheme was established in 1969 and a number of other important steps were taken. These included a public sector minimum wage agreement with the unions. A great deal of control over major enterprises and critical enterprise decisions, however, still lay with managers and foreign TNCs (through technology and, after 1977, marketing and service contracts) and the basis of worker remuneration was not significantly modified. The implementation of a national nonstatutory (public sector) minimum wage agreement together with production bonuses was adversely affected by the endemic public sector fiscal deficit attributable to difficulties in the sugar and bauxite industries. Attempts at worker participation floundered and were shelved when the post-1977 crisis in production struck.

In 1979 the three-year minimum wage agreement, which had been concluded between the government and the TUC in 1977, was effectively suspended. Due to the fiscal crisis, the increases scheduled for 1979 could not be implemented and public sector wages were frozen – although not before the sugar corporation had paid increases to certain workers in the industry with respect to the first five months of the year. Those increases were, of necessity, eventually discontinued and the corporation and the government were taken to court. The court gave judgment against the state. To make matters worse for the government, the Court of Appeal upheld the decision which, in effect, concluded that the increment had been illegally withheld since the Labour Ordinance of 1942, which was mentioned earlier, permitted the regulation of wages rather than their freezing or reduction. However acceptable this decision might have been from the juridical perspective, it was unorthodox logically and an economic nightmare. There followed a number of industrial relations and political problems and the deterioration in government-union relations. The government subsequently passed the Labour (Amendment) Act of 1984 in order to validate the wage freeze. At the same time, by way of a sweetener, it sought to make the TUC the bargaining agent for all public sector workers and to provide for collective labour agreements to be legally enforceable, if the relevant parties desired. Although the sweetener was understood by all to be very dear to the heart of the TUC, the act was challenged by some sugar workers and the High Court struck down the relevant provision. That decision was again upheld by the Court of Appeal. The unions lost, in the process, the legal strengthening that the TUC itself had sought.

By 1980 not only did the state find itself in conflict with labour in all the major industries – now state owned – but the cycle of 'crisis/industrial action/crisis' set in train a downward spiral in productivity and growth from which the economy has yet to fully recover [Greenidge 1982].

Land Policy and Tenure Reform

Tenure reform was to be the lynchpin of land policy in the 1970s. The problems of illegal transfers, subletting, mortgaging, fragmentation and the hoarding of land, to which reference has been made earlier, were seen not as the result of particular relations of production but rather as the specific consequences of inadequate tenure arrangements. Agrarian reform was therefore cast as the provision of the 'machinery' for facilitating a quicker supply of land to the landless [Government of Guyana 1966: xi–5]. In addition, efforts were made to ensure adequate holding sizes.

Settlement of the hinterland by private individuals was to be sponsored by the state, particularly if such settlement was undertaken within the framework of the cooperatives [Hope 1975; Government of Guyana 1972: chs. 8, 9]. Early in the life of the development plan, a study was conducted into land utilization [Naraine 1971]. In its report the committee charged with the study recommended, inter alia, the extension of the life of new leases to thirty-five years with safeguards against abuse and no automatic inheritance. This recommendation was accepted by the government which also agreed to acquire both uneconomic and unoccupied plots [Government of Guyana 1972: 201–4]. Furthermore, in 1975 the prime minister promised, in a major policy statement, to lay before Parliament legislation limiting the size of holdings owned by private individuals and companies [People's National Congress 1975: 20].

In 1978 a committee on land reform again recommended, inter alia, the consolidation of fragmented holdings, the compulsory acquisition of abandoned freehold agricultural land as well as the abolition of landlordism and the subletting of agricultural lands [Sukdeo et al. 1978]. These sentiments were subsequently incorporated in the new constitution [Government of Guyana 1980: 23].

Whilst the intent of all these measures of tenure reform was clear, their impact has yet to be felt. With few exceptions nationalization was confined to TNC assets [Greenidge 1982]. Whilst some of its supporters (including some of the agrarian capitalists who had defected from the PPP) had no problem with this, there were others, including, and especially, small-scale non-rice farmers who wished to see more thoroughgoing reform.

The state was not able to fully deliver the promise on reform for a number of reasons. First of all, politically it could not embark on land reform when nationalization of the nonagricultural and TNC-owned sector was in full swing, partly for fear of upsetting its rural constituents, that is, when it needed their support. Having begun with nationalization, it encountered the problem to which earlier reference has been made, namely, a confrontation with sugar labour that culminated in a debilitating strike which it eventually broke. However, it was a pyrrhic victory and its economic capacity to handle another struggle was severely undermined. Under the critical support compact, the PNC had a free hand in nationalizing TNC assets but nationalization of domestic entities was resisted by the PPP and, more importantly, the action in the agrarian sector for which it could secure support was largely limited to the provision of additional financial and institutional resources for the rice industry.

In place of the land reform, therefore, the government concentrated on new schemes and hinterland settlements. This thrust made such reforms, as had been promised, less urgent. Henceforth, problems with sugar turned on the intrastate relations and the industrial relations conundrum posed by the role of the state as owner of the industry and its role as manager (and tax authority) of the economy [Greenidge 1982]. The respite offered by TNC nationalization was quite short lived therefore. The problems of dealing with domestic agrarian capital and large disparate public enterprises were not grasped. The government was more successful in attempts at land reform in an urban context. Such reform took the form of an ambitious housing programme initiated in the 1970s. The housing leg of the FCH programme sought to add some 60,000 housing units to the stock of housing in five years. Although this target proved to be entirely ambitious, by 1980 the programme, one of the most visible successes of the PNC in office, had brought housing to a wide range of middle and lower income groups.[91]

Some thirty-one subsidized, low-cost housing schemes were initiated between 1970 and 1980. Roughly 2,527 of the total starts were for the benefit of low-income families by means of "Aided Self-Help". It has been estimated that total housing starts amounted to 30,180 between 1970 and 1980 with peaks in 1971–73, 1975–76 and 1979. This represented 3,180 houses per annum compared with an estimated 2,000 in the 1960s and estimated demand of 4,000 units. The estimated cost was some $500 million [IBRD 1970; Government of Guyana 1981]. In addition, the government undertook the development of various stretches of land for house lots. Several housing schemes, including North Ruimveldt, Meadow Brook and Lodge Backlands, were developed through the Central Housing and Planning Authority for this purpose.

This success was partly attributable to the absence of the conflicts so evident in the rural sector. Since the main target group of this programme was urban and because of the heavy self-help element most of the beneficiaries were African. There was also an important rural element in this programme and to the extent that East Indians predominate in rural Guyana they were also beneficiaries. In this regard mention should also be made of the Sugar Industry Labour Welfare Fund (SILWF) which administered a programme under which interest-free loans were made available for sugar industry workers to construct houses on land provided at $1 per lot [Shahabuddeen 1983: 203].[92] Later, the government was to require the nationalized bauxite industry to make similar arrangements for bauxite workers. In the latter case the subsidy was nominally associated with house *construction* as opposed to land acquisition. In this manner the government employed the financial resources at its disposal to reward its supporters and suborn its opponents.

Rice had a more difficult time than sugar in adjusting to the change in government initially. The PPP government had been dubbed a 'rice government' because it had devoted so much of its resources to the rice farmers, who were mainly its East Indian supporters. The new government set out with the aim of redressing this balance. It tried to de-emphasize rice in favour of other agriculture and industrialization to which its own, predominantly urban, supporters were attracted.

First, we may look at the action taken with regard to administration of the rice industry. The PPP dominance of rice politics had long been a matter of concern to the PNC government. Early in its tenure, therefore, the government amended the legislation to remove the RPA, and de facto PPP, control of the RMB. The RMB was itself reorganized, new management was appointed and new vehicles established for developing the rice industry. In place of the RPA, Rice Action Committees (RACs) were established. These committees included administration, rice producers, millers and local authorities (district agencies) concerned with production and infrastructure. The committees were financed by the RMB and they administered district machinery pools and the distribution of subsidized inputs such as fertilizers. Needless to say, the consequential political polarization and pique led to the RPA refusing to serve on either the RACs or the reorganized RMB. In the face of these reactions the industry attracted practically no assistance between 1966 and 1969.

Eventually, notwithstanding this and the problems with respect to the LSSs at BBP (to which we shall turn later), the PNC made strenuous efforts to increase the efficiency of the industry. Without the Cuban contract the market prospects for rice were regarded as being similar to that for sugar – bleak.[93] Rather than facilitating a further increase in the area under rice, it was intended to improve productivity, lower prices and rationalize milling and marketing. Poor husbandry practices, insufficient water utilization, inadequate pest control and insufficient research and development were listed as the prime causes of low productivity [Government of Guyana 1966: xii, 5–9].

In 1969 the Guyana Rice Corporation (GRC) was established absorbing the functions of the Guyana Rice Development Corporation (GRDC) and the RMB which had previously catered for the needs of the rice industry. In that year also the drought in investment in rice was broken and a $26m rehabilitation programme was launched.

Largely with assistance from the US Agency for International Development (USAID), a five-year "rice modernization scheme" was instituted in 1969. Research into new varieties of rice was intensified and fertilizers and pesticides provided. Investment in land was stepped up. Silos for the drying and storage of grain were built, rice mills were modernized to improve the quality of the product and to recover the by-products. Loans were provided by the GCC for this purpose. A rice packaging plant was acquired and installed. Between 1960 and 1980 the number of government-owned mills increased from three to eleven, five of which were established between 1975 and 1978. Throughout the 1980s government-owned multistage mills accounted for 10 to 12 percent of all such mills.

In 1970 the GRC spent $4 million on improving its storage facilities and assistance with ploughing and harvesting, while technical support and other input support were provided to farmers. Considerable progress was made with respect to the adoption of new, higher yielding, long grain varieties such as blue belle and starbonnet over the years 1974–79 in particular.

In addition to the belated revamping of forces of production in the rice industry, considerable attention and resources were devoted to "other agriculture" [Government of Guyana 1973]. Agricultural diversification was to be the basis for future economic growth. This thrust for diversification took on added importance in the context of later efforts to match productive capacity with domestic consumption.

Eventually, the approach to diversifying other agriculture was expanded into a strategy of resource-based industrialization and included the FCH programme. The first phase of this strategy involved import replacement. It was estimated that at the end of the 1960s at least 60 percent of imports were directly substitutable by domestic produce. Those products included foodstuff and forest products [David 1969: 363]. Cognizant of the burden of its food import bill and keen to realize Guyana's potential as the bread basket of the Caribbean, the government implemented a variety of measures aimed at restricting the importation of foodstuff that could be produced locally or for which there were local substitutes in the wider meaning of the term.

The Guyana Marketing Corporation (GMC) was charged with responsibility for providing the marketing infrastructure and supporting facilities on which this diversification was to be had. Farm support prices were set to encourage production of targeted products. Prices were set on the basis of a three-year average with quarterly reviews. Some twenty purchasing locations were established countrywide and marketing outlets were located in the main population centres.

In May 1974 the Accelerated Production Drive was initiated. This programme covered coconuts, papaws, tomatoes, poultry, pineapples, corn, soya beans, blackeyed peas, peanuts, vegetables, running beans, citrus, plantains, bananas and cassava. The programme encompassed loans to finance cultivation of these crops, free plant material and a wide range of other production and cash incentives. In addition, the Guyana Agricultural Products Corporation (GAPC) was established to produce and process several specialized crops such as corn, soya beans, blackeyed peas and peanuts. It also acquired processing facilities for oil palm, fish, citrus and pineapples, tomatoes and papaws, cassava, peanuts, root and vegetable crops. Finally, the Guyana Agricultural Development Bank was established in 1977 to provide development loans and working capital to traditional and nontraditional agriculture, including fisheries and poorer farmers.

Guyana is a traditional supplier of agricultural produce to the Caribbean region. We have already mentioned the importance of rice in this regard. To this might be added fish, beef and plantains up to the early 1950s. Guyana's potential as the "bread-basket of the Caribbean" is well established and widely accepted, if not long anticipated, and the policy of expanding exports rested in part on expanding market access. Creation of a regional market was therefore a logical pillar of product diversification.

The impact of these initiatives and institutions was quite significant. As far as local self-sufficiency in food was concerned, the FCH programme encountered considerable success. According to one estimate, Guyana had achieved nearly 94 percent self-sufficiency in the designated items by the mid 1970s [Nathan Associates1974; USAID 1975]. Production of ground provisions, fruits and vegetables increased substantially and displaced importation of white potatoes, vegetables and fruits in all forms, which were banned. Similarly, local fish, poultry, meat and pork replaced imported equivalents. In addition, consciousness and pride in 'eating local' was developed.

The pursuit of the programme of agricultural diversification was also closely linked to and partly dependent on the success of the promotion of hinterland development or "opening up the interior" [David 1969: 369]. One of the devices intended to facilitate pursuit of this objective was construction of a 400-mile all-weather road to Brazil at an estimated cost of US$25 million. The government had also promised to establish an interior development corporation to coordinate the programme for opening up the interior. This did not materialize. The primary instrument actually employed was national service, an approach first advocated in 1963 [New World Associates 1963]. The specific institutions established in the national service mould were the Youth Corps and, subsequently, the GNS [Standing 1977; Danns 1980: 84–89; Burnham 1974].

The financial cost of this and the programmes aimed at diversification was very high, however. Over the decade 1965–74 some $240 million was spent on such programmes compared with $74 million in the preceding decade. The GMC surplus of G$400,000 had been converted to a deficit of G$600,000 by 1970 primarily because, in addition to being a buyer of last resort, it lacked adequate and appropriate storage facilities. Dumping of spoilt commodities was a constant feature of its operations.

As explained later, the thrust collapsed in 1979 and 1980 with the demise of the GMC and GAPC. The individual institutions involved in the process suffered varying fates.

Settlement Objectives

Whereas the problem of high unemployment was initially a concern insofar as it affected the rural communities, in the 1970s the primary focus was urban. Rural unemployment, however, continued to be a problem. One major factor cited as contributory to the inability to find job places was limited employment opportunities in agriculture. The sugar industry was prevailed upon to provide some relief of the issue by decasualizing the labour force. The cost of this was met from out-of-season work on infrastructure and diversification of land use. The main cause was assumed to be lack of access to land. A prime means of dealing with this problem was therefore identified as easier and quicker access to land. No less than 25,000 unemployed persons were assumed to be ready and willing to engage in farming [Government of Guyana 1966: xlx, 11–19]. Consequently, "at the core of the 1966–72 Plan was the opening up of land for cultivation".

In the preceding chapter, reference was made to the genesis of attempts to settle Guyana's hinterland. The earliest efforts by plantations to secure Caribbean labour for hinterland plantation were blocked by the coastal sugar planters. In 1966 and 1968 efforts to open up the hinterland were revived. The Government of Guyana floated a set of schemes in four areas [Guyana 1966 and 1969b]:

1. Bartica/Potaro – Tumatumari, Mahdia and Konawaruk
2. Rupununi/Kanuku – Moco Moco
3. North West District – Kaituma/Barima
4. Berbice River – Kimbia River

In the late 1960s and particularly in the mid 1970s when the state's financial fortunes rose with improved terms of trade, efforts were made to tackle the urban employment problem directly. The most notable of these devices was the Youth Corps (established in 1967) based at in the hinterland at Tumatumari and in 1968 consisting of over 200 youths. Ostensibly, the objective of the scheme was to familiarize a wide range of urban youths with the potential and lifestyle of the interior and to equip them with the basic skills and drive necessary to 'open up' the interior. In 1973 the GNS was established on a much grander scale than the Youth Corps. At its peak, the GNS employed hundreds of staff to cater for the pioneers at the centres. These two institutions spawned their own LSSs which were to be manned by the graduates of the main institutions. The schemes in question were to be found at Kimbia River (GNS) and Sebai (Youth Corps) [Burnham 1974].

In contrast to those schemes, which were concerned with the young and previously unemployed, other schemes, such as Matthews Ridge, aimed to provide alternative job places for an entire community faced with economic dislocation. When the subsidiary of Union Carbide terminated its operations at Matthews Ridge/Port Kaituma, the state declined to resuscitate it but instead established a development authority (Matarkai) to coordinate the conversion of the entity into a complex of state, cooperative and private livestock, arable farms and orchards. The need to retain people in the area was made more urgent by the existence of US$10 million of otherwise unutilized infrastructural facilities. These facilities included a thirty-two-mile railway track and rolling stock as well as 277 kw of electric power (far in excess of the needs of the resident community). The objective then was to protect existing jobs of primarily PNC supporters.

The hinterland schemes were an important device for furthering the goal of import replacement. The goal had two dimensions – the production of noncoastal or new commodities and the production of those in high demand which had formerly been imported ["Population and development", *Sunday Chronicle,* 21 December 1975: 6, 43]. The most notable example was solanum (or white) potatoes cultivated on a pilot scheme/state farm at Cato in the Rupununi [Mittleholzer 1973]. The other crops of this nature actually grown on LSSs were cotton, which was produced at the Kimbia settlement, and oil palm, produced at Wauna.

It should also be noted that the hinterland schemes were intended to demonstrate the viability of and act as change agents for the diffusion of new techniques of production and the adoption of nontraditional crops. We have already pointed to the unfamiliarity of coastal dwellers with farm technologies other than those of sugar, rice and flatland cultivation. The LSSs were intended to expose farmers and settlers to some other technologies and forms of management, particularly commercial production, namely:

    i. smallholder satellite farms linked to agro-processing facilities
    ii. large-scale mechanized production

6.2 Glass factory, 1979.

The schemes were also charged with large scale mechanized cultivation of traditional crops, including new varieties of these crops. Their success was to serve as a catalyst for the adoption of such systems by private farmers. Large-scale mechanized production of cassava, cotton and black-eyed peas are worthy of mention in this regard. The GNS/Youth Corps and Peoples' Temple Agricultural Project (PTAP) schemes were intended to perform these types of function.

LSSs were also supposed to facilitate the rationalization of small farm settlements. Potter, for example, has argued that the main objective of the scheme along the Soesdyke-Linden Highway was to ensure orderly land settlement [Potter 1979b]. It was supposed to forestall squatting and haphazard peasant settlement of the lands opened up by the intercity link. However, whilst this is a plausible contention, it is not sustainable. The rationalization of the urban dairy industry through localization was certainly an explicit objective of the Moblissa section of the Soesdyke-Linden Scheme. But the Moblissa scheme was part of a programme aimed at upgrading peasant dairy production in Georgetown and its environs through their incorporation in a state/private agro-industrial complex located outside of the urban area. In fact, the important and explicit objective of the six Soesdyke-Linden settlements was the resettlement of returning Guyanese and immigrant West Indians desirous of farming. It was one of the schemes devoted to this purpose [Government of Guyana 1974].

Several other attempts had been made to settle foreigners [Burrowes 1984: 293]. We have already made reference to the case of the Jews. The concern to provide a refuge for Jews fleeing Nazi persecution led to the first serious efforts to explore the agricultural potential of the hinterland areas.[94] As a result of the outbreak of the Second World War nothing came of these efforts, but the seed that had been planted germinated. The objective of LSSs devoted to settlements for persecuted or minority groups from abroad did not die. In 1947, following two resolutions by the Standing Conference of the Anglo-American Commission, the British government appointed a commission to "consider the possibilities of land settlement in British Guiana and British Honduras". Unlike previous efforts, however, on this occasion consideration was to be given to the settlement of refugees from the war as well as of West Indians [Government of Guyana 1966]. Once again, nothing of substance materialized.

Later, burgeoning restrictions in the UK, in the form of the 1962 Common-wealth Immigrants Act, as well as restrictions in Canada and the US made the attractiveness of this enterprise more evident both to Guyana and the West Indies. Approaches to the US and Canada for assistance to finance a scheme yielded no fruit. In 1974 permission was granted to a group of settlers who, though not Jews, were foreigners in search of a better life. The settlers were members of the People's Temple, an American sect led by Jim Jones. It has been said of these (predominantly African American) settlers that "the community itself had a seemingly comprehensive and progressive social programme. Through such a programme, the hope was to build and sustain a very unique socialist community in a society whose dominant ideology was cooperative socialism" [Matthews and Danns 1980: 78].

There were other attractions associated with the PTAP. Lack of strongly motivated labour was regarded by the government as a major barrier to its efforts at hinterland settlement. The foreigners of the PTAP commended them-selves because they appeared to be strongly motivated and highly skilled.

In addition to being "well organized", they were well endowed with financial resources. The organizers had ambitious plans to establish a large community serviced by an airport, holiday resort as well as agricultural and industrial activities.

PTAP was granted some 2,000 ha in the first instance at Jonestown, near Port Kaituma, in the North West District. At the time of the well-known tragedy they had built many houses and established a thriving mixed farm, culti-vating corn, ground provisions, wing beans, cassava and livestock. Further-more, the quality and capacity of the medical centre and communication facilities were not only well known but without parallel in the country [Matthews and Danns 1980: 78]. These facilities were established with no direct financial assistance from the Government of Guyana. At the same time, the group was apparently sympathetic to the government's aims and frequently rendered assistance of a material and ideological kind to the government.

The notorious and tragic mass murder and suicide that took place on 16 November 1978, which in the process claimed the life of US congressman Leo Ryan, as well as the lives of some 1,000 persons resident at the PTAP at the time, has given rise to a library of its own, both in books and film [see, for example, Harris 1996 and the film *Guyana Tragedy – The Story of Jim Jones*, starring Powers Boothe and James Earl Jones]. This PTAP was in many ways an irony, for although it was not born of the sugar industry, it shared many of the latter's characteristics. Like the sugar plantation, it was totally self-contained but tightly articulated to the state. In its labour management it can be characterized as an atavism. In the words of one commentator, "it is clear that Jonestown was an experiment in human organization involving a migrating people searching for a 'better life' and encouraged by officials of a state struggling to conquer the problem of underdevelopment" [Matthews and Danns 1980: 78]. One could as well add the struggle to discourage preemptive military action by a neighbour.

The Framework of Settlement Administration

Whereas during the 1960s the administration of the LSS had been gradually centralized, by the early 1970s the administration that evolved was more diffuse and decentralized. The LDD continued to exercise control over the existing coastal and pre-1964 LSSs not yet incorporated.

By the 1970s most of the older surviving LSSs had achieved the self-governing status of Bush Lot, as may be seen from Table 1. On those schemes the factional rivalry catalogued by Silverman had become commonplace as was the case in most villages. It has been argued that the PPP and PNC sought to control these villages because they did not believe that much would be done in the absence of such control. Indeed, this is not an entirely unreasonable position. From 1967 the PNC sought to infiltrate traditional PPP strongholds, exploiting in the process "political, economic and religious cleavages and, in so doing, was to alter the local level" [Silverman 1980: 161]. The cleavages were especially intensified in the case of Bush Lot. Here, as elsewhere, the chairman of the village council was allotted the role of 'middleman' with access to patronage which enabled him to extend his influence. Insofar as this chairman now had resources far beyond those that had been formerly available, for mobilizing support, the factional competition became more extreme. Very early in the process the PPP retaliated and violence was directed against PPP opponents [Silverman 1980: 159–60].[95]

For schemes not incorporated into the local government system, there was no clear locus of control. Moco Moco, Marudi and New River came under the control of the Interior Department. Matthews Ridge, established as a special project during the course of the same year, was administered by the Ministry of Agriculture. Sebai, settled in 1972, was the 'responsibility' of the Youth Corps management but the Matthews Ridge administration was responsible for providing it with assistance by way of machinery services. The Kimbia River settlement fell under the aegis of the GNS.

With this diffusion of control came diverse terms and conditions. As a consequence, the inputs to the schemes varied in direct relation to resource capacity of the overviewing authorities. In the cases of Matthews Ridge and Sebai, these inputs could be equated in terms of quantity with those provided by a local government authority on the coast. However, the quality and quantity of the communal facilities available to Matthews Ridge and the GNS settlers had no parallel in LSSs on the coast. Elsewhere, settlements suffered from the state's preoccupation with minimizing investment in new, particularly agricultural, infrastructure such as drainage.

Prospective settlers to these new LSSs were provided with pre-settlement training. The nature of the training was reasonably uniform. At Matthews Ridge, settlers were not given formal training but were exposed to on-the-job training on the state farms – 'worker/settler programmes'.[96] Settlers intended for the other schemes were exposed to an imaginative programme. Wives and unmarried women, for example, were trained in communications, masonry and welding. Men were given military training as well as training in agricultural practices, land development, cooperatives, and maintenance and operation of agricultural equipment.

A second novelty was the payment of allowances to settlers during the initial year of settlement. Settlers at GNS, Moco Moco, Marudi and New River, inter alia, received allowances in kind and in cash. Single settlers at Kimbia received $420 while married couples received $2,760. The allowances were terminated after two years in the case of Kimbia settlers. Although this was a novelty in pre-1960s Guyana, settlers on the rain-fed schemes in Kenya, such as Makeweni and Machakos, were usually provided with food until the first harvest [Ruthenberg 1966: 54]. These arrangements stood in marked contrast to those extended to the settlers on the Soesdyke-Linden Highway. In the case of these settlers the brochure stated, "it is essential that migrants have enough money to support themselves and families for a minimum period of one year . . . an amount of not less than $3,000 will be able to support a husband, wife and four children up to the time of harvesting of the first crops" [Government of Guyana 1974: 8].

During the initial five years of settlement on the LDD-administered schemes, ultimate decision making powers lay with the department. Subsequently, titles to land could be issued if the scheme was deemed successful. In the interim, the cooperatives, into which settlers were grouped, were supposed to be responsible for land acquisition, banking, savings and credit facilities, procurement and supply of inputs, organization of land preparation, harvesting, and marketing [Payne 1976a, 1976b].

The GNS settlers were less autonomous. The settlement was supposed to be administered by the management of the GNS until the scheme achieved viability. Day-to-day administration was the responsibility of a settlement authority which included two settlers' representatives. Cultivation was to be conducted on a cooperative basis and there was the promise of an eventual element of private ownership and operation. The land was issued to settlers on the basis of a long-term lease at an initial rental of $1.23/ha and $2.47/ha, ultimately. Basic and communal facilities, such as potable water, electricity, stores, schooling, land preparation, clothing and supply of input, were the responsibility of the settlement authority. Cultivation was intended to be the responsibility of a twenty-five-man cooperative [Guyana National Service 1975a; 1975b].

The Matthews Ridge project authority also had responsibility for communal facilities but its input into the operations of the cooperatives was considerably less than that of the GNS. Here and on all the other schemes except the GNS-run Kimbia River scheme, state agencies, such as the agricultural extension service, the GAPC and the marketing board, were intended to play a prominent role. In other words, as far as extension and marketing were concerned the settlements were treated no differently from the remainder of the agricultural sector.

In contrast with the foregoing schemes, settlers on the Soesdyke-Linden highway were required to take on responsibility from the time of settlement for securing their twenty-five-year (with the right to a further twenty-five-year renewal) lease. Assistance was provided by the LDD but the responsibility for seeing the exercise through lay with the settlers themselves. Matters pertaining to the farming system, such as crop selection for example, lay entirely with the settlers.

By far the most autonomous of all the schemes was the PTAP at Jonestown. In the words of one commentator, "Jonestown, as far as we know, had minimum interference from the Guyanese government, enjoyed an autonomy as no other foreign or Guyanese community did, and flourished in its material developments" [Matthews and Danns1980: 80]. The state provided the settlers with land, some technical advice, as well as seed and planting material.

In the light of this diverse pattern of assistance, the contention by some authors [Matthews and Danns 1980] that the schemes and the settlers' initiative were stifled by the heavy hand of the state could only be applicable to some schemes, if it is relevant at all. The debate on the role of state in the context of agrarian modernization and the peasantry has of course raged far outside of Guyana and we do not propose to settle it here.[97]

Underlying Issues and Paradoxes

The politics of rice

Early during the tenure of the new government, considerable attention was devoted to correcting some of the abuses that had developed in relation to LSSs. Thus the political consequences of the PPP's land settlement policies and the PNC's reaction were to haunt and influence the shape of agricultural policies for the next two decades. One obvious result was the inability of the state to go through with land reform measures aimed at consolidation and enhancing beneficial occupation. They sought, for example, to enforce the collection of rents and to evict recalcitrant tenants. BBP was the focus of a good deal of these efforts, and in 1969 the three cooperative mills were sold because of the extensive indebtedness of the settlers to the GCC. As a result of the political uproar attendant on these efforts, the government dropped pursuit of these initiatives.

Infrastructure – strategic considerations and cost minimization

As may be seen from Map 2, most of the schemes established between 1968 and 1975 were located in the hinterland. In 1969 a government memorandum explained the issue thus: "events have taken place which have created a new urgency for settlement in the interior and have caused the Government of Guyana to embark upon a scheme for interior development without waiting upon outside participation". Of these events the most outstanding have been "the closing down of the Manganese Co. . . . and the externally promoted uprising in the Rupununi in January this year" [Government of Guyana 1969a: 20]. Earlier in the same report the authors made the point more expli-citly: "the occupation of the larger part of the interior is essential for national security. It is unwise for there to be such large tracts of Guyanese territory unoccupied and unexploited."

Within a year of these events, LSSs were established at Moco Moco, Marudi Valley and New River. The primary aim behind these settlements was territorial occupation dictated by strategic considerations. It would hardly be surprising, therefore, to find that the agricultural objective was relegated to second place in such circumstances. In fact, it was in recognition of the importance of economic development in facilitating the primary task that the subsidiary objective, namely, production of agricultural commodities, was pursued. In this context priority was given, wherever possible, to items not produced on the coast ["Population and development", *Sunday Chronicle*, 21 December 1975: 6, 43].

As a result of the haste with which these hinterland schemes were established, planning, establishing the technical feasibility and formulating financing arrangements had to be cursory. In these circumstances the most important task was to settle and secure the land. This probably explains why the settlers at Moco Moco were called upon to construct the access link to Aishalton, the nearest airstrip, before any cultivation commenced. This exercise involved the opening up of a twenty-seven-mile track and the construction of twenty-one bridges and was a particularly heavy undertaking given the limited number of settlers [Government of Guyana 1970a]. The provision of agricultural infrastructure, on the other hand, attracted relatively low priority. Thus, although the net area available for cultivation at Matthews Ridge was some 7,094 ha, in 1969 only 243 ha were cleared. Similarly, at Marudi a mere 4 ha were cultivated in 1970.

An important determinant of the location of schemes was the overwhelming concern to minimize settlement costs. The 1966–72 plan indicated that LSSs would be located close to other communities or to access roads, or markets, in order to minimize new infrastructural investment. Furthermore, the inclusion of the six schemes in the Soesdyke-Linden Highway project went a long way towards making the cost/benefit ratio of the road more attractive. In this context the Matthews Ridge scheme may also be mentioned, for the farms on that scheme were intended to be established along the Kaituma road. The location of the schemes was symptomatic of the manner of establishment and operation of the LSSs.

This emphasis was also evident from the rudimentary state of the marketing arrangements. Few of the schemes had what may be considered adequate facilities for the storage or processing of produce. At the same time, arrangements had not been made for the marketing agencies to make special provision to address these problems. The buying agents (like the markets) were often not only located inordinate distances from most of the hinterland schemes, but their visits to the buying points were few and irregular.

As a consequence of these factors, losses resulting from spoilage and pilfering were excessive. Those associated with the shipment of tomatoes from Moco Moco, for example, were as high as 50 percent. On that very scheme, farmers lost a significant proportion of their 1972 crop as a result of their inability to secure appropriate containers for the shipment of their produce. Whilst it cannot be denied that even on properly planned schemes these mishaps sometimes occur, it is undoubtedly the case that haphazard and incomplete planning was a significant contributory factor to these unfavourable experiences. Indeed, it may even be argued that in some cases these were costs that the government was prepared to bear. For example, the New River Development Plan projected annual revenues of $21,480. Although transport costs alone, amounting to $27,000, far exceeded total revenues [Government of Guyana 1970b], settlement proceeded notwithstanding these projections. In other words, cost considerations were secondary.

The strategic imperative was also reflected in the number of schemes and their occupants. The bulk of the post-1965 schemes attracted far fewer settlers than did the pre-1965 schemes. Some idea of the small scale of operations on these schemes may be had from Table 1. In other circumstances, only one or two schemes would have been established given such numbers. At Tumatumari/Konawaruk in 1969, hardly 8 ha had been cleared. At Moco Moco, where there was an estimated 80,935 ha, only 40.47 ha had been cleared for occupation by an estimated forty settlers. During the same year, settlers had cleared only 600 out of 6,070.2 ha allocated. The total population of the latter area was only 4,000 persons (640 families) [Government of Guyana 1966].

There can be little doubt that the scattering of small numbers of settlers over so many schemes compounded the burden of overheads involved in interior land settlements. Indeed, it may well have undermined their ability to succeed, for there is fairly widespread agreement that for optimal results an LSS should cater for at least 500 and preferably 1,000 settlers [IBRD 1985: 122–24].

The financial costs associated with uneconomic schemes were largely absorbed by the state. In some instances inputs were provided free of charge to settlers. New River settlers, for example, were supplied and assisted by the Guyana Defence Force (GDF) administration at nearby Camp Jaguar. The same was true of the arrangements for Sebai and Kimbia settlers who were carried financially by the Youth Corps and GNS, respectively.

This aspect of the LSS operations endowed their finances with a high degree of indeterminacy, especially as far as costs were concerned. It was difficult, in other words, to ascertain the profitability of the venture in narrow financial terms. However, as the state's capacity to extend such assistance contracted during the latter half of the 1970s, the transfer of the full costs to the settlers imposed intolerable financial burdens on the latter, most of whom eventually abandoned the ventures.

Urban employment, ethnicity and scale

Another issue weighing heavily on the schemes of this era was their catchment area. The attempt to draw on urban unemployed resulted in the schemes becoming associated with Afro-Guyanese [see, for example, Matthews and Danns 1980]. Furthermore, the induction of females into the GNS as a precondition for university entrance led to a vocal, middle class and predominantly East Indian opposition to that institution. LSSs became caught up in the consequential politicization of the GNS. While it has been common to treat such reactions as typically cynical political byplay, some aspects are worthy of comment.

One of the contentions of the PPP during the 1950s was that the employment opportunities in the police and paramilitary were monopolized by Guyanese of African origin. The training of the intake of the Youth Corps and the GNS in particular was provided by the GDF. In the case of the GNS scheme, only persons who had completed at least one year's training with the GNS were eligible to be considered for a place on the Kimbia scheme [Guyana National Service 1975a: 3]. So, in addition to the participants being recruited predominantly from the urban community, the military orientation of the training compounded this perception of an Afro-Guyanese bias.

In reality, the schemes, other than those of the GNS and Youth Corps, were far more balanced racially than any that had gone before. If there were consistent and marked imbalances in these schemes it was in the representation of the sexes. There was a relative paucity of women, with all the attendant consequences, as may be seen at New River. Nonetheless, these perceptions coloured attitudes towards the schemes and went a long way towards denying them the number and range of applicants, and therefore settlers, that they may have otherwise attracted. This compounded the burden of the overheads associated with hinterland settlement.

Another dimension of the problem was the appropriateness of urban recruits. It has become fashionable to regard the African element of the Guyanese populace as not being agriculturally inclined [see, for example, Matthews and Danns 1980]. However, a perusal of the censuses over the last century does not support this view. Occupational and geographical mobility have been characteristics of both East Indians and Africans in Guyana. Such mobility is attributable to factors other than social trauma or genes, as may be gauged from the first section of this book.

Information available from elsewhere suggests that there may be rational, though not obvious, grounds on which urban dwellers opt out of rural agricultural jobs [Greenidge 1975]. Relatively low product prices and uncertain yields often contrast unfavourably with higher urban informal sector earnings and a low probability of employment. It is clear that the problems experienced by many of the settlers were such as to make for lower expected incomes in rural than in urban areas. Furthermore, the techniques/tools of production on many of the schemes were such as to render settlers little more than subsistence producers. As such, settlement would be of little attraction to anyone who hailed from an urban environment, whatever their race.

On the better endowed GNS and Matthews Ridge schemes a somewhat different contradiction might be noted. The training provided to prospective settlers took place on large state farms which were heavily mechanized and characterized by a relatively extensive division labour. Furthermore, few, if any, of these farms were commercially viable. This would not appear to have been the most appropriate training ground for future small-scale farmers, especially constrained as many would be with regard to fixed and working capital. This, may well be the reason for the often observed phenomenon of settlers leaving the schemes at the end of the wage-employment phase.

Fiscal incidence

A major contradiction emerged with respect to fiscal incidence and the agricultural sector in general and LSSs in particular. There should be no underestimating the political significance of the issue. We have already indicated that it was a rallying point for opposition to the PPP government in 1962–64 (see chapter 5). In fact, the very high politicization of this issue tends to cloud reasoned analysis. We shall touch briefly on three aspects of fiscal incidence that are pertinent with regard to agriculture and LSSs in Guyana: taxation, the direction and bias of public expenditure policy, and other transfer instruments such as pricing policies.

Starting with the latter issue, the available information confirms the continuation of the pattern established in the nineteenth century with respect to rents, D&I rates and other charges. In no year of the 1964–80 period had the state collected enough from settlers to cover the costs either of maintaining the facilities on the LSSs or of delivering the services required. Over the years 1970 to 1980, total current revenues actually fell, namely, from $970,000 in 1975 to $730,000 in 1980. Arrears, net of write-offs, amounted to $1.19 million for the period 1960–80. When both D&I rates and rents are taken into account the arrears in 1968 and 1969 were $2–2.3 million and $1.9 million, respectively.

These deficits have been incurred and arrears accumulated in spite of a standing 20 percent government subsidy on D&I charges, grants and periodic write-offs. On average, arrears in 1969 were equivalent to 54 percent of the assessments and a cursory examination of the data unearthed no correlation between arrears and viability of the schemes [Government of Guyana 1969a].[98] A subsequent study of the water rates system in the main agricultural areas, including D&I schemes, reveals that the problem of arrears continued into the 1980s [Optima Technical Services 1991: pt. 4].

In relation to product prices, the situation is less clear and not unidirectional. As has already been indicated, the GMC, for a good deal of its existence, transferred resources to farmers particularly because it was the buyer of last resort in a situation where the farmers were not obliged to offer the corporation first option [Nathan Asscociates 1974].

It is in the case of rice, however, that the most controversy exists. Paddy prices were set by the GRB which, as sole buyer and exporter of rice during that period, controlled about 25 percent of milling capacity and determined retail and processing margins. It has often been assumed that in executing this role as statutory, monopoly buyer it transferred resources from farmers to urban consumers. This is not supported by the figures and is certainly not true of the entire period in question. The view persists, however, and probably owes its origins to the first steps taken by the PNC government in 1964 to rationalize pricing policy. In the words of an International Monetary Fund (IMF) report,

since 1964, concealed subsidies to farmers through prices higher than justified by market conditions, made it impossible for the Board to meet its expenditures and compelled it to borrow from the government and the commercial bank amounts of more than G$4 million each in 1965 and 1966. In order to ease the deficit, the Board reduced in late 1966 the price paid to farmers from G$18 to G$16 for a 180 pound bag of milled rice . . . prices available to the Board are G$31, fob, per bag under an agreement with the West Indies; G$20 per bag for domestic sales and G$14 fob, per bag in the world market. [IMF 1967: 11]

In fact, farmers received $14 per bag, net of milling costs. Looked at another way, the price change meant higher prices for better varieties. Even in the case of the less preferred varieties, however, it was not all reduction, for subsidies were still being provided through the GDC. By 1968 the deficit had been eliminated and a surplus of $3.5 million recorded. In addition to the 12 percent price reduction to farmers, improved export prices also contributed to this outcome. This performance by the Guyana Rice Board (GRB) was not sustained into the 1970s. By 1980 the board was again recording heavy losses.

After 1978 direct and indirect subsidies, in the economy as a whole had been reduced and price controls were liberalized. Rice inputs, such as fertilizers, had been halved in 1978 but the level of the subsidies increased up to 1980. At the same time, after 1971 periodic price increases were implemented. In 1980 prices increased twice to the tune of 19 percent. It has been estimated, however, that over the years 1975–80 real returns to farmers fell [IBRD 1982; IMF 1981]. Notwithstanding this, in the political arena a strong perception remains that the government has pursued anti-rice policies since 1964.[99]

It is instructive to juxtapose the rice price policy with fiscal policy and the issue of arrears. In keeping with experience throughout the world, it has been notoriously difficult to collect income taxes from the agricultural sector. In addition, the agricultural sector has since 1956 been spared the main indirect taxes – import duties and consumption taxes on imported machinery, equipment and spares.

The main device with the potential for lifting the contribution of the industry, the Sugar Levy Act of 1974, was emasculated when after a year of operation the tax was remitted. After nationalization of the industry, the 135-day strike effectively killed the prospects of this as a viable tool of taxation and the contribution of the industry to the fiscal effort again fell well behind that of bauxite. There is a remarkable asymmetry between this experience of pricing and taxes and that of investment financing.

The post-1964 government has been unwilling or unable to recoup either the maintenance or investment costs by way of user charges or income taxes. Even the marketing board, a traditional means of taxing farmers [Bauer and

Yamey 1968; Bauer 1989], has, as a whole, turned out to be not very effective in that regard.

Postwar development programmes, on the other hand, have been dominated by the agricultural sector. In these programmes, rice and D&I in particular have been paramount. Notwithstanding its initial pronouncements, the post-1964 government had itself become a rice government [Hanley 1987].

Over the years 1970 to 1980 some $313 million was devoted to D&I and sea defence projects. In 1980, 17 percent of GNP was devoted to the central government's capital investment programme. Major D&I projects alone accounted for 31 percent of that programme. In regard of this, nearly one-quarter of a million acres or over 91,000 ha, including the Tapakuma Irrigation Scheme and the Mahaicony/Mahaica/Abary Scheme, were either being drained and irrigated for the first time or rehabilitated. Agriculture as a whole attracted 42 percent of the funds [Bank of Guyana 1980]. Furthermore, the Draft Agricultural Development Plan of 1986–89, which in part incorporated 1986 programmes, proposed a total capital expenditure on public sector agriculture of G$121.5 million, of which some $31.2 million would be devoted to water control systems and $14.9 million to rice. Six major D&I schemes including those mentioned were slated for these funds [Government of Guyana 1985b].[100]

In summary, the fiscal flexibility enjoyed by pre-1953 administrations was lost to the successor administrations with the political realignments that had taken place. The bulk of the foreign aid secured was not only devoted to infrastructure but to agricultural infrastructure. It may be added that the likely returns to the investment can only be regarded as questionable. One study of the Incremental Capital Output Ratio (ICOR) in agriculture has suggested that over the years 1977 to 1983 the ICOR value was very erratic [Government of Guyana 1991]. Being unable to recoup the returns from the investment by way of taxes or any other fiscal instrument, the government was forced to rely on urban-based (personal and corporate income) taxes, indirect taxes and public enterprise transfers. When the enterprises encountered difficulties there was increasing reliance on indirect taxes again.

Cooperative management and commercial farming

One of the most serious disappointments of this era was undoubtedly the failure of the cooperative societies to make a significant positive impact on the management of the schemes. Both the PNC government and its predecessor, the PPP, put a great deal of store by the Cooperative Society as a device for overcoming the main handicaps of small-scale farming in a physical and institutional environment that appeared to favour large-scale operations. Land societies, credit societies and buying societies were all promoted with great zest.[101] Farmers bred in a capitalist or plantation economy framework have a well-known animosity or wariness towards cooperatives. It was not, however, such animosity that posed the most intractable of problems.

Initially, on the earlier schemes such as BBP, cooperatives were not established at all or involved only a few settlers, or collapsed soon after being established. On many of the post-1964 schemes, however, a significant number of societies were actually established and became operational (see Table 9). In 1969 some 800 societies with a total membership of some 60,000 persons were registered in the country. Subsequently, there was a marked expansion on the LSSs. The special privileges enjoyed by the cooperatives and LSS cooperatives gave rise to a great deal of envy by less privileged entities. The settlers at Sebai and the Soesdyke-Linden LSSs were cases in point. Studies in other countries, such as Dominica, also found that the cooperatives were envied by the rest of the community [Nunes 1989: 58–64].

There is some evidence that the cooperatives enjoyed some advantages in the business arena. A study of cooperatives on the coast concluded that creditors and lending agencies regarded cooperative societies as preferred customers for they reduced the administrative cost of lending to a given number of small farmers and they also covered the creditors against the risk of loss by guaranteeing those loans [John 1977].

Given this initial success of the cooperatives it is important to understand why the movement has been regarded as a failure. First of all, the facilities enjoyed by the societies were so widely abused that the state, the sponsor of cooperatives, was forced to exercise tighter control of the societies and to temper the enthusiasm with which these activities were pursued [Payne 1976b].

In essence, some members used the vehicle of the cooperative to secure access to land on more favourable terms than would have otherwise been possible. It was the common practice for members of land cooperatives to sell their membership rights to such cooperatively acquired land in order to realize a capital gain. This was probably responsible for the nonissuance by the Interior Department of titles to settlers within the first five years of settlement. At the end of that period the titles were only issued to cooperatives which were deemed to have been successful in retrospect. As a consequence, the establishment of agricultural land cooperatives eventually declined.

Similarly, many of the societies rapidly incurred substantial debts which could not be serviced. Indeed, such debts were often not properly authorized and in many cases members refused to acknowledge them. This reflection of weak and inadequate management and control of the societies was compounded by less than adequate supervision and monitoring by the Cooperative Department, which had a responsibility for ensuring that the practices of these societies were consistent with the rules and regulations under which they were established.

In order to make up for this inadequacy on the part of its field officers, the department sought to secure some collateral from the societies. Apparently, in the case of unregistered cooperatives, it was the common practice for the crop or output to be taken as collateral. In the case of Matthews Ridge, for example, the project authority reaped and disposed of the cooperatives' crops in order to recoup its advances and fees for the services extended to settlers. From the time of the establishment of the Cooperative Society in January 1971, the proceeds from the sale of settlers' produce was held by the chief interior development officer.

The reaction of the cooperators to these attempts at safeguards, further undermined the farmers' standing and credit-worthiness in the wider sense of the term. In order to evade creditors and their liens, settlers resorted to the disposal of produce through agencies other than the official channels such as the GMC, the state marketing board. The consequences of these developments for the relationship between the state and its protégé were predictable.

Within the societies, morale declined over the years not only in response to these 'external' developments but as a result of weak decision making and lack of controls and accountability within the societies themselves. These organizational inadequacies were also a reflection of the type of resources, human and institutional, from which the cooperatives drew and on whom they depended, for example, low and uneven educational levels among farmers, unfamiliarity with complex corporate transactions, the prevalence of ascriptive status and so on. Thus, the personalization of issues and the reluctance or failure of members to regularly and systematically monitor the activities of officials were commonplace in all societies [John 1975]. With overreliance on a single leader the scope for unauthorized individual initiative, misappropriation and fraud was great. In reality fraud frequently took place. In this regard the cooperatives might be said to have facilitated transfers of income to the educated and articulate, who were frequently the perpetrators of frauds against other members.

Some of the problems were a consequence of the collectivist ethic to which the societies subscribed. An important disincentive to the successful operation of some societies was the 'free-rider' problem. The common practice of dividing proceeds equally among members provided no incentive for individual members to make a positive contribution to the group's efforts. Far from that, such a method of reward provided a positive incentive to pre-emptive misappropriation which could take any form from theft of funds to the unauthorized use of equipment and materials for personal gain.[102]

The results of these problems were soon evident. There was a loss of confidence in cooperatives in general. At Matthews Ridge, twenty-four land cooperatives societies were established between 1968 and 1973. By 1975 all but one or two of these existed in name only. On the Soesdyke-Linden Highway the number of societies fell from seventeen to seven over the decade 1970–80, while the number of members declined by about one-third. The same story might be related for BBP, Cane Grove, La Bonne Mere and Anna Regina. Generally speaking, only the buying societies, that is, those formed to take advantage of bulk purchasing of inputs and land acquisition, have been able to successfully survive these trials.

Some commentators have portrayed the cooperative problem as one of the "Collectivist-Ship-Awash-in-a-Capitalist-Sea" [Soloman and Friedman 1982: 233]. Some of the preceding observations lend credence to this perception. It needs to be acknowledged that the underdeveloped economic context also compounded the problems of the societies. However, the foregoing problems surface in one guise or another in all businesses. By and large they are not peculiar to cooperatives and their solution or resolution ought to be within the capacity of any competent management unit. The fundamental and intractable problem with the cooperatives may well lie, however, with the process of decision making by management.[103]

It can and has been argued that the problem lies not so much with the contradictions of collectivist ethics versus underdeveloped capitalist context but rather with the failure of the management units to adhere to at least one key imperative of good management. That imperative is the need to always be able to resort to a mechanism that would enable resolution of conflicts and interpersonal rivalries. Within an egalitarian institution, such a mechanism is imperative and needs to be employed in a manner and with such dispatch that the effective decision making capacity of the institution and its operational integrity are protected.[104] Nunes, in a study of the Castle Bruce estate in Dominica, highlights lack of a conflict resolution mechanisms and "hyperdemocratization" [Nunes 1989: 58–70] as giving rise to expulsion and frequent conflicts.

This is, however, not unusual, even in cooperatives operating in the developed countries.

The agricultural cooperatives, least of all those on LSSs, and their problems in Guyana have not been exhaustively studied and there may well be other relevant aspects of this experience that need to be examined.[105] One interesting phenomenon in this regard is the extent to which farmers exercise the so-called exit option. We have already referred to the practice or tendency of farmers to withhold surplus production from official marketing channels and the loss or 'defection' of settlers when they ceased to receive wages. One attempt at an holistic explanation of these factors[106] has been offered by Hyden [1980]. This may be a line of examination worthy of being pursued as a separate study, particularly since it would seem to have some relevance to the urban unemployed.

Results

So few LSSs survived to the end of the period that it is easy to conclude that the schemes were unambiguous failures. Most of the problems mentioned in the context of preceding phase continued into the period from 1965 to 1980. By the late 1970s absenteeism, sharecropping and subdivision of plots was prevalent in BBP. Subsidized inputs were widely sold to nonsettlers.[107] The few Africans at BBP were encountering labour problems because of the relatively small size of their households. This affected their ability to market their products and therefore tended to force them to switch to less perishable activities or leave land underutilized. Competition between rice and livestock was a widespread problem and on BBP alone 13,000 cattle were impounded in 1973. The GAPC canning facility began to encounter difficulties; there was no cold storage and the varieties of tomatoes produced appeared to be inappropriate for the form of processing envisaged.

It is rather difficult to gauge the extent to which the schemes aimed at territorial occupation were successful. Indeed, it seems to be fairly widely accepted that the diplomatic initiative may well have been the only effective counter to the Venezuelan threat [Fauriol 1984].

Employment

In terms of employment, the main contribution of the schemes was to generate demand for wage labour. Moco Moco, for example, drew heavily on coastal dwellers for its settlers. This was also especially evident in the GNS case. Some

80 percent of the GNS intake were formerly unemployed urban youths. In addition almost an equal number of persons was employed to staff the service. On the other schemes where settlement farming was actually undertaken, a significant number of administrators and support staff were employed to help with the establishment and management of operations. Furthermore, the bulk of the administrators and settlers were from the coast.

As a serious stimulus to self-employment or own-account farming, however, the contribution of the schemes was insignificant, as may be seen from Table 1. Doubtless, the low levels of production and the absence of vertically integrated operations severely restricted the multiplier effect of the schemes. In this context the schemes for emigrants were perhaps the most successful, initially. It has been estimated that between 1968 and 1971 some 6,500 applications, mostly from abroad, predominantly other West Indians, were received [Downer 1979: 3]. In 1976, 61 percent of the settlers were non-Guyanese (of whom 86 percent were Jamaican) and 68 percent of the non-Guyanese were from the UK [Payne 1976a].

Attracting settlers

These schemes may, in this sense, be considered to have been considerably successful. Not only did many West Indians and Guyanese come (or return) to Guyana to settle but also to help build a major hinterland road (Mahdia). Many individuals settled of their own volition in the Tumatumari-Mahdia area and took up farming (livestock and crops) as well as mining.[108] However, rather than establish an LSS at that location, the government chose the apparently cheaper option of settlements on the very difficult soils along the Soesdyke-Linden Highway.

In the post sugar price boom era the settlers were faced with declining government financial assistance and support. Although many settlers still remain on the schemes, many more, indeed most, have succumbed to difficult economic conditions and the agronomic problems.

Agronomic issues

On the Soesdyke-Linden schemes, as on the large-scale state farms at Matthews Ridge, attempts were made to tackle new crops or traditional activities in difficult agronomic circumstances. At Soesdyke-Linden and Kimbia, conditions were specially difficult. The soil consisted primarily of white sand and was not flat as is the topography of the coast. Natural and improved pastures exhibited marked protein deficiency. The other contributory factor to agronomic problems was the fact that some of the crops, such as cotton, tumeric and black-eyed peas, were relatively unfamiliar to most Guyanese, and even today a great deal of work still remains to be done on the selection of appropriate varieties, pest control and fertilizer regimes.

Given the unfamiliarity of most coastal dwellers with hinterland farming, these agronomic problems loomed quite large on the LSSs. Technical support by way of preliminary trials was a dire necessity. Little was actually undertaken. In recognition of this problem Hooker [1973] in his report on the intermediate savannas had recommended that government provide Bookers or Sanbach Parker with incentives to establish pilot farms to help fill this lacuna. By 1976, however, both had been nationalized and the task proved to be beyond its successor, GAPC, as indeed did survival! Settlers were provided with some agricultural training prior to settlement but this could be no more than rudimentary. Frequently, cultivation had to commence in the absence of advice from extension staff, for example, at Moco Moco and New River. In the latter case the settlers arrived before the survey was completed and the agricultural officer arrived after the crop was planted! It is hardly surprising, therefore, to find frequent reports of poor land preparation, incorrect timing and application of fertilizers, soil erosion, and contamination of waterways [Potter 1979b: 13–14; Downer 1979: 7–9]. Clearly, these factors heightened the uncertainty associated with earning a living from agriculture on these schemes.

Infrastructure

The belief that infrastructural requirements on hinterland schemes would be relatively cheap because costly water control systems, such as sea defences and irrigation, and expensive land clearing would not be needed were factors commending their establishment [David 1969: 369]. It appears that in reaction to the inordinate investment in D&I on coastal schemes, the government decided that no significant investment was warranted in land development in general or D&I in particular. This approach could perhaps be represented by the advertisement for Budget Cars which invites prospective clients to "drive first class, pay economy". This was, of course, not an appropriate approach. Drought and flooding were just as much features of agricultural activity in, say, Matthews Ridge as the coast. The hinterland settlements were therefore frequently rendered inaccessible during the wet season. On one scheme, chronic shortages of feed for pigs during the rainy season resulted in the loss of many animals.

Considerable costs could indeed be incurred in land preparation. One estimate put the cost of land clearance in Matthews Ridge, the activity to which most funds were devoted, at twice the cost of preparing a similar acreage of marginal land on the coast [IBRD 1970]. While ease of mechanical operations was a characteristic of brown sand operations, considerable quantities of inorganic fertilizers and limestone were occasioned by low levels of soil fertility and unpredictable rainfall.

In pursuit of its preoccupation with minimizing investment in infrastructural costs, schemes were supposed to be sited along existing or proposed roads [Government of Guyana 1966b: xi–7]. This approach and rationale is now widely supported by recent research [see IBRD 1985b: 46–48]. The schemes at Moco Moco and Marudi Valley depended on the Mahdia Road (to Linden and coastal markets) but this was never completed [Government of Guyana c. 1972: 141–44]. Reference has been made to the nexus between the Matthews Ridge scheme and the Port Kaituma road and the Soesdyke-Linden scheme and the Linden Highway [Government of Guyana c. 1972: 141].

At the end of the day, when one of the roads on which some of the schemes depended did not materialize, the settlers had to depend on air transportation to move their produce to the coastal markets and to import inputs. At the prices prevailing in the early 1970s and with rising fuel costs (even with a freight subsidy in the case of the national airline) few products could financially justify this mode of transport.

Recapitulation and Conclusions, 1965–1980

During this most controversial of eras the alliances that had been forged during the preceding periods underwent major shifts. The economic and social interests represented by the state differed somewhat from the previous era, particularly that of pre-1954. In this case the PNC administration controlled an alliance of predominantly urban-based middle and lower income groups together with some rural African farmers, some East Indian landlords and businessmen, particularly Muslims, as well as a changing mixture of other elements. The nature of this alliance, its stability and, most importantly, its class interests are a matter of heated and continuing controversy.

The government was still faced with unhelpful external forces ranging from Suriname to the US but had initially dealt with these by a variety of measures varying from alliances to military force. As was the case with the internal politics, the relationship with these forces varied over time depending in part on the relationship between the state and the TNCs. In the longer term the government sought protection from these actors in a variety of international fora including the Caribbean Community (CARICOM) and the Non-Aligned Movement [see Ferguson 1995 for a more extensive discussion of the international environment and its impact on domestic policies]. This battle and the nationalization of primarily TNC assets lent some support to the case for the label 'non-capitalist' sometimes ascribed to the period.

Domestically, the old battle between sugar and the labour movement was transformed into a struggle with different actors – the same struggle was now being waged on the LSSs. The pursuit of an essentially statist policy, especially after 1975, was intended and did largely succeed in weakening the power of private big businesses locally. However, state ownership brought with it certain consequences including confrontation between the state and its managers on the one hand and the 'proletariats' on the other. However, this was neither a straightforward nor a continuous process. Alliances were forged and broken, reconstructed and refashioned. Hence the other appellation – intermediate regime – forever juggling ethnic, class and economic interests in pursuit of the political goal which included a weak Opposition. The dependence shifted from patrons in capital to the state as the patron. This shift is well demonstrated in the case of agriculture, rice and LSSs.

Initially, the PNC administration, frequently perceived as an antirural alliance, had considerable difficulty coming to grips with the rice industry controlled by the main Opposition party. Urban-rural politics clouded attempts to reform the rural sector and terminate abuses on LSSs. In a sense, the rice industry may be said to have won out but it was a pyrrhic victory akin to that won by the government in sugar. The attempt to diversify output and the location of production spawned, for the second time, policies that came close to providing guaranteed markets for commodities other than rice. A plethora of supporting agencies and facilities were established which, whilst facilitating responsiveness of supply, were costly to the Treasury. From 1977, under the pressure of the fiscal crisis, the quantum of financial support began to be steadily reduced and by 1980 the arrangements were being dismantled. By the end of the era the programmes and free market policies being promoted by the multilateral financial agencies undermined the viability of smallholder rice production and exposed them to the power of the millers, landlords and machinery owners.

Inevitably, these changes affected the LSSs, for the attempted diversification was dependent on hinterland settlement and a major pillar of that thrust was LSSs. Closely wedded to these policies was the objective of reducing urban unemployment. Unemployment had been rearing its head since the 1960s and was now urban in its incidence, and it was primarily an African problem. The problem of rural unemployment was apparently expected to be solved by agrarian and, particularly, tenure reform. The politics of rural Guyana, however, constrained the feasibility of this option. LSSs were therefore the main, if not the sole, means of providing 'land to the tiller'. In that regard, whilst many novel approaches were pursued, it does appear that the financial cost of that exercise was considerably underestimated. At the same time, the settlement models may well have been inappropriate with respect to scale, commercialization and mode of management.

A military focus on some of the schemes may have been dictated by the strategic considerations which had given rise to the establishment of schemes along the borders, particularly with Venezuela and Suriname. In the words of one observer, "loyalties and control of the interior could no longer be taken for granted" [Manley 1982]. However, on the GNS and Youth Corps schemes, the mainly urban intake and the consequential predominance of Africans along with the compulsory induction of university students and public service scholarship beneficiaries combined with the military emphasis to revive the spectre of ethnicity. Ethnicity, that is, not so much in the old sense of exclusiveness but in cultural orientation. In their multiracial focus, the schemes were perceived as socially inappropriate at best and a tool of cultural dominance at worst.

Attempts to attract foreigners for hinterland development were both spectacular and tragic. They offer several lessons in the responsibilities of government, ranging from sensible selection of location to the pitfalls of abdicating government by trading supervision for political support. The cooperative experiences proved to be disappointing both ideologically and materially. The fragility of the embrace of the collectivist ethic by members was one aspect of the problem. The inherent weakness of cooperatives as a decision making unit was another.

Today, many of the ideas around which the settlements were fashioned or conceived have been endorsed as having some virtue. The need for careful and integrated planning and support cannot be overemphasized; it was not always provided. It also needs to be recognized that settlement is a costly undertaking. So, material and financial resources need to be directed where they might be most effective. In addition, clearly defined areas need to be left for the proper exercise of individual entrepreneurial initiative.

It may well be concluded that the enthusiasm for the LSSs in this era outstripped the agronomic, logistical and managerial capacity of the administration. Noncapitalist or intermediate, the regime lost sight of the importance of economics in attaining and maintaining its political goals.

It may be argued, however, that what was distinctive about the LSSs of this era was not so much these forgoing factors but the attempt to sidestep the problem of coastal land tenure, with its latent and not-so-latent tensions, via strategic hinterland settlements. Actually, a pursuit of such a policy may itself have fired the popular – national and regional – imagination as had the construction of the Mahdia road. But some of the schemes had an explicit ideological and pedagogic purpose. And the latter did not only include the promotion of racial tolerance and of the socialist creed. The party's allies along with many of its enemies viewed this approach, already facing stiff resistance from senior managers in the public sector where it was being pursued, as part of a package of unacceptable cultural and political indoctrination.

For a second time a national government had contrived to generate sectional resistance to a tool that ought to have been a national rallying point.

CHAPTER 7

THE END OF COLONIZATION, 1981-1985

"You will never know," he said graciously, "how hard we tried to make it work. I did not wish to leave . . . In the end, I had no choice but to go. But many of us desperately wanted it to succeed. We preferred the idea of social justice even to our own freedom. What you are talking about so enthusiastically is the death of a great dream for us."

Pauline Melville, *The Ventriliquist's Tale*

Economic Crisis

In periodizing the PNC era into three periods, 1965 to 1975, 1976 to 1980 and 1981 to 1985, two factors have been taken into account. First, as far as LSSs are concerned the 'experiment' in colonization came to a close between 1980 and 1985. Second, a new constitution promulgated in 1980 was viewed by many commentators as a formalizing of, if not a change in political direction that began in the late 1970s, then confirming the authoritarian nature of the administration.

For Guyana, the late 1970s and 1980s were periods of serious economic dislocation and disequilibrium. Whereas per capita income rose by some 4 percent per annum in real terms during the first half of the 1970s, not only did it fall between 1975 and 1983 but in spite of positive growth in 1984 and 1985, recorded output in the latter year was some 15 percent less than the level in 1980. Guyana's terms of trade declined dramatically after 1979, and in spite of IMF programmes in 1978, 1979 and 1981 the decline was not reversed. The contraction in overall economic activity left sugar and bauxite accounting for almost 90 percent of foreign exchange earnings in 1985 but those two sectors were also the source of poor output performance. After 1981 the financial performance of the public enterprises, led by sugar and bauxite, compounded the traditional deficit on the central government's current account and public sector savings became negative. The resource gap which stood at 2 percent in 1971–75 was initially kept at a reasonable level by holding down imports. It slipped, however, to 12 percent of GDP for the period 1975–80. Subsequently, the government allowed external payments arrears to accumulate resulting in the closing off of access to balance of payments resources, suspension from access to IMF resources and the drying up of trade credit. External payments arrears accumulated to US$702 million by 1985, in addition to which current debt service obligations alone were equivalent to 133 percent of the annual exports of goods and nonfactor services. Debt service obligations could not be met, and in spite of a number of innovative attempts at barter, debt swaps, forward sales and the like, the capacity to service these debt declined and arrears loomed very large in the debt stock. It has been estimated that in the productive sectors utilization was on average some 40 percent of effective capacity due to the chronic shortage of foreign exchange and the consequential shortage of spares and inputs.

Measures to correct the situation including the devaluation of the Guyana dollar in June 1981, January 1984 and periodically after October 1984, when the currency was tied to a basket of currencies, only had passing effect. Due to continuing poor export performance and inflation the currency continued to depreciate. Investment declined from 33 percent of GDP in 1981 to 22 percent in 1985 and within that period private investment fell from 22 to 10 percent of GDP. By then the public sector deficit stood at a staggering 61 percent of the GDP [IBRD 1985b, 1986; Government of Guyana 1985b, 1986].

All of this had a number of adverse implications for the FCH programme in particular, the programme that was the primary pillar on which the 'small man' was to be fashioned into a 'real man'. Under this policy, medical care, education, some basic transport and the utilities were either provided free of charge by the state or at controlled prices which rarely moved and then bore no relation to cost of delivery. Additionally, controlled prices covered a wide range of basic items encompassing some thirty-five products or product groups accounting for 15 percent of the Consumer Price Index (CPI).

The capacity of the public sector to deliver these services, to which the government was committed, could have been expected to decline in line with the deterioration of the fiscal situation. It was in fact acutely compounded by the growth of a burgeoning parallel market. The growing inability of the state to meet the Basic Needs Set it had brought the populace to expect was evident. But the parallel market activities gave rise to calls for government to involve itself in more and more activities, and by 1985 some 90 percent of import and export trade was in its control. The ever increasing extension of the state administration into areas that required resources with which the public sector was not equipped caused the administration to buckle even as it needed to be more effective.

Public sector wages had to be frozen in 1982 and 1983, and subsequently across-the-board increases were restored on the basis of annual negotiations. There were attempts to link the increases in some part to improvements in productivity via incentive schemes under the supervision of a national, broad-based planning body, which included TUC representatives – the National Economic and Social Council, an organ of the State Planning Commission. It was of limited value.

Other elements of the state's programme are of relevance to our story. First is the restructuring of the state corporations under the plan devised by Kuhn Loeb, Lehman Bros, Warburg et al. in 1984. This plan involved the grouping of the enterprises under one supervisory authority for purposes of political/policy direction. There was also to be the use of performance contracts and arrangements to permit the enterprises the freedom to respond to market signals and the granting of more autonomy to the managers. Second, the Guyana Rice Board, the statutory marketing authority for the rice industry, was split into three new entities [Greenidge 1983].[109] These entities were basically built around the provision of milling, marketing and grading services. It was felt that the GRB was absorbing an inordinate proportion of the surplus of the industry and it was doing so primarily by financing a bloated and inefficient bureaucracy. The IBRD estimated that in 1981–82 the board absorbed some 64 percent of the industry's surpluses and that the net returns to paddy under high yielding varieties fell by some 40 percent. The numbers can doubtless be disputed, but the point of relevance here is that there was perceived to be a conflict of interest of sorts between two of the beneficiaries of the nationalization process, the farmers on the one hand and the bureaucracy and consumers on the other.

Agricultural Policy

Attempts to bring relief to the productive enterprises in public and private sectors would have to depend heavily on external financial support. But, for the economic reasons stated above as well as the fractures arising from the government's political stance, this was not forthcoming. After 1982, the only donors from whom continuous, and significant, support was being received were the Inter-American Development Bank (IDB), Canada, the European Union and Japan. The purpose of much of that aid was primarily to restore the market. Under the IDB's Agri-sector Loan Programme, the agricultural and land policies of Guyana returned to problems of pricing, restricting state involvement in marketing especially in non-rice and non-sugar areas. But the macroeconomic imbalances which reflected themselves in shortages of inputs and consumer goods undermined much of that assistance. A recent study reminded us that with extensive rationing in the consumer market, peasants' supply response to price incentives tend to be relatively weak or even negative [Eriksson 1993]. Guyana's experience attests to this, particularlyin the case of rice.

As far as LSS projects were concerned, the IDB, the main crutch in agriculture, showed little interest in settlement of the colonization type. Instead, resources were provided for the existing major D&I schemes to be rehabilitated, starting with the Tapakuma on the Essequibo Coast – primarily a rice and mixed farming area. Phase I of the massive Machaica/Mahaicony/Abary (MMA) Scheme was completed during this period. The old BBP scheme was rehabilitated and three small schemes were redesigned or rehabilitated at Buxton/Friendship, Noreed Hoop/La Jalousie and Craig/Relief in 1984. All of these areas were already colonized to a large extent, including the MMA, where the allocation of state lands by the regional administration continues to pose a problem, as regards small versus large and East Indian versus African farmers.

Agricultural research activities of the National Agricultural Research Institute (NARI) were supported by regional institutions such as the Caribbean Research and Development Institute (CARDI) and the Inter-American Institute for Cooperation in Agriculture (IICA) but these entities all had their own financial and management problems over the period and this restricted the extent of support which could be provided. Non-rice agriculture by way of vegetables and ground provisions, fruit orchards and copra/vegetable oil were largely without adequate extension services and the necessary marketing facilities remain a backwater, both technologically and agronomically. The GMC continued as a buyer of last resort for some commodities until 1985 but high losses due in part to the unreliability of electricity supply eventually brought even that to an end.

In 1981 agricultural processing enterprises accounted for some 28 percent of all the industrial enterprises in Guyana. The bulk of these were state owned but very much on a medium to small-scale base due to constraints on the acquisition of inputs and lack of investment. Attempts to establish joint ventures bore little fruit. Refined vegetable oil provided a good insight into the dilemma.

Output had reached a level of 600,000 gallons in 1980 but had fallen to 15,000 in 1984, a mere 25 percent of domestic demand [Optima Technical Services 1990].

The main losers in this decline and restructuring, therefore, were non-rice and non-sugar agriculture. The hinterland beef and tobacco industries centred in the Rupununi were practically destroyed, being devoid of transport to coastal markets and short of inputs and imported staples.

All of these developments served to accentuate wealth and income disparities between urban and rural labour, the African and East Indian communities. Wage labour and government-sponsored colonization were giving way to other activities especially trading. It may be safely concluded then, that by 1985, the era of LSS had come to an end. Indeed, 'cooperative socialism' itself as envisaged by its founder, was about to breathe its last.

Labour/Industrial Relations

In reaction to all of these developments, the relationship of the state and its labour allies, which had become increasingly difficult after the minimum wage agreement was suspended, deteriorated. That relationship itself is complex enough to warrant a study in its own right. For purposes of our discussion, suffice it to note that in the face of the above-mentioned constraints on the bargaining position of the government-affiliated unions they lost considerable ground and, to make matters worse, they did so to Opposition unions, primarily to GAWU of the PPP.

In a number of industries government supporters preferred to be represented by Opposition unions rather than GLU, MPCA, GMWU and other PNC unions. The reason is not difficult to find. Being Opposition unions, the National Association of Agricultural, Commercial and Industrial Employees (NAACIE) and GAWU could be expected to prosecute their interests assiduously, if only to make political capital. Nonetheless, when one bears in mind quite how inept the GAWU in particular has proven over the years [Pierce 1984] and the damage inflicted on it (and the Treasury) by the 135-day 1977 sugar strike, the faith of the workers is surprising. It is of course possible that such behaviour may be more of a statement about their perception of the nonmilitancy of the government unions rather than one of faith in the GAWU. Eventually, this weakened the position of the PNC and smaller unions in the TUC, but when they could not be dislodged a rival to the TUC was established, the Federation of Independent Trade Unions of Guyana (FITUG). The labour movement again mirrored the political/racial divide.

Other elements of the political alliance managed by the PNC also became less reliable although they remained in place. Many established and traditional businesses were closed, having been displaced by those that had made a success of parallel market activities, including smuggling and trading in currency. The main support base of the party became restless and considerable political effort was required to maintain it. The defection of strongholds, such as Linden and elements of the army, in between elections was made embarrassingly evident by the political activities of the Working People's Alliance (WPA) led by Walter Rodney. The government's reaction to these events lost it many friends. That loss which began in the 1970s accelerated after 1980.

Local Government Reforms

In 1980 a new constitution was adopted. Among the changes that the new constitution introduced was a local government system which provided for the extensive devolution of power to the regions. Each part of the country, including LSSs, was to be the responsibility of a local authority, a cooperative, which was the base of the system [see Hamilton 1986 for outline and references]. There can be little doubt that the government recognized that this proposal could have removed from its direct control a considerable portion of the system – an outcome, as we have shown earlier, it had gone to great lengths to avoid. It was probably felt, however, that the loss of control would be acceptable because a considerable degree of executive power, particularly as regards implementation, would be devolved to local communities rather than to political parties, including the PNC. In a sense, it could be seen as intended to compensate for the loss of direct representation associated with proportional representation in general elections.Under this regime, the centre would no longer be able to dominate all corners of the country by virtue of its monopoly of executive functions and its control of revenues.

It is also probable that at that time the leadership of the PNC anticipated the successful conclusion of discussions on a merger with the PPP. Such an eventuality or even fear of an electoral loss to the PPP may have informed this approach. Devolution of this sort, which is similar to that being pursued by the British Labour Party after the Thatcher era, would protect the PNC from the kind of complete political exclusion suffered by the British Labour Party at the hands of the Conservatives in all regions, even those where it was considered a majority. The system was partially implemented in 1985 but was so complex and costly in terms of its human resource requirements that it could not be fully implemented as conceived.

If true, as we have argued, it is an irony that such an initiative should have fallen foul of demographic and bureaucratic constraints for in this system, which allows for an inclusive regional/communal political participation, lies one element of the possible resolution to the conundrum of governance in Guyana.

CHAPTER 8

SUMMARY AND CONCLUSIONS

At school they were prepared to take possession of the future, so that the world which raged outside, the presence of race riots, local political intrigue and power struggles were viewed as fictions.
Jancie Shinebourne, *Timepiece*

I

This study sought to:

i. provide the background against which settlement schemes were established and developed in Guyana;
ii. identify the objectives of these schemes;
iii. trace the manner in which they changed in relation to the unfolding modes of production;
iv. assess their success in terms of the objectives, stated and implicit.

Given all that has been said in the foregoing about LSSs and their place in the political economy of Guyana, it should come as no surprise to find that assessment is not an unambiguous exercise. The objectives of the schemes did not only vary over time but also with different groups at any given point in time. Beneficiaries themselves, for example, may attribute a higher priority to some set of objectives than that envisaged by the government in establishing the schemes. We see in Momsen's study of the Caribbean [1987] a useful examination of the problems arising from this dichotomy between peasants' attitudes and the state's intentions. There is also an important dichotomy between the stated objectives and the 'real' objectives dictated by the logic of the system. This latter dichotomy may have been of special import in Guyana's case.

The study of Guyana's schemes is rather interesting and shows that there are many senses in which Guyana's schemes differ from those established elsewhere. We have largely excluded from consideration urban land reform as well as unsponsored schemes. The urban schemes were quantitatively unimportant prior to 1970 and therefore their omission does not unduly bias the findings. Unsponsored schemes, such as those characterized by the village movement have, of course, been quantitatively important and, while not considered LSSs, have been used to a limited extent as a point of reference for our study.

The schemes to which we have turned our attention for most of the period of our coverage have been profoundly influenced by the economics and politics of sugar and the 'plantation' and subsequently what we may call, for want of a more appropriate term, the intermediate regime of cooperative socialism.

One of the most noticeable features of the schemes has been the bifurcation of large- and small-scale agriculture and the problems of the different organizational forms found in the agrarian sector. Another concerns the intended beneficiaries – the choices of and reactions to – the explicit ethnic dimension, the urban/rural dichotomy, the coastal/hinterland dilemma as well as colonization versus tenure reform. A third feature is the significant influence of strategic factors in the decision to establish such schemes and their location.

Many of the problems specific to named schemes are well known though not necessarily well documented. Systematic analysis of some of these issues has not been undertaken however. Indeed, some dimensions of analysis, such as farm planning with optimization techniques, have been almost entirely neglected.[110] One ubiquitous problem which has attracted attention is inadequate infrastructural facilities.

The provision of infrastructural facilities seems to have been a critical factor frequently exerting a baleful influence on the schemes. The literature on the subject is not definitive on the issue of the appropriate range of facilities necessary to underpin successful operation of the schemes. Ali [1974], for example, citing Lewis, Finnes and Fisk, lists nine activities which in effect require 'adequate' provision of all facilities ranging from the organization of group activities to housing. Matthews and Danns [1980], on the other hand, point to the stifling impact of closely supervised schemes. In this review, 'successful' settlements are found with and without extensive facilities. Inevitably, assessment will turn on the objectives. If the emphasis of the schemes is on smallholder production the basic infrastructural needs will be considerably more than that required of schemes providing a purely custodial function. Clearly, it is with regard to the latter that Ruthenberg was referring when he observed that LSS were "highly economic measures of social relief" [1966: 60].

Developments in the formulation and implementation of land policy have left an indelible mark on the direction and nature of LSSs in Guyana. We have seen some of the reasons for, and some of the implications of, land and labour policies. We have outlined the implications of asymmetrical land policies as between village and LSS and have observed the factors contributing to the frustration of the efforts to create African as well as East Indian peasantries.

This study has sought to explain the evolution of the approach to LSSs in Guyana with reference to the nature of Guyana's political economy, specifically the dependent nature of the plantation mode (its articulation to that of the metropole). It has been argued that policies which reflected fractures in the relations between articulated modes of production led to problems for the planters. At the outset the sugar industry was in effect being invited to make a reluctant transition from chattel slavery to agrarian capitalism. In reaction to those problems the early schemes (1865–1905) were established. They represented an attempt by the dominant sugar interests to manage access to land in such a manner as to further control the supply and price of labour available to sugar plantations. Pricing and fiscal policies as well as the other instruments of the state were mobilized to attain these ends. The policies served not only to widen the racial mix of the society but to underpin the divisions and conflicts of interest between the races by way of labour market segmentation. Worthy of mention also is the manner in which immigration was financed.

It has been assumed that these early LSSs were failures. In terms of the stated objectives this is a justifiable conclusion. But whatever the rationale, the effects of the earlier schemes were twofold. First, they helped to keep labour on or close to the sugar industry and also to keep the wages of sugar labour down. Initially, the schemes merely involved the distribution of land to settlers. Given the opportunity-costs facing the 'settlers', little development actually took place on these LSSs. Although the settlers controlled their own labour power and land, they were coerced to offer this labour to the sugar industry when the latter required labour. In effect, therefore, they constituted a reserve of labour on which the sugar industry could draw.

Second, with the land provided and the financial resources available, the majority of settlers could manage little more than subsistence. Many were forced to sell the land to make ends meet and in the process contributed to accelerated private accumulation and the growth of a stratum of domestic landlords. One effect of LSSs was therefore the establishment of petty capitalist producers via the uneven distribution of land among East Indian immigrants. When this era comes to be more thoroughly researched, it is likely that the rise of many East Indian families to prominence during the interwar years will be traced to the opportunities provided by way of the land and capital accumulated from these LSSs. In terms of their contribution to developing agrarian capitalism, the LSSs of this era could be considered quite successful.

During the second phase (1906–47), there were again several fractures in the metropolitan-cum-sugar plantation alliance as well as some between the latter and their local allies such as the merchants. In the face of these reverses associated with the termination of indentureship, the depressions and the Second World War, there was a most comprehensive public rethinking of the role of LSSs. The access of different groups to such schemes and the function of the schemes, especially vis-à-vis the supply of labour to the sugar industry, were therefore redefined. The process of change was far from smooth because the sugar industry still held its own in the face of the reverses but enough changed to enable policy alterations over time, some of which would mean new rules of play.

In this way there emerged other rationales for the LSSs and the policies affecting smallholders and the prospects of the peasantry also. More attention was paid to the development of the *forces of production* on the schemes as they were needed to provide not merely labour but commodities. However, little attention was devoted to the *relations of production* unless they appeared to be directly inimical to capitalist development in the rural areas. Hence the limited attention to tenure reform.

The second wave of fractures was associated with the spread of nationalist politics and the establishment of political parties closely linked to the labour movement, the most effective of these spanning the rural/urban, East Indian/African divide. During this era (1948–64) the emasculation of sugar as a political as well as economic force was intensified. This did not necessarily spawn a revolution in the attitudes to peasant farming for, in the approach to independence, the domestic alliance (the PPP) was removed from office and a local representative of the colonial state ensconced. When the PPP was re-elected to office it was an emaciated PPP shorn of most of its non-Indian collaborators. In this way the country moved towards independence. The associated struggles with the colonial power had at least two consequences. First, it left the colonial administration in a stronger position than before and it used that advantage to thwart the PPP in their attempt to pursue radical and allegedly communist objectives based on the strength of a peasant/proletarian alliance.

Resources were therefore devoted to the forces of production in order to resolve the conflicting demands of rice and sugar to promote more rapid economic growth. For the first time there were serious attempts to promote the establishment of an independent peasantry but consistent policies to implement this objective only emerged after 1957. Given the racial segmentation of the society, the pursuit of basically agrarian policy focusing almost exclusively on rice and its infrastructural needs led to further problems in the country. Rapid differentiation of the peasantry was associated with the development of the forces of production. Capitalist relations became just as deeply entrenched on the new LSSs as on the old, in spite of increasing intervention by the state, partly because of the failure of the state to implement comprehensive agrarian reform. The programme of modernization which had accompanied the new thrust to promote a peasantry did not solve the problem of a viable smallholder economy. Indeed, it might be argued that it contributed to a further shift by settlers from dependence on landlords to dependence on capital. By the time a new government took over the levers of the state, both the administrative weakness and the inability of the state to deal with the enormous backlog of land settlement problems were quite evident.

The utilization of LSSs as a device to reward party supporters did not only reinforce the divisions in the rural sector but it also turned LSSs into a national political issue. This helped to thwart the emergence of any peasant/proletarian/worker alliance, if that was indeed the government's intention. The colonial power capitalizing on the forces that were now arraigned against the PPP government engineered the latter's fall.

The struggle left the owners of the plantations with an opportunity to reduce their dependence on Guyana. If in the 1860s Guyana could have been considered to be a plantation economy tied economically to the metropole, by the 1960s it had clearly undergone a major change. The preceding represented the most important of these – political independence and the declutching from the metropolitan sugar industry. Not that these alone were dramatic but when taken alongside the diversification of the economic structure they could be seen as very important. The shadow of totality, for example, cast by the plantation over the economy and the society as a whole had been largely removed. The cultural legacy of racial stratification had been somewhat unravelled, bauxite, rice, forestry and fisheries were prominent contributors to GDP and employment. The high degree of urbanization reflected these changes and was an indication of the political and related industrial relations struggle that lay ahead.

However we care to portray the 'new mode' of production, the sugar plantation was not its motive force, nor was ascribed status its feature. In this era the state shared the role of the entrepreneur with private business. The manner of its operations was to moderate the workings of the economy and in turn to determine the political superstructure. At the same time, those developments would intervene in the local polity–factional politics. Tensions and fractures were not peculiar to the old mode so tensions and fractures there were after 1964 and 1976. Fractures, that is, between national and foreign as well as between domestic and domestic. We see that these fractures affected in their own way the approaches to land and labour policies.

Initially, the new government, with an urban base and a more complicated agenda arising from a mixed alliance, neglected LSSs in reaction to the racially partisan policies of its predecessor. Eventually, confronted with international threats to the country's territorial integrity and a hinterland uprising with ethnic overtones and implications for its alliances, the PNC's interest in LSSs was kindled. The LSSs offered at once an opportunity to beneficially occupy land with trusted and trained settlers and to alleviate the problem of urban unemployment. It was grasped.

During the ensuing phase, the post-sugar or statist era as it were, the geographical location of the schemes shifted completely. The new settlement schemes were no longer preoccupied with freeing themselves from the embrace of sugar. They were caught up in other problems, one of which was the struggle for national territory. Whilst this in itself need not have been an undesirable development, it can be justifiably argued that such involvement of the settlements was premature and contributed in large measure to the limited development of the forces of production and the limited longevity of the schemes.

Both the urban-oriented schemes (for example, GNS) and the others (Moco Moco) can be said to have raised new conundra. For an explanation of these it is necessary to view the attempt to build LSSs on cooperative societies in the context of an administered but unplanned and subsequently an ailing economy. The latter features and the difficulty of establishing cooperatives to run complex enterprises with underdeveloped manpower were primary causes of the problems and disappointments experienced.

And yet, some schemes of this period may well have been successfully established and operated if the racial undercurrent, which had always characterized the schemes, had not emerged as such a strong factor. As a result of this factor (first the exclusive East Indian tenancy of the earlier schemes and their subsequent attempts to use them as a device for curing urban unemployment) LSSs have been seen by many as a zero sum game in racial terms. In this latter period in particular, their association with urban, and therefore essentially Afro-Guyanese, settlement hampered the emergence of a national consensus that may have helped to attract adequate numbers of settlers so necessary to spread the overheads associated with the very expensive activity of interior settlement.

In attempting to fashion new tools with which to overcome some of the earlier handicaps such as diseconomies of small-scale production, both pre-independence and postindependence governments set a great deal of store by the cooperative movement. But the cooperative management was weak and the problem of government involvement and control all added to the problems of management at times.

In a sense, the weakness of the cooperative societies pointed to the fact that the hard-won advances in agrarian development dating from the late nineteenth century were still to be consolidated. The development of human resources and the fashioning (or, more accurately, the retention) of a cadre of technically competent staff remain missing elements in the mosaic of agrarian reform. The dilemmas on this front reflect the hazards of attempting to fashion and operate cooperatives in an administered but basically unplanned economy. Tackling the issue of comprehensive agrarian reform, which has been evaded and glossed over in the past, will need to be coterminous with the promotion of LSSs, peasant or small-scale agriculture, as well as cooperatives, if the type of experiences outlined above are to be avoided. It remains to be seen whether the lessons have been learnt, for post-1980s fiscal crises have precluded further attempts at such settlements. Whilst earlier settlements left their recruits coerced first by the plantation, then landlords and subsequently capital, under cooperative social-ism their patron was the state.

In its drive towards modernization the state had attempted to employ the LSS as a multifaceted instrument – productive, pedagogic and strategic. Some goals were achieved, but along the way the longevity of the settlements was sacrificed. The urban-dominated state, often insensitive to, if not contemptuous of the primacy of the economy in the achievement of its political goals, was economically fragile and without external patrons of its own in the long term. It eventually succumbed, therefore, to economic factors along with its domestic and foreign enemies.

II

. . . there was no point in trying to do anything about everyday life. It was an illusion behind which lay the unchanging reality of dream and myth. 'We look for the mask behind the face", he said, shaking his finger and laughing.

Pauline Melville, *The Ventriliquist's Tale*

The contradictions referred to in the preface can be found in many aspects of Guyana's history and its politics. Today, Guyana is a country about which very little is known outside its borders and what is known tends to be unflattering. Sir Walter Raleigh's obsession with finding the beautiful empire of Guyana cost him his head. Subsequently, in 1763, one of Guyana's counties, Berbice,[111] was the site of the first major slave revolt in the Western hemisphere, a revolt that was the most important until the Haitian Revolution. Conan Doyle's *The Lost World* and Henry Hudson's *Green Mansions*, it has been said, were inspired by Guyana's hinterland. Yet today, more of the world's citizens are likely to recall Guyana, if they recognize the name at all, for the Jonestown tragedy than for its physical features – real or fabled.

The contradictions of LSSs are set to continue with the ending of the colonization of new lands for settlement. Unless the problem of modernization and development is approached in a less dysfunctional way than has been the case to date, real empowerment will remain elusive not only for small farmers. What the study of LSSs shows is not that there is any special economic or agronomic obstacle to empowerment. The empowerment of the small farmer and the creation of a peasantry requires that over time, clear and consistent economic and political policies be pursued on behalf of the beneficiaries.

The process of empowerment is dynamic and for it to be maintained, it will need to be constantly rejuvenated. The obstacles to empowerment seem to lie with the impact of the political process on the social relations of production and the influence of the latter on polity. Economic policy should be fashioned as a process that is less antagonistic and competitive, less of a zero-sum game. Political and social cohesion is a prerequisite for a package of consistent and mutually reinforcing policies.

The story we have outlined, whether that of the plantation economy or of local party politics (both with class interests superimposed on marked racial divisions) is obviously not one of political and social cohesion. For such stability one should turn to the polity itself.

Land is such a highly political commodity that the policies related to it will reflect the vagaries of national politics. Empowerment of those having access to land therefore requires either that some "politics be taken out of land or that land be substantially taken out of politics". Taking politics out of land could be done by ensuring that land allocation targeted at prospective small farmers is not determined primarily by ethnicity and filtered by party allegiance. The exercise should not be treated as part of the spoils of election and should not be extended to communally owned lands, especially if such land is the object of squatting. This is the major source of the lack of consensus over land allocation and it is intractable because of its historical coincidence with ethnic divisions, as explained earlier.

To take the land out of politics would require that small farmers' representatives be seen to prosecute their collective interests in their own right. The dependence on representative organizations, which are not only ethnically based but are also the poodles of one political party, leaves small farm policies susceptible to radical swings when governments change. Of course, this is not a position peculiar to the small farmer, for as we have outlined, it is in the mould of much of Guyana's politics. But additionally, by being allied to a political party, heavily influenced by rural capital, which is quite "allergic to taxation", and sugar workers who see themselves as the rightful owners of the profits of the nationalized sugar corporation, they run a special risk in an arena that is so divided. For in order to respect the predilections of the two dominant rural strata in the party and at the same time to attenuate the vagaries of differentiation, which inevitably accompany marketization and modernization, the party tends to seek resolution of this dilemma in non-rural and (frequently) urban-based taxes. We have already highlighted the consequences of such a scenario. The peasantry or small farm sector thereby becomes potential prey, twice over, to the zero-sum perception of the political game. Clearly, the resolution of the dilemma or conundrum does not lie solely in the hands of these small farmers.

To confront that challenge would enable Guyana to remove its mask and to put an end to the flight of its citizens from an empty land to overcrowded shores in search of tranquillity and prosperity. Their plight was well portrayed in Melville's description of the capital city, Georgetown, itself, which, confronted by the frightening land mass at its back, "smiled out to sea, believing that its future lay beyond the horizon, and ignored the lands behind it and the people who lived there" [Melville 1997: 36].

APPENDIX

TABLES

1. Land Settlement Schemes Established in Guyana, 1865–1980
2. Technology Employed in Production of Paddy on LSSs, 1906–1980
3. Statement of Terms of Acquisition of Land by Settlers (selected schemes)
4. Cumulative Arrears in Payments of Rents and D&I Rates in Recent years ($000)
5. Cost of Acquisition, Reconditioning and Laying out of Plantations Acquired by the State ($)
6. Schedule of the Number of Rice Mills for 1906–1980 (inclusive)
7. Rice Yields on Selected LSSs in Stated Years (bags/ha [average/annum])
8. Land Settlement Schemes: Estimated Capital Investment
9. Cooperative Membership on Selected LSSs

Table 1: Land Settlement Schemes Established in Guyana, 1865–1980

Name and location of scheme	Year Established[A]	Total Net Area (ha)	No. of Settlers Planned[B]	Actual	Initial Holding Size/Family (ha)	Main Activities Planned	Date Ceased Being LSS	Status at 1980
1865–1905								
Hopetown, Camoenie Creek, Demerara	1865	370	na	800	na	charcoal and shingles	1905	local authority (village)
Nooten Zuil, EC Demerara	1872	123	225	na	0.67	not specified	"	local authority (village)
L'Amitie ('Broke Pot') Mahaica Creek, EC Demerara	1879/80	40.5	na	4	"	"	"	local authority (village)
Huis t'Dieren, Essequibo	1880	243	350	53	0.81	"	1905	"
Cotton Tree, WC Berbice	1882	na	na	na	0.8	"	"	"
Helena, Mahaica Creek, EC Demerara	1897	600	1,200	1,206	0.5	"	"	"
Whim, Corentyne River Berbice	1897/98	1,448.7	na	574	0.5	rice, coconuts coffee and fruit trees		"
Bush Lot, WC Berbice	1897/99	528.7	755	1,227	0.5	rice	1905	"
Maria's Pleasure, Essequibo	1902	70.4	na	152	0.5	rice and coconuts	1905	"
1906–47								
Windsor Forest cum annexis[C]	1910–12	1,538	na	755	1.2–2.02	rice and dairy	1960	"
Clonbrook, EC Demerara[D]	1911	na	na	144	0.4	not specified	1918/19	"
Triumph, WC Demerara	1913	na	na	268	0.4	"	1960	
Lancaster/Unity, EC Demerara	1912/13	168	239	na	0.4	"	1960	"
Craig, EC Demerara	1915	192.2	na	na	na	"	1960	
Anna Regina cum annexis Essequibo[E]	1923	3,540	750	623	0.8–4.05	rice	1960	
(Bush Lot)	(1930)	93.4	(100)	(85)	(1.2)	—	1960	
Charity-Amazon, Pomeroon Essequibo	1944	69	180	79	2.02	township	1966	township
Vergenoegen cum annexis, WC Demerara[G]	1946	1,457	150–200	328	1.2–6.1	rice and dairy (initially cane ground provisions)	1961	local authority (village)

1948–64

Location	Est.					Crops/products	Year	Status
Cane Grove cum annexis, Mahaica Creek[H]	1948	2,922	500	545	1.2–6.1	rice, dairy cotton	1960	local authority
Onverwagt, WC Berbice	1955	2,084 (2,104)	408	419	4.0–6.1	rice and coconuts	1970	being extended local authority
Garden of Eden, EB Demerara	1956	486	77	76	3.1–20.3	tree crops and dairy; subsequently cane	1960	local authority (1968)
Mara cum annexis, Berbice[I]	1957	1,161.5	130	32	6.1	rice, cocoa poultry, vegetables and tree crops	1970	Lidco scheme
Black Bush Polder, Berbice	1959	10,926	1,550	1,441	6.1	rice and green vegetables	–	
Tapakuma, Essequibo	1962	1,659.2	500	4.05	4.05	rice and cattle	–	being executed
Wauna-Tarikita, Essequibo[J]	1962	607	50	34	6.1–20.2	citrus, pineapple, oil palm and coffee, cattle, provisions	na	state farm
Brandwagt-Sari, Berbice	1964	4,775	500 (2)	84	2+	cattle	na	state farm

1965–8

Location	Est.					Crops/products	Year	Status
Matthews Ridge, Essequibo[K]	1969	18,900***	na	na	10–20	–	1978	development
New River, Corentyne Berbice (Youth Corps)[L]	1969	81	100	30	21.1	plantains, tubers and legumes	1971	absorbed by GNS in 1976
Moco Moco, Kanuka Mts, Essequibo[M]	1969	162	30	16	4.05	tomatoes, cassava, onions, legumes, carrots and poultry	1974	defunct
Marudi Mountain, Essequibo[N]	1969	na	60	55	na	tomatoes, cabbage and carrots	1971	defunct
Soesdyke/Linden cum annexis, EB Demerara[OP]	1971	13,300	2,935	1679	4.05	pineapples, cashews, citrus and poultry	–	ongoing
Sebai, NWD, Essequibo (Youth Corps)	1972	1,113	100	2	10.1	ground provisions and plantains	1974	defunct
Cato, Upper Mazaruni, Essequibo	1972	na	na	na	not applicable	Solanum potatoes	na	state farm
People's Temple Agricultural Project (Jonestown), NWD, Essequibo	1974	1,000	na	na	7,000	corn, ground provisions, wing beans, cassava and livestock	1978	defunct
Kimbia, Berbice (Guyana National Service)[Q]	1975	3,237	150	35	(8.1)	cotton, peanuts, blackeyed peas, cashew nuts and orchard crops	–	defunct since 1992

Sources and Notes for Table 1

Sources: Bayley 1919: 69, 71; British Guiana 1953a: 11; British Guiana 1911–12: 8, 9; British Guiana 1930: 138–41; Guyana 1966: ii–3; Beachell and Brown, 8; British Guiana 1960a: 8; British Guiana 1964: 107–8, 116; *Rice Review* (April–June 1962): 23; Nathan Associates 1974: 277, Table S1; Young 1958; Nath 1950; Government of Guyana 1968; Ministry of Agriculture – File # LSI6/2/1II.

A For 'year established' the date of allotment to settlers has been used in this study whenever possible. Some other publications employ the date of government acquisition, allotment to settlers or invitation to apply, hence the dates indicated may differ from those found elsewhere.

B On the pre-1902 schemes 'numbers of settlers' pertain to 'official' settlers for the year 1897. On the other pre-1964 schemes, the numbers related to 'official' settlers in the year 1964.

C Cum annexis refers to the neighbouring plantations of La Jalousie and Hague. Also called 'Government Estates'.

D This scheme had 286 cultivation lots but the total area of the scheme is not available although it would have been in excess of 144 ha.

E Prior to the implementation of the Tapakuma scheme to which the third depth, amounting to 1871 ha gross, was transferred.

F Cum annexis refers to the neighbouring plantations of Reliance, Bush Lot, Henrietta, Richmond, La Belle Alliance, Lima, Devonshire (second depth only).

G Cum annexis refers to the neighbouring plantations of Philadelphia, Greenwich Park and Barnwell.

H Cum annexis refers to the neighbouring plantations of La Bonne Mere.

I Cum annexis refers to the neighbouring plantations of Germania, Vryberg, Shepmoed, l'Enterprise and Ma Retraite.

J This pilot scheme was intended to precede the development of the entire 13,759 ha of land between Wauna Creek and Yarakita.

K Area actually cleared in 1969 was about 260 ha.

L The initial allocation was actually 0.2 ha and was intended to be 1 ha subsequently and 12.1 ha eventually.

M On this scheme the figures pertain to the year 1977.

N On this scheme the figures pertain to the year 1970.

O Cum annexis refers to the neighbouring plantations of Kuru-Kuru, Yarrowkabra, Low Wood, Long Creek, Dora, Clemwood and Moblissa.

P On this scheme the figures pertain to the year 1976.

Q On this scheme the figures pertain to the year 1975.

Table 2: Technology Employed in Production of Paddy on LSSs, 1906–1967

Period	Land Preparation Levelling/Planting	Transportation	Weeding	Fertilizing	Harvesting	Irrigation
1905	hand/manual land preparation; later land levellers and cultivators	canal punts for farm-to-mill paddy movement; oxcart for road transport	hand	no manuring or hay	sickle/hand cutting sun-curing bull-mashing hand-winnowing	practically nonexistent
1920–28	oxen-hired, harrow and board, broadcast sowing	"	"	"	"	"
1949–54	oxen	"	"	introduction of sulphate and super sulphate	use of dryers and storage bonds; winnowing by tossing on screen; 2 percent of farmers cut 17 percent of paddy with combines	availability of rudimentary water control; minimal maintenance
1954–64	tractor-ploughing, broadcasting of pre-sprouted seeds (no. of tractors rose from 390 in 1959 to 777 in 1960)	utilization of road system and internal combustion-engine, trucks, tractors and trailers	"	volume of fertilizers rose by more than 60 percent; introduction of new varieties of rice	increase in combines from 21 in 1959 to 128 in 1960	improvement in water control; provision of flood control and some irrigation facilities
1965–80	tractor-ploughing etc., as per 1954–64	road trucks, tractors and trailers	pesticides	increasing fertilizer use; introduction of several new varieties including starbonnet	exclusively by combines	considerable increase in irrigated acreage; 1970–80 commencement on additional quarter of a million acres

Sources: Beachell and Brown, n.d.: 3; British Guiana 1931b: 141; British Guiana Annual Report 1964; British Guiana Census in 1952 (1953): 23; Caffey and Efferson 1965: 5; British Guiana Administrative Report 1932; British Guiana 1960a.

Table 3: Statement of the Terms of Land Acquisition of Land by Settlers (selected schemes)

Name	Lease (yrs.)	Rental and Cash Price if Stated
Huis t'Dieren	99	$14.83 per ha. Outright purchase.
Bush Lot, WC Berbice	99	$21.15 per ha. Outright purchase.
Windsor Forest (Cum annexis)	99	$14.83 per ha; $21.15 per ha for outright purchase.[A]
Clonbrook	–	$23.88 per ha. Outright purchase.
Triumph	–	$49.00 per ha. Outright purchase.
Unity/Lancaster	–	$0.49 per ha. Outright purchase.
Craig	99	1st year free then $14.83 per ha. Thereafter annually.
Anna Regina	25	$14.83 per ha. Outright purchase.
Bush Lot, Essequibo	99	$0.39 per ha. Outright purchase after three years' rental.
Charity/Amazon	99	$0.27 per ha. Outright purchase.
Vergenoegen	21	$0.49 per ha. Rental.
Cane Grove (La Bonne Mere)	21	$0.49 per ha. Purchase price.
Onverwagt	Lease	$25 per ha. Rental.
Mara	sale	$124 per ha. Purchase price.
Black Bush Polder	25	Right of renewal for another 25 years. Rental $25/ha pa.
Tapakuma	25	Right of renewal for another 25 years. Rental $25/ha pa.
Soesdyke/Linden	25	
Kimbia River	25	Right of renewal for another 25 years. $23/ha and $2.47/ha ultimately.

Sources: British Guiana 1914–15: 337; British Guiana 1941–42; British Guiana 1912: 8; British Guiana1964c: 102; Ministry of Agriculture and National Resources (1966).

A   Actual terms were $1 per acre for the first year and $6.00 per acre thereafter annually, whilst at Hague rental was $3 per acre for one year and $5 per acre per year subsequently.

Table 4: Cumulative Arrears in Payments of Rents and D&I Rates in Recent Years ($000)[A]

	1966	1967	1968	1969
Anna Regina	–	–	1,600	15
Vergenoegen	–	–	1,800	–
Cane Grove	–	–	300	–
Onverwagt	8	10	900	–
Garden of Eden	8	4	300	–
Mara	12	13	820	–
BBP	123	130	1,330	137
Wauna/Tarakita	–	–	–	–
Tapakuma	24	26	na	na

Source: Ministry of Agriculture, Annual Reports.
NB: – indicates negligible.
A   Net of write offs.

Table 5: Cost of Acquisition, Reconditioning and Laying out of Plantations Acquired by the State ($)

Scheme	Acquisition cost	Reconditioning Cost	Layout Cost
Nooten Zuil	15,000	–	–
Unity/Lancaster	800	6,378	1,150
Craig	25,084	–	–
Bush Lot	14,420	48,168[A]	–
Cane Grove	60,100	303,000	24,000
Onverwagt	100,000	973,229	–
Garden of Eden	120,000	–	34,000
Mara	180,000	–	–
Black Bush Polder	–	16,153,000[B]	–
Wauna/Yarakita	–	226,459	–
Brandwagt/Sari	–	102,39	–

Sources: Bayley 1919: 69–71; British Guiana 1930: 143; British Guiana 1947: 35–36; British Guiana, Administrative Reports of the Director of Agriculture 1932–65; British Guiana 1964: 108; Nath 1950; Young 1958.

A   At the end of 1961.

B   Development expenditure for 1964 construction work.

Table 6: Schedule of Number of Rice Mills for Period 1906–1980 (inclusive)

Period	No. of Multi-stage Mills Established	Total No. of Mills	Government-owned Mills
1906–7	–	44	
1907–8	1	56	
1909–10	1	62	
1917	1	86	
1927	1	na	
1930	7	na	
1936	2	na	
1938–39	–	197	
1940	3	na	
1957	–	215	
1958	3	218	
1959	1	219	
1960	2	224	3
1961	2	198	
1965	2	na	
1970	4	211	11
1976	3	na	
1978	4	na	
1980	–	162	17

Sources: British Guiana 1907–8; British Guiana 1939c; British Guiana 1939c; British Guiana 1960a; Guyana Rice Milling and Marketing Authority's files.

NB: At the beginning of 1960, there were 212 mills of which 210 were privately owned and the remainder owned by the British Guiana Rice Development Company.

Table 7: Rice Yields on Selected LSSs in Stated Years (bags^A/ha [average/annum])

	1941	1945–48	1950	1955	1959	1960	1970	1980	1985
National Average		40.8			37.8	35.8	28.4	46.2	52.6
Windsor Forest		44.5	44.5	na	46.9	36.1^B	49.4^C	na	56.8
Anna Regina			28.5	47.8	53.8	50.4	27.7	45	54.4
Vergenoegen	24.7	na	na	26.2	47.8	25.6	na	45	na
Cane Grove		na	na	39.5	33.8	29.6^A	37.1^C	60.7	56.8
Onverwagt		—	—	—	20.9	19.3	28.9^C	33.1^C	52.1
Mara		—	—	—	—	26.9^B	—	—	—
Black Bush Polder			—	—	—	19	17.3	31.2	46.0
Tapakuma (Tapacooma)			—	—	—	34.1	32.1	57.3	58.6

Sources: Government of Guyana: Department of Lands and Mines, Internal file #L.S. 16/2/2; Annual Report, Lands and Mines Department 1977; Annual Report, Lands and Survey Division 1978; Annual Report, Lands and Mines Department 1979 (Appendix II); Annual Report, Lands and Survey Division 1981; Annual Report, Lands and Mines Department 1982; Annual Report Lands and Mines Department 1967; Guyana Rice Marketing Board Report for the year ending 30 Sept. 1972; Beachell and Brown, n.d.; British Guiana 1931b; British Guiana Annual Report of the Commissioner of Lands and Mines 1956; British Guiana 1960c; *Rice Review* (April–June 1962); British Guiana 1950; British Guiana, Annual Report, Commissioner of Lands and Mines 1951.

A Bag = 140 lb.
B Guyana Rice Milling Marketing Authority's estimate.
C Figure represents 1966 yield.

Table 8: Land Settlement Schemes: Estimated Capital Investment

Name of Scheme	Construction Period	Capital Expenditure	
		Total ($m)	Per Family[A] ($)
Onverwagt	1954–55	0.03	54[B]
Garden of Eden	1961	0.5	6,233
Mara	1954/9 and 60/3	3.7	
Black Bush Polder	1957–61	16.15	11,207
Tapakuma	1961–62	14.6	10,814
Wauna/Yarakita	1961–65	0.43	13,000
Brandwagt/Sari	1964–65	0.33	6,470

Sources: Gyanchand 1963; ICJ 1965; Ministry of Agriculture, Annual Reports 1954–67; British Guiana 1964b: 22; British Guiana 1925–34: 17; Estimates of Guyana 1978.

A   Actual families.

B   Only for years in question. This amount represents the cost of fencing; up to 1969 no monies had been approved for a capital programme.

Table 9: Cooperative Membership on Selected LSSs

Scheme	No. of Cooperatives 1960	1970	1980	Functioning in 1980	No. of Members 1960	1970	1980	Comment
Bush Lot		1		?	2,000	10		c. 1967
Anna Regina	40	50	6					
Charity/Amazon		1		?		28		1967 figs.
Vergenoegen	1		6	6	106	148	176	1961 figs. for 1960
Cane Grove	1		7	4	325	200	1–200	1961 figs. for 1960
La Bonne Mere	1	4	2	2	15	150	75–100	1964 figs. for 1960
Mara	1			?	52			1964 figs. for 1960
Black Bush Polder	18	20	4	4	317	2,000	700	1964 figs. for 1960
Tapakuma		1		?		68		1967 figs. for 1970
Wauna Yarakita	1			?	32			1964 figs. for 1960
Brandwagt Sari	1			—	68			1964 figs. for 1960
Matthews Ridge	8	34	8	1	52	200	100	1969 figs. for 1970
Moco Moco			2	1		12		
Marudi		1	2	—		48	10	
Soesdyke Linden		17	7	7		1,860	600	

Sources: British Guiana 1964c: 107; British Guiana 1953a: 18; Government of Guyana 1969a; Government of Guyana 1968, *Official Gazette*, 11 November 1967; Government of Guyana 1967, Annual Report of the Ministry of Agriculture, p. 7; British Guiana Rice Producers Association 1961, *Rice Review* 3, no. 1 (January–March); Ministry of Agriculture files.

NOTES

Notes to Chapter 1

1. Throughout the text the term Guyana is used not in a historically specific sense but to refer to the three counties, Demerara, Berbice and Essequibo, that now constitute Guyana and which were formerly (during part of the period covered) known as British Guiana. The latter was, until 1966, a British colony.
2. These took place in 1838. For an interesting personal account of the significance of the latter event to one of Guyana's most famous sons, see S. Ramphal, "Some in light and some in darkness: the long shadow of slavery", *Third World Foundation Monograph* 12 (1983).
3. See the bibliography in D. Hulme, "State-sponsored land settlement policies: theory and practice", *Development and Change* 18, no. 3 (July 1987), for example. Many of these publications are, however, too country-specific to be of global value. Hulme's contribution aims to frame generalization which are "applicable to state-owned land settlement schemes throughout the Third World" (415).
4. One reason for this lacuna may be the paucity of published information on Guyana's LSSs in general and the post-1960 schemes in particular. Most of the empirical data included in this study, for example, relate to the pre-1960 schemes and much of that had to be garnered from not easily accessible primary and archival material.
5. This aspect is usually treated under housing policy. See also E. Fitzgerald, "Land reform", in *Economic Development: the New Palgrave*, edited by J. Eatwell et al. (London and New York: Norton, 1989). Some reference is made to it in that context later.

Notes to Chapter 2

6. Formal abolition took place in 1834 but was followed by a four-year-long period of 'apprenticeship'. The extent of the resulting 'freedom' of labour may be gauged from M. Shahabuddeen 1986b. The term African has been employed here in a generic sense as have Chinese and Portuguese. Other comparable descriptions are black and Afro-Guyanese.
7. Including attorneys, agents and a myriad of professionals and the merchant classes. The main plantations were owned by British companies such as Booker Bros, J. McConnell, the Colonial Co., Thomas Daniel and Sons and James Ewing and Co.
8. There were also a few Dutch, North Americans and "a handful of Jewish families". See B. Moore, "The culture of the colonial élite in nineteenth century Guyana", in *The White Minority in the Caribbean*, edited by H. Johnson et al. (London: James Currey, 1995), 97.
9. In keeping with the practice in Guyana, the terms 'plantations' and 'estates' are used interchangeably.
10. See also W. Rodney, "Guyana: the making of a labour force", *Race and Class* 22, no. 4

(1981); and A. Adamson, *Sugar without Slaves: The Political Economy of British Guiana, 1838–1904* (London: Yale University Press, 1972).

11. The term plantation, except when defined otherwise, refers to the organizational form or agricultural unit concerned with the production of sugar. The form, modelled by Best and subsequently analysed by Beckford, has dominated Guyana's economy for nearly 200 years. We have treated it here as a 'mode of production' for purposes of exposition. The very different forms that it took over the last 200 years or so does indicate that the uniqueness that this widely employed nomenclature implies may be misplaced. For recent insights and a critique of the concept of the plantation, see F. Pryor, "The plantation as an economic system", *Journal of Comparative Economics* 6, no. 3 (September 1982).

12. Among these entrepreneurs was Quintin Hogg whose prominence in the country was partly attributable to his role as innovator. Hogg, probably the largest plantation owner in the British West Indies at that time and owner of Bel Air and De Kinderen plantations, inter alia, was later to become a renowned philanthropist. See *Daily Argosy*, "Historical notes of sugar estates" (1883): 5, 6.

13. One author has characterized this propensity as follows: "In truth, however, historians have been more eager to follow the freedom out of the estates than they themselves were to have" (K. Haraksingh, "Control and resistance among overseas Indian workers: A study of labour on the sugar plantations of Trinidad, 1875–1917", *Journal of Caribbean History* 14, no. 2 [1981]).

14. See also Adamson, *Sugar without Slaves*, for a summary of this trend first analysed by Farley and termed the 'village movement'.

15. In the words of one author, "within very wide limits the local legislature was allowed free reign to regulate legal conditions that governed the deployment of labour. This meant that the political hegemony of the planter class guaranteed that the class struggle at the point of production would be conditioned primarily by legal sanctions rather than by the generation of market forces as such" (Rodney, "Guyana").

16. See for example, Rodney, "Guyana"; Adamson, *Sugar without Slaves*; C. Bourne, "Review article on the plantation economy of Guyana", *Social and Economic Studies* 24, no. 4 (December 1975); P. Fraser, "The immigration issue in British Guiana", *Journal of Caribbean History* 14 (1981): 28–29; and M. Cross and G. Herman (eds.), *Labour in the Caribbean* (Warwick: Warwick University, Caribbean Studies, 1988).

17. This is not to suggest that all the ills afflicting the villages could be properly laid at the door of 'king sugar' or the 'plantocracy'. The inappropriate size of smallholder decision-making units, a general shortage of working capital and the drawbacks of the traditional system of land tenure – 'children property' – also contributed to the precarious financial existence of the villages. See also F.H. Ramsahoye, *The Development of Land Law in British Guiana* (New York: Ocean, 1966); Adamson, *Sugar without Slaves*; A. Young, *The Approaches to Local Self-government in British Guiana* (London: Longman, 1958); British Guiana, "Report of a Small Farmers' Committee and Legislative Council" (No. 9, 1931).

18. These pieces of legislation provided for the imposition of penal sanctions for breaches of work contracts and, in the words of one author, "jail was not infrequently the alternative to failure or refusal to work" (M. Shahabuddeen, "Slavery and histiographical rectification" [Guyana Commemoration Commission, Georgetown, 1984], 11).

19. Around 341,000 indentured labourers were imported from India (70 percent), Madeira, and the Azores (Portugal), 1835–82, China, 1853–79 and a number of other (non-African) countries by the time this policy was terminated in 1917 (see Adamson, *Sugar without Slaves*). See also Haraksingh, "Control and resistance", for the Trinidad case, a mirror of

the Guyana experience. The author also provides a thoughtful analysis of the reasons why such immigrant labour would have been more susceptible to 'control', a characteristic so important to the planters.

20. The equivalent of 10s and £2.46.

21. One estimate put the number of acres of land acquired by freed slaves at 9,049.5 on which 25 communal villages were established. Additionally, 13 settlements were founded on Crown lands.

22. See Fraser, "The immigration issue".

23. The homogenous geographical region bounded by the rivers Amazon, Negro and Orinoco to the south and west and the Atlantic to the north.

24. It needs to be noted that both extensive and intensive water control are imperative within the coastal strip of Guyana most of which is both below sea level at high tide and subject to heavy rainfall. Such control was realized during the eighteenth and nineteenth centuries through the combined use of abundant slave labour and Dutch hydrologic skills. Settlement and cultivation of the coast was permitted by the empoldering of the flood plains of the river and the tracts of land facing the sea. Plantations were laid out in protective blocks of over one hundred hectares each with a sea frontage of one hundred Dutch rods (roughly 376 metres). Most plantations required one wall to restrain the water and another to hold back the swamps and savannah rivers that lay at the back of the plantations. Where the foreshore was low, drainage could be effected by gravity but a sturdy set of sea defenses was an absolute necessity. High foreshores, the result of coastal accretion, did not normally require massive sea walls but on the other hand in such places pumps were needed for drainage. Unduly heavy rains either on the coast or inland could inundate flood plains or cause breaches of the back dams. Heavy seas could sweep away sea walls and the silt-laden coastal current frequently necessitated the abandonment of riverain plantations.

25. See T. Bottomore et al. for a summary of the debate surrounding the use of the concept of the 'state' as employed in this study (*A Dictionary of Marxist Thought* [Cambridge, MA: Harvard, 1983] 464–68).

26. See Cross and Herman, *Labour*, pp. 298–99 for some indication of the subsequent fiscal system.

Notes to Chapter 3

27. See chapter 2.

28. A similar resolution was adopted in neighbouring Suriname in 1884. See J. Adhin, *Development Planning in Suriname in Historical Perspective* (Utrecht: Drukkerij, 1961) 44, M. Shahabuddeen, *From Plantocracy to Nationalization* (Georgetown, Guyana: Guyana Printers, 1983), 235, quoting Laurence, places the date of this policy change at 1893. See also J. Mandle, *The Plantation Economy: Population and Economic Change in Guyana* (Philadelphia: Temple University Press, 1973); and Bourne, "Review article".

29. Also spelt Nooten Zueill or Nootenzuill. See also Table 1 and Map 2 for the main features and the locations respectively, of all the schemes cited in the text. According to Shahabuddeen, *From Plantocracy*, 235, the first proposal involved Plantation Best on the west coast of Demerara.

30. Some indication of the preoccupation of the Immigration Agent General's (IAG) Office with the planters' labour supply may be had from an examination of the IAG's reports, for example, in 1919 he reported that, "the reaping of a good rice crop further detracted from the inadequate labour supply available for work on sugar plantations. Every effort was made

to attract labour . . . there was great demand for labour. Inconvenience was suffered by estates as a result."

31. This contrasts with an actual average daily wage of some 2–4 cents for agricultural labour!
32. Some periodic supervision was also provided by visiting district commissioners and their subordinates (Gavin Kennard, pers. comm.).
33. This change has given rise to some confusion in the literature. J.W. Vining, in his "Site development and settlement scheme failure in Guyana", *Journal of Tropical Geography* 42 (1976): 86, for example, has included in his list of defunct schemes those which under-went this change in status.
34. The term peasant as employed in this study refers to a small-scale farmer with title to part of the land he or she cultivates, who sells part of the farm output and purchases inputs and/or sells his or her labour. There are more complex definitions and the relationship between peasants and the mode of production within which they operate is the subject of endemic controversy. See also, for example, Bottomore, *Marxist Dictionary*, 85, 363–65; N. Stern, "Peasant economy", in *Economic Development: The New Palgrave*, edited by J. Eatwell et al. (London and New York: Norton, 1989); and T. Shanin (ed.), *Peasants and Modern Sociology* (Harmondsworth: Penguin Modern Sociology, 1971).
35. In the arena of banking the involvement of the state in support of sugar interests was also apparent. In 1895–96, for example, the local administration guaranteed the liabilities of the British Guiana Bank after a 'run' on it which was largely triggered by the crisis in the sugar industry. The significance of this issue is often overlooked and analysis of the nationalization of agricultural land in the Caribbean is rather rare. See also A. Brown, "Issues of public enterprise", *Social and Economic Studies* 30, no. 1 (March 1981); B. Coard, *The Role of the State in Agriculture in Grenada* (Mona, Jamaica: Caribbean Public Enterprise Project and Institute of Social and Economic Research, 1980); P. Emmanuel, *An Overview of Public Enterprise in the West Indies Associated States*; and P. Reno, *The Ordeal of British Guiana* (New York: Monthly Review Press, 1964), 77–78. See M. Odle, *The Evolution of Public Expenditure. The Case of a Structurally Dependent Economy: Guyana* (Mona, Jamaica: Institute of Social and Economic Research, 1976) for some idea of how the earlier national-izations in Guyana served the interests of the sugar industry. However, it should be noted that not all the estates so acquired were former sugar plantations. Whim on the Corentyne river grew cotton before being abandoned, after 1862.
36. Some of these lands such as Windsor Forest, La Jalousie and Hague were acquired at 'sales of execution' when owners defaulted on payment of sea defence levies. These estates could, of course, have simply been auctioned, as was the case with village lands, and the proceeds set off against the debts incurred by their owners.
37. The importance of this latter factor in reducing the costs of LSSs is now widely recognized. See also IBRD (Report No. 5625, Washington, DC, 1985), "The experience of the World Bank with government-sponsored land settlements", 26, 48.
38. A former cotton plantation.
39. In this regard, reference has already been made to the withdrawal of administrative support when market conditions improved at the turn of the century.
40. In the cases of Lancaster and Clonbrook, the land was parcelled into house-lots and only sold as such to settlers.
41. Hardship assistance on schemes could have stemmed the loss of good settlers from many schemes. See IBRD, "The experience of the World Bank", 39.
42. This is also the consensus with regard to schemes globally. See also Hulme, "State-sponsored land", 413–14.

43. For some additional insights into Mr O's (Wu's) flight, see M. Crawford, *Scenes from the History of the Chinese in Guyana* (Georgetown, Guyana: Marlene Kwok Crawford, 1989), 43–50 and M. Kirkpatrick, *From the Middle Kingdom to the New World,* Vol. 1 (Georgetown, Guyana: Marjorie Kirkpatrick, 1993), 45–47.

44. See R. Frucht, "A Caribbean social type", *Social and Economic Studies* 16, no. 3 (1967), for a discussion of the characteristics of the Caribbean small farmer vis-à-vis the theoretical construct of a peasant.

45. See P. Pierce, *Non-capitalist Development: The Struggle to Nationalize the Guyana Sugar Industry* (Ottowa, NJ: Rowman and Allanheld, 1984), for example, for an instance of the persistence of view that "race first took on political significance during the fight for independence" (88).

Notes to Chapter 4

46. In fact, the similarity with the sugar industry is so striking that the bauxite operation has been termed an 'urban plantation'.

47. Discussions of some of the explicit policies and other factors giving rise to the social division of labour by race are contained in Shahabuddeen, *From Plantocracy*; B. Moore, *Race, Power and Social Segmentation in Colonial Society; Guyana after Slavery* (New York: Gordon and Breach, 1987); and D.E. Danns, *The History of the Bank of Guyana* (Georgetown, Guyana: Bank of Guyana, 1990).

48. Indeed, Ken Post, *Arise Ye Starvelings* (The Hague: Martinus Nijhoff, 1978) argues that the working class movement was constantly betrayed by the its leadership which was drawn from middle class elites.

49. In 1938 the League of Nations appointed a commission to report on the feasibility of such a settlement. Nothing materialized from the commission's report but in 1939 the British government extended an offer of land for the settlement of Jews in Guyana. See Government of Guyana, Aide de Memoire from the Government of Guyana, 1969.

50. Charity/Amazon which was established at that time is not of concern to us in this study because it was not intended to undertake agricultural development. It was rather a township, an *entrepot*, to the upper and lower Pomeroon.

51. In this regard Silverman reported that settlers in Bush Lot, West Coast Berbice (WBC), who benefited from the adoption of the recommendations in this report, moved to the Abary River to occupy their grants. Others maintained farms in both places. Some of those who moved continued to sell their labor to the plantations whilst still undertaking subsistence farming. The settlers at Bush Lot also benefited from a windfall of 1,000 acres (405 ha) made available as a result of the failed Varey Scheme (Mo Silverman, *Rich People and Rice: Factional Politics in Rural Guyana*, Monographs and Theoretical Studies in Sociology and Anthropology in Honour of Niels Anderson 16 [Lieden: E.J. Brill]).

52. Settlers at Cane Grove, Vergenoenen and La Bonne Mere were also provided with communal pastures and the house lots were converted to leasehold in 1950.

53. For reasons to which reference has already been made, Anna Regina may have been considered a special case.

54. One of the main reasons appears to have been a notion that working in flooded rice fields made workers susceptible to elephantiasis, or 'big foot', an affliction of which most Africans were mortally afraid (Kennard, letter to author, 1988).

55. Although it should be noted that Silverman has observed that free paddy seed was made available to Bush Lot (WCB) farmers in 1922 (45, 958).

56. Ironically, the low prices concluded under this agreement precipitated a fall in the acreage

sown to rice. See IBRD, *The Economic Development of British Guiana* (Baltimore: Johns Hopkins, 1953); Caribbean Commission 1947, No. 3.

57. Work on schemes established in other countries during the 1960s and 1970s suggests that cost per family range from US$5,000–$20,000. See IBRD, "The experience of the World Bank", iii, 4b.

58. For some other possible reasons see G. Ablasser, "Issues in settlement of new lands", *Finance and Development* 24, no. 1 (March 1987); and IBRD, "The experience of the World Bank".

59. In 1930 the 77 families amounted to 278 persons (Administration Report of the Director of Agriculture for 1930, British Guiana 1931, 139–41).

60. The price of such balancing was very high for settlers as we shall see later.

61. This phenomenon was first noted by Young who pointed out that over the period 1953–55 alone, the number of villages with exclusively African council membership had fallen from 18 to 13 whilst those consisting of East Indians only had risen from 3 to 8, particularly in villages with elected councils.

62. Recent experience suggests that more often than not the proximate cause of such action is usually a dispute over the 'illegal' or unauthorized sale of part of all of collectively owned land, children's property, to outsiders. The other part-owners frequently find themselves involved in expensive litigation to protect their interests – litigation that the buyer usually is in a better position to afford. Sometimes the process is triggered by an informal loan of the land and eventually squatters rights are then claimed on the death of the person who authorized the deal. Such disputes cause much bitterness both within families in African villages and between one village and another since frequently they escalate.

63. Subsequent schemes had to await the implementation of the Marshall Report ("Report on local government in British Guiana" [May 1955, Georgetown]) in 1969 before being converted. See chapter 5.

64. The name the author assigned to the village studied, Rajgahr, does not appear anywhere in the official records. The *Guyana Gazette*, which is an authoritative source of place names and changes, also makes no reference to it. The reason for the substitution, of an admittedly more Indian-sounding name, is not mentioned but there is no doubt that it is Bush Lot since its precise location and the names of its prominent residents are provided.

Notes to Chapter 5

65. For a readable and reasonably balanced summary of this period see R. Manley, *Guyana Emergent: The Post-independence Struggle for Non-dependent Development* (Cambridge, MA: Shukman, 1982). See also H. Green, *From Pain to Peace: Guyana 1953–1964* (Georgetown, Guyana: Tropical Airways, 1987); Sallahudin, "Guyana: The struggle for liberation" (Georgetown, Guyana: Guyana National Printers, 1994); and Latin American Bureau, *Guyana: Fraudulent Revolution* (London: LAB and World Council of Churches, 1984) for contrasting views. Many of the references in the chapter also cover this period.

66. Although compulsory education was introduced in 1876, this requirement was in force since 1907 and later removed.

67. In the case of Bush Lot, farmers received second and third depth lands in the Abary and this facilitated the establishment of a cattle industry in WCB.

68. See G. Rohlehr, *Calypso and Society in Pre-independence Trinidad* (Trinidad and Tobago: Gordon Rohler, 1990), 502–7, for the placement of these events in a Caribbean context as well as the popular perception (in addition to his own) of events as articulated by the calypsonians of the day, in and out of Guyana. Among the most well known of such songs

was Melody's "Indian Party" and "Apan Jaat". The appeal to race as such was, it should be stressed, by no means unique to the nationalist movement. See P. Beatty, *A History of the Lutheran Church in Guyana* (Berbice, Guyana: Paul Beatty, Jr, 1970).

69. At which point there was the displacement of the PPP by an Opposition coalition of the People's National Congress/United Force (PNC/UF).

70. The country was granted full internal self-government in 1961; independence in 1966 and opted for republican status in 1970. It stayed out of the 1958–62 West Indian Federation.

71. It has since been contended that the programme of mechanization was financed entirely from the sugar industry's special funds, which were intended in part to finance improved conditions for sugar workers. In the words of C.Y. Thomas ("Sugar economics in a colonial situation", *Ratoon Studies in Exploitation* 1 [1969]: 26), "the industry modernized itself at the expense of Guyanese and other resources".

72. However, it was acknowledged that throughout the world indebtedness and ignorance of scientific farming practices jeopardized the independence and viability of the peasantry.

73. The Black Bush Polder (BBP) and Boerasire are discussed in this paper since they also involved the reallocation of land and fall within our definition of LSSs.

74. See E. Hobsbawm, "Peasants and politics", *Journal of Peasant Studies* 1, no. 1 (1973); and H. Alavi, "Peasant classes and primordial loyalties", *Journal of Peasant Studies* 1, no. 1 (1973) for a glimpse into the complexities involved in peasantry politics.

75. This latter criterion could be anticipated to favour rural families and East Indians in particular. See ICJ, "Report of the Commission of Inquiry on 'Racial problems in the public service'", October 1969, Geneva.

76. Formerly the property of the Colonial Company.

77. In some instances the state directly undertook the supply of these machinery services; for example, the Land Development Division established a machinery pool at Mara and a fleet of combines was based at BBP to harvest settlers' rice.

78. For example, discriminatory hiring of machinery was often practised against ethnic as well as religious minorities in rural areas.

79. The IBRD report also observed that, "existing ordinances regulating tenant/landlord relations and fixing minimum prices for paddy and rice do not appear to be effectively enforced" (146).

80. It does appear that in the selection of settlers, political favouritism was not an unusual occurrence globally in the 1960s and 1970s. IBRD, "Guyana: A framework for economic recovery" (Report No. 5592-GUA, 15 May 1985, Washington, DC), 12.

81. Brandwagt Sari had been a sugar plantation during the Dutch era whereas the Mara Land Development Scheme was established on land acquired from the owners of Houston Estates Ltd, the only locally owned private sugar plantation operating in the country today.

82. It needs to be borne in mind that Garden of Eden and Brandwagt Sari were initially established as pilot schemes.

83. This experience seems to stand in marked contrast with those elsewhere where settlement authorities have only tended to withdraw from LSSs with great reluctance. IBRD, "Guyana: A framework", 32. It should be added that although Cane Grove was converted to a local authority in 1960, no titles could be issued to settlers because the surveys had not been completed. They remained incomplete as late as 1965. Ministry of Agriculture, Annual Report 1965, 92.

Notes to Chapter 6

84. Indeed, the establishment of the African Society for Cultural Relations with Independent Africa (ASCRIA) by one of its more radical leaders helped to bring pressure to bear on the PNC to implement policies of interest to its core supporters.
85. Pierce, *Non-capitalist Development*.
86. Silverman has alleged that, "in addition, public works benefitting entire villages, were used to subvert [PPP] support" (*Rich People and Rice*, 159–70).
87. At that time Africans accounted for some 41 percent of the population.
88. The "pressure" referred to partly manifested itself in Venezuela's seizure of Guyana's portion of territory on Ankoko Island in 1968. In addition to this, in the following year an armed confrontation took place between Guyana and Suriname over the New River Triangle. See Odle, *The Evolution of Public Expenditure*, ch. 5; D. Nath, *A History of Guyana*, Vol. 3 (London: D. Nath, 1976), ch. 12; F. Burnham, *A Destiny to Mould: Selected Discourses by the Prime Minister of Guyana*, compiled by Nascimento and Burrowes (London: Longman Caribbean, 1970).
89. Although the PNC's well-publicized financial support to the liberation movements of South Africa was not directed to this end, there can be little doubt that it did not hurt the defence of Guyana's case for its current borders abroad.
90. With the assistance of the Caribbean neighbours a protocol was signed with Venezuela in 1970. This did not stop aggressive Venezuelan pursuit of their case in the international fora. See Manley, *Guyana Emergent*, chs. 3 and 4.
91. It should be noted that a recent study has concluded that "there has not been a recognizable housing policy in Guyana since Independence in 1966", Peake ("From cooperative socialism to a social housing policy", in Potter and Conway 1997). But this conclusion is one of several contradictory statements in the study. This particular one seems to stem from the author's view that the targets of the programme were inappropriate.
92. Peake, "From cooperative socialism", has noted that over the years 1954 to 1964 the SIWLF built 10,785 housing units compared to 3,900 by the government.
93. This assessment is not universally accepted. It has been observed that behind the apparently attractive prices of the Cuba contract were equally uncompetitive prices for the imports of cement and paper bags, inter alia, under the barter arrangement (Kennard, letter to the author, 1988).
94. Rohlehr, *Calypso and Society*, suggested that the intention was to receive re-migrants from the UK, where the government feared that the long-term settlement of large numbers of Jews would have generated hostility.
95. Although it should be noted that such violence, including bombing, predated 1967 and was not only associated with PPP-PNC matters but also with the 'politics of rice', for example.
96. This pre-settlement wage employment was not without its hazards, however. See IBRD, "Guyana: A framework", 34.
97. For one view leaning on the side of the non-inevitability of the state's escalating role in this debate, see J. Jiggins, "Beyond Ujamaa in Tanzania: A review article", *Third World Quarterly* 3, no. 1 (January 1981): 94.
98. Rents and charges are only collected and shown separately in the Annual Estimates of Expenditure and the Annual Reports of the Ministry of Agriculture for those schemes established between 1923 and 1962 and the Soesdyke-Linden Scheme.
99. An idea of just how extreme and partial such analysis may become can be had from a publication on ethnicity (S. Debiprashad and D. Budram, "Participation of East Indians in

the transformation of Guyanese society", in *India in the Caribbean: Special Commemorative Edition 1838–1988*, edited by D. Dabydeen and B. Samaroo [Warwick: Hanslib and University of Warwick, 1987]) which deemed the periodic market-inspired pricing policies to be racist and anti-East Indian!

100. Camacho et al. ("The use of input-output analysis to estimate secondary economic benefits of irrigation schemes", paper presented at International Commission on Irrigation and Drainage, Tenth Congress on Irrigation and Drainage, Athens, Greece, 1978) have argued that for every dollar earned on these D&I schemes, an additional dollar may be earned in the economy as well as an additional off scheme worker for each one employed on the scheme.

101. See K. Hope, "Strengthening rural cooperatives in Guyana", *Journal of Rural Cooperation* 6, no. 2 (1978) for an outline of some problems and suggested solutions. See Mitchell et al. 1979; Hope 1975–76 for a background to the recent history and expansion.

102. Although in the light of this the popularity of employee share ownership is somewhat puzzling.

103. For more discussion of this aspect in an African context see J. Platteau, "Land reform and structural adjustment in sub-Saharan Africa: controversies and guidelines" (FAO Economic and Social Development Paper no. 107, Rome, 1992), especially 244–97.

104. For a most interesting and quite detailed analysis along these lines in connection with a well-known cooperative-type organization with implications of a wide nature, see "The real paper", in *Life and Death on the Corporate Battlefield: How Companies Win, Lose and Survive* by P. Soloman and T. Friedman (New York: Signet NAL, 1982), 212–36.

105. See I. Sukdeo, "Labour mobility in land development schemes" (ILO Labour Moblity Project, IDS, University of Guyana, 1978), ch. 6, for a sketch of the early history of cooperatives and their problems. For a longer historical perspective, see H. Jeffrey, "Cooperative socialism: A critical review" (Staff Discussion Paper, IDS, University of Guyana, 1977).

107. Opting out of surplus production for the market and refusing to cooperate on 'self-help' projects without bribes or other goods and services which are in effect 'wages' (see Jiggins, "Beyond Ujaama", 96).

107. Sukdeo, "Labour mobility", 47, cites racial discrimination by LSS administration as a problem in this era. The direction of this discrimination on an overwhelmingly East Indian–settled and administered scheme is not clear from the text. It is just as well to note, however, that the state marketing agency initially became involved in the provision of machinery services in some districts in order to provide services to those groups against whom these practices were employed. See also C.B. Greenidge, "The problems and prospects of agro-industry as a transformation agent in plantation-type economies", *Public Enterprise* 3, no. 1 (1982).

108. Tumatumari is the site of a former gold mining operation by Consolidated Goldfields Ltd.

Note to Chapter 7

109. The authority had already been reformed on at least three occasions since its establishment in 1946 and all took place under the PNC administration: 1965, 1969, 1973 and then in 1984.

Notes to Chapter 8

110. Such as the works of E. Clayton, *Agrarian Development in Peasant Economies* (Oxford: Pergamon, 1964) and *Economic Planning in Peasant Agriculture* (London: Wye College, University of London, 1965), which have spawned a range of studies on East Africa. The single exception is a study by P.J. Hooker, "A preliminary study of economic potential of beef cattle, grain and legume-seed production in the intermediate savannas of Guyana using a linear programming model", *Economic Report* 51 (1973).

111. At the time a Dutch colony and a separate country.

BIBLIOGRAPHY

Official Documents: National Archives and Relevant Ministries

British Guiana. 1897. Report of the West India Royal Commission (C. 8655).

British Guiana. 1904. Report of the Immigration Agent General with Appendices including Report of the Superintendent of the East Indian Settlement.

British Guiana. 1907. Report of Committee Appointed to Give Effect to Proposals of the Land Settlement Commission Report (in continuation of Sessional Paper no. 849). Annual Session Combined Court no. 889, no. 4127.

British Guiana. 1907–8. Administrative Report of Immigration Agent General.

British Guiana. 1912. Report of the Land and Mines Department for the Years 1911–12, Argosy Co. Ltd.

British Guiana. 1914–15. Administrative Report of Immigration Agent General.

British Guiana. 1917a. Report of Committee Appointed to Enquire and Report as to the Effect of Leasing Crown Lands, and as to the Grounds, If Any, Which Exist to Warrant the Revival of the Policy of Selling Crown Lands to Small Cultivators.

British Guiana. 1917b. Report of Committee on the Sale of Colony Lands together with the Colony Report. Combined Court no. 908. Second special session (GSO No. 3704/17).

British Guiana. 1918. Annual Report of the Immigration Agent General, 1917.

British Guiana. 1919a. Report of Sub-committee of the Colony Development Committee to Consider the Question of East Indian Immigration Generally. Combined Court no. 11 (GSO No. 5214/18).

British Guiana. 1919b. Speech by the Hon. C. Clementi, CMG, Government Secretary on the subject of local colonization: delivered in Combined Court on the 6th February. Combined Court no. 9 (GSO No. 1084/19).

British Guiana. 1919c. Report on the Conditions during the First World War and Problems Awaiting Solution.

British Guiana. 1919d. Precis of the History of Immigration into British Guiana from Barbados. Combined Court. First Special Session 1919. Combined Court no. 15/1919 (GSO No. 7239/14).

British Guiana. 1924. Governor's Memorandum on the Colonization of British Guiana, 24 October.

British Guiana. 1925–34. Colonial Estimate no. 16483. Comparative Statement of Expenditure.

British Guiana. 1925. Report of the Committee Appointed to Enquire as to the Desirability of Setting up a Permanent Board of Colonization and Development (GSO No. 370/24).

British Guiana. 1928a. Governor's Memorandum of 20 October 1928 on the Colonisation of British Guiana.

British Guiana. 1928b. Governor's Annual Message to the Legislative Council. December.

British Guiana. 1929a. The East Bank Essequibo (paper prepared by J. Mullins). Appendix to Colonisation Report.

British Guiana. 1929b. Governor's Memorandum no. 3 (20 November 1928). Revised 21 January 1929. Control of Colonisation (MP 424/29).

British Guiana. 1929c. Leaflet advertising particulars of land settlement of Plantation Hampton Court, Essequibo, 2 January 1929.

British Guiana. 1929d. Governor's Memorandum no. 3, 20 November 1928 (Revised to 21 January 1929). Control of Colonisation.

Btitish Guiana. 1929e. Governor's Memoradum no. 4, 6 February 1929. On Land Settlement at Bush Lot, Essequibo District. MP 828/29 Georgetown.

British Guiana. 1929f. Governor's Memorandum no. 5, 7 February 1929. On Preparation of Henrietta as an Agricultural Station and Land Settlement. MP 828/29.

British Guiana. 1930. Report on the Sugar Industry of the West Indies and British Guiana, 1929–30 (Cmd. 3517).

British Guiana. 1930–35. Administrative Reports of Director of Agriculture.

British Guiana. 1931a. Report of a Small Farmers' Committee and Legislative Council (No. 9).

British Guiana. 1931b. Administrative Report of the Director of Agriculture for 1930. Argosy Co. Ltd.

British Guiana. 1932. British Guiana Sugar Producers' Association: Letter reporting finding of sub-committee appointed to consider government's land settlement and colonization proposals and forwarding estimates of costs from Plantations Wales, Philadelphia, Vergenoegen and Diamond, 3 September. Appendix XI.

British Guiana. 1933. Report of a preliminary agricultural survey of areas suitable for land settlement and Colonisation by West Indians by the Hon J. Mullins and Capt. F. Burnett. Legislative Council no. 8. CSO 3660/32.

British Guiana. 1934–35. Report by Brigadier-General J.R. Browne and Dr G.R. Giglioli on his mission to British Guiana (District Rupununi).

British Guiana. 1938–39. Report of the Committee Appointed by His Excellency, the Governor to Consider or Advise "What steps are practicable to expedite the development of the colony". Economic Council, Fourth Session.

British Guiana. 1939a. Report of the British Guiana Commission to the President's Advisory Committee on Political Refugees. Third Legislative Council, No. 11/1939 with Appendices (LC Paper No. 12/1939).

British Guiana. 1939b. Report of the Land Settlement Committee. Third Legislative Council, Fourth Session, 1938–39. Legislative Council No. 2 (GSO No. 57/5).

British Guiana. 1939c. Third Legislative Council. Fourth Session 1938–39. Report of the Essequibo Coast Rice Committee.

British Guiana. 1939d. The Development of Transportation Routes under the Projected Colonization of Refugees in British Guiana by Lt. Col. R.U. Nicholas, Corps of Engineers, US Army.

British Guiana. c. 1939. Note on the Possibilities for the Agricultural Settlement of Involuntary Refugees from Central Europe in the Hinterland of British Guiana by Sir G. Evans.

British Guiana. 1941–42. Third Legislative Council. Seventh Session. Report of the Rice Farmers' Committee.

British Guiana. 1943. Interim Report of the Land Settlement Committee. Third Legislative

Council, Ninth Session 1943 (LC No. 12, GSO 57/II).

British Guiana. 1947. Annual Report for Year 1947.

British Guiana. 1948. Papers Relating to Development Planning. Vol. 2. Reports of the Subcommittee of the Main Development Committee of the Legislative Council (LC Paper No. 11).

British Guiana. 1949. Colonial Reports, 1947. HMSO.

British Guiana. 1950. Annual Report of the Director of Agriculture.

British Guiana. 1952. Agriculture in British Guiana. Census 1953, Vol. 1, No. 1 by O.P. Blaich.

British Guiana. 1953a. Annual Report of Cooperative Development.

British Guiana. 1953b. Report by the Agricultural Adviser of the Secretary of State for the Colonies. F. Brown. 24 December 1953.

British Guiana. 1951–54. Annual Reports of the Director of Land Settlement.

British Guiana. 1955. British Guiana Annual Report 1955.

British Guiana. 1957a. Annual Report on British Guiana for the Year 1956.

British Guiana. 1957b. Annual Report of the Ministry of Agriculture.

British Guiana. 1960a. Annual Report for Year 1960.

British Guiana. 1960b. Second Legislative Council under the British Guiana (Constitution) Temporary Provisional Orders in Council 1953 and 1954. Fourth Session, No. 10.

British Guiana. 1960c. Annual Report of the Director of Agriculture.

British Guiana. 1961. Annual Report of the Director of Agriculture.

British Guiana. 1962. Annual Report for Year 1961.

British Guiana. 1964a. Papers relating to development planning.

British Guiana. 1964b. Development Estimates as Passed by the Legislative Assembly.

British Guiana. 1964c. Annual Report of the Ministry of Agriculture.

British Guiana. 1964d. Annual Report of the Director of Agriculture.

British Guiana. 1965a. Annual Report of the Ministry of Agriculture.

British Guiana. 1965b. Annual Reports for the Years 1960 and 1964.

Caribbean Commission. Committee on Agriculture, Fisheries and Forestry of the Caribbean Research Council. 1946. Caribbean Land Tenure Symposium. Washington, DC.

Caribbean Commission. Committee on Agriculture, Fisheries and Forestry of the Caribbean Research Council. 1947. Grain Crops in the Caribbean. Crop Enquiry Series, no. 3. Washington, DC.

Colonial Office. 1942. Colonial Development and Welfare in the West Indies: Agriculture in the West Indies.

Government of Guyana. n.d. Production of Paddy on Black Bush Polder from Inception. Land and Mines Department (File No. LS 10/2/2/).

Government of Guyana. 1966a. "Migration". paper presented at the Commonwealth Caribbean-Canada Conference. Ottawa, 6–8 July, Guyana delegation.

Government of Guyana. 1966b. *British Guiana (Guyana) Development Programme: 1966–72*. Georgetown, Guyana: Government Printery.

Government of Guyana. 1968. Annual Report of the Ministry of Agriculture and Natural Resources for the Year 1967.

Government of Guyana. 1969a. Ministry of Economic Development. Report of Chief Cooperative Officer.

Government of Guyana. 1969b. Aide de Memoire from the Government of Guyana. Visit of Governor N. Rockefeller to Guyana, 4–5 July.

Government of Guyana. 1970a. Department of Land Settlement. File on Marudi Pioneer Cooperative Land Society.

Government of Guyana. 1970b. Development of the New River Area Plan. Interior Department.
Government of Guyana. c. 1972. Second Development Plan 1972–76. Draft. Ministry of
    Economic Development. Georgetown, Guyana.
Government of Guyana. 1974. The Soesdyke/Linden Highway Project. Agriculture
    Development Programme. Ministry of National Development and Agriculture. May.
Government of Guyana. 1977–79. Annual Reports, Lands and Mines Department.
Government of Guyana. 1978–81. Annual Reports, Lands and Mines Department.
Government of Guyana. 1981. Guyana's Housing Drive, Ministry of Public Welfare (Housing).
Government of Guyana. 1985. Draft Agriculture Development Plan. 1986–89. Ministry of
    Agriculture, Coop. Republic of Guyana. Georgetown. October
Government of Guyana. 1985. Budget Speech. Session Paper No. 1, Fourth Parliament of
    Guyana. Third Session 1983–85. National Assembly, Georgetown.
Government of Guyana. 1986. Budget Speech. Session Paper No. 1, Fifth Parliament of
    Guyana. First Session, 26 February. National Assembly, Georgetown.
Government of Guyana. 1991. The Incremental Capital-output Ratio of Guyana's Agricultural
    Sector: 1977–1980. Planning Department, Ministry of Agriculture. 8 January. Georgetown
Guyana National Service. 1975a. Kimbia Settlement Prospectus. GNS Planning Division,
    Georgetown, Guyana.
Guyana National Service. 1975b. Settlement Programme – Kimbia. Office of the Director
    General. Internal Communication.
HMSO. 1954. Colonial Office Report on British Guiana for the year 1952. CO London.
HMSO. 1955. Colonial Office Report on British Guiana for the year 1953. CO London.
Laws of British Guiana: East Indian Land Settlement Regulation Ordinance, 1901.
Laws of British Guiana: East Indian Land Settlement Regulation Ordinance, 1905, No. 8.
Laws of British Guiana: Crown Lands Resumption Ordinance No. 30 of 1905.
Laws of British Guiana: 1953. Rice Farmers Security of Tenure Amendment Ordinance.
Laws of British Guiana: 1957. Acquisition of Land (Land Settlement) Ordinance No. 13.
West Indies Royal Commission. 1946. Report of the West Indies Royal Commission. Lord
    Moyne: Chairman, HMSO (Cmd. 6607).
West Indies Sugar Commission Report. 1930. (Cmd. 3517.)

Books and Articles

Ablasser, G. 1987. "Issues in settlement of new lands". *Finance and Development* 24, no. 1
    (March).
Adamson, A. 1972. *Sugar without Slaves: The Political Economy of British Guiana, 1838–1904*.
    London: Yale University Press.
Adamson, A. 1984. "The impact of indentured immigration on the political economy of British
    Guiana". In *Indentured Labour in the British Empire 1834–1920*, edited by K. Saunders.
    London: Croom Helm.
Adhin, J. 1961. *Development Planning in Suriname in Historical Perspective (With Special
    Reference to the 10 Year Plan)*. Utrecht: Drukkerij J.J. Smits. Oude Gracht 231.
Alavi, H. 1973. "Peasant classes and primordial loyalties". *Journal of Peasant Studies* 1, no. 1.
Ali, R. 1974. *Land Settlement Planning in Trinidad and Tobago. A Study of the Dairy and Pig
    Project*. Working Paper no. 2. Mona, Jamaica: Institute of Social and Economic Research.
Ambursley, F., and R. Cohen, eds. 1983. *Crisis in the Caribbean*. London: Heinemann.
Amerasinghe, N. 1973. "Resource use and production possibilities on settlement schemes in

Ceylon (a case study)". Staff Research Workshop. Wye College, University of London.

Andic, F.M., and T.G. Matthews. 1965. *The Caribbean in Transition: Papers on Social, Political and Economic Development.* Rio Pedras, Puerto Rico: Institute of Caribbean Studies, University of Puerto Rico.

Anglo-American Caribbean Commission. 1946. Caribbean Land Tenure Symposium. Committee on Agriculture, Nutrition, Fisheries and Forestry of the Caribbean Research Council, Washington, DC.

Baber, C., et al. 1986. *Guyana: Politics, Economics and Society.* Marxist Regimes Series. Boulder, CO: Frances, Penter and Lynne Rienner.

Bacchus, M. 1970. *Education and Socio-cultural Integration in a Plural Society.* Occasional Paper Series, no. 6. Montreal: McGill University.

Bank of Guyana. 1980. *Annual Report 1980.* Georgetown, Guyana: Bank of Guyana.

Bauer, P., and P. Yamey. 1968. *Markets, Market Control and Marketing Reform: Selected Papers.* London: Weidenfeld and Nicholson.

Bauer, P. 1989. "Marketing boards". In *Economic Development: The New Palgrave*, edited by J. Eatwell et al. London and New York: Norton.

Bayley, G. 1909. *Handbook of British Guiana.* Georgetown: Permanent Exhibitions Committee. (Printed by Argosy Co. Ltd. Later editions published as *The British Guiana Handbook* by J.H. Stark, Boston.)

Beachell, N., and O.B. Brown. n.d. *Report on Mechanisation and Organisation of Rice in British Guiana.* London: Colonial Office.

Beatty, P. 1970. *A History of the Lutheran Church in Guyana.* Berbice, Guyana: Paul Beatty, Jr.

Beckford, G. 1972. *Persistent Poverty: Underdevelopment in Plantation Economies of the Third World.* Oxford: Oxford University Press.

Bernstein, H., ed. 1973. *Underdevelopment and Development: The Third World Today.* Harmondsworth: Penguin.

Berrill, K. 1961. "Comments on 'The economic future of British Guiana' by P. Newman". *Social and Economic Studies* 10, no. 1.

Bertram, M. 1992. *The Birth of Anglo American Friendship. The Prime Facet of the Venezuelan Boundary Dispute. A Study of the Inter-reaction of Diplomacy and Public Opinion.* Lanham, New York and London: University Press of America.

Besson, J., et al., eds. 1987. *A Paradox in Caribbean Attitudes to Land. Land and Development in the Caribbean.* Warwick Caribbean Studies Series. London: Macmillan.

Best, L. 1968. "Outlines of a model of pure plantation economy". *Social and Economic Studies* 17, no. 3 (September).

Bhaduri, A. 1977. "On the formation of usurious interest rates in backward agriculture". *Cambridge Journal of Economics* (December).

Boesen, J. 1979. "On peasantry and the 'modes of production' debate". *Review of African Political Economy* 15–16 (December).

Bolland, O. 1981. "Systems of domination after slavery: the control of land and labour in the British West Indies after 1838". *Cooperative Studies in Society and History* 23, no. 4 (October).

Boodhoo, M.J. 1971. "The role of public enterprises in the economic development in Barbados, Guyana and Trinidad and Tobago". PhD diss., University of Leeds.

Boodhoo, M.J., et al. 1981. *The Impact of Brain Drain on Development: A Case Study of Guyana.* Georgetown: University of Guyana.

Boserup, E. 1965. *The Conditions of Agricultural Growth.* London: Allen and Unwin.

Bottomore, T., et al. 1983. *A Dictionary of Marxist Thought.* Cambridge, MA: Harvard University Press.

Boulding, K. 1961. "Social dynamics in West Indian Society". *Social and Economic Studies* 10, no. 1 (March).

Bourne, C. 1975. "Review article on the plantation economy of Guyana". *Social and Economic Studies* 24, no. 4 (December).

Brewster, H. 1969. "The pattern of change in wages, prices and productivity in British Guiana 1948–62". *Social and Economic Studies* 18, no. 2 (June).

Brookfield, H. 1975. *Interdependent Development*. London: Methuen.

Brotherson, L. *c.* 1969. "Land utilisation study: A preliminary report on the economics of land use on the coastlands". Ministry of Economic Development, Georgetown, Guyana.

Brown, A. 1981. "Issues of public enterprise". *Social and Economic Studies* 30, no. 1 (March).

Browne, E.A. *c.* 1910. *British Guiana as a Holiday Resort*. Demerara, British Guiana: Sprostons Limited.

Browne, E. 1954. *Colonial Office Report on British Guiana for the Year 1952*. London: Colonial Office.

Brown, F. 1954. "Land settlement problems in British Guiana". *Daily Argosy*, 13–15 April.

Burnham, F. 1970. *A Destiny to Mould: Selected Discourses by the Prime Minister of Guyana*. Compiled by Nascimento and Burrowes. London: Longman Caribbean.

Burnham, F. 1974. *L.F.S. Burnham on National Service*, vol. 1, no. 1. Georgetown, Guyana.

Burrowes, R. 1984. *The Wild Coast: An Account of Politics in Guyana*. Cambridge, MA: Schenkman.

Caffey, R., and J. Efferson, 1965. "An appraisal of rice production and market problems in British Guiana". Produced under the provisions of contract AID/1a–269–270, USAID. April.

Camocho, R., et al. 1978. "The use of input-output analysis to estimate secondary economic benefits of irrigation schemes". International Commission on Irrigation and Drainage, Tenth Congress on Irrigation and Drainage. Athens, Greece.

Carew, J. 1994. *Ghosts in Our Blood – with Malcolm X in Africa, England and the Caribbean*. Westport, CT: Lawrence Hill.

Chambers, R. 1969. *Settlement Schemes in Tropical Africa*. New York: Praeger.

Chase, A. 1964. *A History of Trade Unionism in Guyana, 1900 to 1961*. Ruimveldt, Guyana: New Guyana Co. Ltd.

Clayton, E. 1964. *Agrarian Development in Peasant Economies*. Oxford: Pergamon Press.

Clayton, E. 1965. *Economic Planning in Peasant Agriculture*. London: Wye College, University of London.

Coard, B. 1979. *The Role of the State in Agriculture in Grenada*. Mona, Jamaica: Caribbean Public Enterprise Project and Institute of Social and Economic Research.

Craig, S. 1977. Afterword. In *Labour in the West Indies* by W.A. Lewis. London: New Beacon Books

Crane, A.V. 1938. "A proposal for a land settlement scheme in British Guiana". Georgetown, British Guiana. Mimeo.

Crawford, M. 1989. *Scenes from the History of the Chinese in Guyana*. Georgetown, Guyana: Marlene Kwok Crawford.

Crookall, L. 1898. *British Guiana; Or, Work and Wanderings among the Creoles and Coolies, the Africans and Indians of the Wild Country*. London: T.F. Unwin.

Cross, M., and G. Herman, eds. 1988. *Labour in the Caribbean*. Warwick Caribbean Studies Series. London: Macmillan.

Cummings, L. 1973, ed. "Essequibo islands, land tenure and land use". Occasional Paper no. 2, Department of Geography, University of Guyana.

Dalton, H.G. 1855. *The History of British Guiana comprising a general description of the colony, in*

2 Volumes. London: Longman, Brown, Green.

Daly, V. 1975. *A Short History of the Guyanese People.* London: Macmillan Education.

Das, M. 1977. *I Want to Be a Poetess of My People.* Georgetown, Guyana: GNS Publishing Centre.

Danns, D.E. 1990. *The History of the Bank of Guyana.* Georgetown, Guyana: Bank of Guyana.

Danns, G. K. 1978. "Militarization and development. An experiment in nation-building". *Transition* 1, no. 1.

Danns, G.K., and L. Matthews. 1989. "Perspectives on the development and underdevelopment of communities in Guyana: A socio-historical analysis". In *Studies of Development and Change in the Modern World,* edited by M. Martin and T. Kandal. Oxford: Oxford University Press.

Dash, J. 1935. "Livestock problems in British Guiana". Address delivered by Prof. the Hon. J.S. Dash, Director of Agriculture, to the Chamber of Commerce, Berbice, 5 April.

David, W. 1969. *The Economic Development of Guyana 1953–64.* London: Oxford University Press.

de Kadt, E. 1972. *Patterns of Foreign Influence on the Caribbean.* London: Oxford University Press.

de Wilde, J., ed. 1967. *Experiences with Agricultural Development in Tropical Africa.* Baltimore: Johns Hopkins University Press for the IBRD.

Debiprashad, S., and Budram, D. 1987. "Participation of East Indians in the transformation of Guyanese society, 1966–79". In *India in the Caribbean: Special Commemorative Edition 1838–1988,* edited by D. Dabydeen and B. Samaroo. Warwick: Hanslib and University of Warwick.

Dorner, P. 1972. *Land Reform and Economic Development.* London: Penguin.

Downer, A. 1979. "Settlement on the white sands". Paper presented at the Fifth Commonwealth Conference on Development of Human Ecology. Georgetown, Guyana.

Dulfer, E. 1974. *Operational Efficiency of Agricultural Cooperatives in Developing Countries.* Washington, DC: FAO.

Dumont, R. 1963. "Planning agricultural development". Report to the Government of British Guiana. FAO Expanded Programme of Technical Assistance, no. 1706, Georgetown.

Dunham, D. 1982. "Politics and land settlement schemes: The case of Sri Lanka". *Development and Change* 13.

Eatwell, J., et al., eds. 1989. *Economic Development: The New Palgrave.* London and New York: Norton.

Emmanuel, P. 1980. An Overview of Public Enterprise in the West Indies Associated States. Mona, Jamaica: Caribbean Public Enterprise Project and Institute of Social and Economic Research.

Eriksson, G. 1993. *Peasant Response to Price Incentives in Tanzania: A Theoretical and Empirical Investigation.* Research Report 91. Uppsala: Nordiska Afrikaanstitutet.

Farley, R. 1954. "Rise of a Peasantry in British Guiana". *Social and Economic Studies* 2.

Farley, R. 1964. "Rise of village settlement in British Guiana". *Caribbean Quarterly* 11.

Fauriol, G. 1984. *Foreign Policy Behaviour of Caribbean States: Guyana, Haiti and Jamaica.* Lanham, New York and London: University Press of America.

Fenty, A., ed. 1984. *Twenty Years in Government. A Chronicle of Achievement.* Georgetown, Guyana: PNC.

Ferguson, T. 1995. *Structural Adjustment and Good Governance. The Case of Guyana.* Georgetown, Guyana: Public Affairs Consultancy Enterprise.

Fernandes, R. 1990. *The Guyana Mosaic.* Georgetown, Guyana: Guyana Stores.

Fitzgerald, E. 1987. "Land reform". In *Economic Development: The New Palgrave,* edited by J. Eatwell et al. London and New York: Norton.

Forte, G., and R. Maguire. 1988. "Qualifying success: The case of the Marouca Transport Cooperative Ltd". *Grassroots Development* 12, no. 3.

Fosbrooke, H., et al. 1960. *Land and Politics among the Luguru of Tanganyika*. London: Routledge.

Fraginals, M., et al., eds. 1985. *Between Slavery and Free Labour:The Spanish-speaking Caribbean in the 19th Century*. Baltimore: John Hopkins University Press.

Fraser, H. 1935. "Dairy cattle in British Guiana". *Agricultural Journal of British Guiana* 2 and 3.

Fraser, P. 1981. "The immigration issue in British Guiana: The economic and constitutional origins of racist politics in Guyana". *Journal of Caribbean History* 14.

Frucht, R. 1967. "A Caribbean social type: Neither 'peasant' nor 'proletarian'". *Social and Economic Studies* 16, no. 3 (September).

Gellner, E. 1969. *Populism: Its Meaning and National Characteristics*. London: Weidenfeld and Nicholson.

Ghai, D., et al., eds. 1979. *Agrarian Systems and Rural Development*. London: Macmillan.

Girvan, N. 1967. *The Caribbean Bauxite Industry*. Mona, Jamaica: Institute of Social and Economic Research.

Graham, S., and D. Gordon. 1977. *The Stratification System and Occupational Mobility in Guyana: Two Essays*. Mona, Jamaica: Institute of Social and Economic Research.

Green, H. 1987. *From Pain to Peace: Guyana 1953–1964*. Georgetwon, Guyana: Tropical Airways.

Greene, E. 1974. *Race vs Politics in Guyana. Political Cleavages and Political Mobilization in the 1968 General Election*. Mona, Jamaica: Institute of Social and Economic Research.

Greenidge, C.B. 1975. "After school, what? Employment, incomes and prospects of Kenya's rural youths three years out of primary school". Discussion paper, University of Guyana (March).

Greenidge, C.B. 1976a. "Country proposal: An overview of public enterprises in Guyana". Caribbean Public Enterprise Project, Universities of the West Indies and Guyana (March).

Greenidge, C.B. 1976b. "The marketing problems of settlement schemes in Guyana". Mirev. Planning Unit, Ministry of National Development. Georgetown. Mimeo.

Greenidge, C.B. 1978. "Book review: Gladstone Lewars' *Small Farm Financing in Guyana 1968–70*". *Social and Economic Studies* 27, no. 3 (September).

Greenidge, C.B. 1980. "The state as entrepreneur: An overview of the state and public enterprises in Guyana". Caribbean Public Enterprise Project, University of the West Indies and University of Guyana.

Greenidge, C.B. 1982. "The problems and prospects of agro-industry as a transformation agent in plantation-type economies". *Public Enterprise* 3, no. 1.

Greenidge, C.B. 1993. "Privatization under structural adjustment". In *Privatization: A Global Perspective*, edited by V. Ramandham. London: Routledge.

Greenidge, C.B., et al. 1978. "Report on a survey of associative forms of production". Compiled for the Inter-American Institute of Agricultural Services, Georgetown, Guyana (May).

Gyanchand, 1963. "Report of the three-year plan 1964–66 for British Guiana". Central Planning Division, Georgetown.

Hamilton, S. 1986. "The regional system. Principles and structures: A historical review and analysis". *Guyana Journal of Public Administration* 1 (March).

Hanley, E. 1975. "Rice, politics and development in Guyana". In *Beyond the Sociology and Development*, edited by I. Oxaal et al. London: Routledge.

Hanley, E. 1987. "The Guyanese rice industry and development planning – the wrong solution for wrong problem". In *A Paradox in Caribbean Attitudes to Land: Land and Development in the Caribbean*, edited by J. Besson et al. Warwick Caribbean Studies Series. London: Macmillan.

Haraksingh, K. 1981. "Control and resistence among overseas Indian workers: A study of labour on the sugar plantations of Trinidad, 1875–1917". *Journal of Caribbean History* 14, no. 2.

Harris, D. 1979. "Labour in the West Indies: The birth of a workers movement?" *Transition* 2, no. 1.

Harris, W. 1996. *Jonestown*. London and Boston: Faber and Faber.

Harriss, J. 1982. *Rural Development: Theories of Peasant Economy and Agrarian Change.* Hutchinson University Press.

Hart, R. 1988. "Origin and development of the working class in the English-speaking Caribbean area: 1897–1937". In *Labour in the Caribbean*, edited by M. Cross and G. Herman. Warwick Caribbean Studies Series. London: Macmillan.

Henfrey, C. 1972. "Foreign influence in Guyana: The struggle for independence". In *Patterns of Foreign Influence in the Caribbean*, edited by E. de Kadt. Oxford: Oxford University Press.

Heuman, G. 1981. *Between Black and White, Race and Politics, and the Free Coloureds in Jamaica 1792–1865*. Westport, CT: Greenwind Press.

Hindess, B., and P. Hirst. 1975. *Pre-capitalist Modes of Production*. London: Routledge.

Hintzen, P. 1989. *The Costs of Regime Survival: Racial Mobilization, Elite Domination and Control of the State in Guyana and Trinidad*. Asa Rose Monograph Series. Cambridge and New York: Cambridge University Press.

Hobsbawm, E. 1973. "Peasants and politics". *Journal of Peasant Studies* 1, no. 1.

Hooker, P. J. 1973. "A preliminary study of the economic potential of beef cattle, grain and legume-seed production in the intermediate savannas of Guyana using a linear programming model". *Economic Report* 51.

Hope, K. 1975. "Cooperative socialism and the cooperative movement in Guyana". *Review of International Cooperation* 68, no. 2.

Hope, K. 1976. "Cooperativism and cooperative socialism in Guyana". *Yearbook of Agricultural Cooperation.*

Hope, K. 1978. "Strengthening rural cooperatives in Guyana". *Journal of Rural Cooperation* 6, no. 2.

Hubbard, H.J.M. 1969. *Race and Guyana: The Anatomy of a Colonial Enterprise*. Georgetown, Guyana: Hubbard.

Huggins, H.C. 1935. "Seasonal variation and peasant agricultural credit in British Guiana". *Agricultural Journal of British Guiana* 2, no. 3.

Hulme, D. 1987. "State-sponsored land settlement policies: Theory and practice". *Development and Change* 18, no. 3 (July).

Hyden, G. 1980. *Beyond Ujamaa in Tanzania: Underdevelopment and an Uncaptured Peasantry.* London: Heinemann.

IBRD. 1953. *The Economic Development of British Guiana. Report of a Mission Organized by the IBRD at the Request of the Government of British Guiana*. Baltimore: Johns Hopkins University Press.

IBRD. 1970. "Current economic position and prospects of Guyana". Report No. CA-4a (October). Washington, DC.

IBRD. 1978. "Agricultural land settlement". World Bank Issues Paper, Washington, DC.

IBRD. 1982. "Guyana: Recent developments and short-term prospects". Report No. 3951, Washington, DC.

IBRD. 1985a. "The experience of the World Bank with government-sponsored land settlerments". Report No. 5625. Washington, DC.

IBRD. 1985b. "Guyana: A framework for economic recovery". Report No. 5592-GUA (15 May). Washington, DC.

IBRD. 1986. "Guyana: A proposal for economic recovery". Report No. 6591-GUA (24 December). Washington, DC.

ICJ. 1965. "Report of the British Guiana commission of inquiry. Constituted by International Commission of Jurists: 'Racial problems in the public service'". Geneva (October).

IMF. 1981. "Guyana: Recent economic developments". Washington, DC.

IMF. 1967. "Guyana: Recent economic developments". Washington, DC (31 March).

Im Thurn, E. F. 1883. *Among the Indians of Guiana; Being Sketches Chiefly Anthropologic from the Interior of British Guiana*. London: Keegan Paul, Trench and Co.

Jagan, C. 1966. *The West on Trial: My Struggle for Guyana's Freedom*. London: Michael Joseph.

Jagan, C. 1977. "Guyana: A reply to critics". *Monthly Review* (September).

Jameson, K. 1980. "An intermediate regime in historical context: The case of Guyana". *Development and Change* 11, no. 1.

Jeffrey, H. 1977. "Cooperative socialism. A critical review". Staff Discussion Paper. IDS, University of Guyana, 1 November.

Jiggins, J. 1981. "Beyond Ujamaa in Tanzania: A review article". *Third World Quarterly* 3, no. 1 (January).

John, E. 1975. "The cooperative sector of the Matthews Ridge/Kaituma agricultural project". Student paper, University of Guyana. Mimeo.

John, E. 1977. "The economies of farm cooperative societies along the coastlands of Guyana with particular reference to cane farming". Student paper, University of Guyana. Mimeo.

Johnson, H. 1978. "The political uses of commissions of enquiry: The imperial colonial West Indian context". *Social and Economic Studies* 27, no. 3 (September).

Johnson, H., et al. 1995. *The White Minority in the Caribbean*. London: James Currey.

Jonas, J. 1990. *Anancy in the Great House: Ways of Reading West Indian Fiction*. New York: Greenwood Press.

Joseph, C. 1998. *Anglo-American Diplomacy and the Re-opening of the Guyana-Venezuela Boundary Controversy, 1961–66*. Georgetown, Guyana: Free Press.

Killick, T. 1982. *Adjustment and Financing in the Developing World: The Role of the IMF*. Washington, DC: IMF/ODI.

Kirby, J. 1973. "Essequibo Islands: Analysis of land use patterns". Occasional Paper 3. Department of Geography. University of Guyana.

Kirke, H. 1898. *Twenty-five Years in British Guiana*. London: S. Low, Marston.

Kirkpatrick, M. 1993. *From the Middle Kingdom to the New World*. Vol. 1. Georgetown, Guyana: Marjorie Kirkpatrick.

Kitchin, G. 1982. *Development and Underdevelopment in Historical Perspective. Population, Nationalism and Industrialization*. London: Methuen.

Klein, H., et al. 1985. "The transition from slave to free labour: Notes on a cooperative economic model". In *Between Slavery and Free Labour: The Spanish-speaking Caribbean in the 19th Century*, edited by M. Fraginals et al. Baltimore: Johns Hopkins University Press.

Lacey, G. 1953. "Report on water control legislation and drainage and irrigation rates". Office of the Secretary of State for the Colonies, London.

Landis, J. 1971. "Race relations and politics in Guyana". PhD diss., Yale University.

Latin America Bureau. 1984. *Guyana: Fraudulent Revolution*. London: LAB and World Council of Churches.

Laurence, K. 1965. "The establishment of the Portuguese community in British Guiana". *Historical Review* 5, no. 2.

Lavarre, W. c. 1935. *Gold, Diamonds and Orchids*. New York: Fleming H. Revell.

Layne, N. 1970. "The plural society in Guyana". PhD diss., University of California, Berkeley.

Leechman. A., ed. 1913. *The British Guiana Handbook*. Georgetown, British Guiana: The Argosy the Permanent Exhibitions Committee, Argosy Co. Ltd.; London: Dulau and Co.

Lewars, G. 1977. *Small Farm Financing in Guyana 1968–70*. Mona, Jamaica: Institute of Social and Economic Research.

Lewis, G. 1968. *The Growth of the Modern West Indies*. New York: Monthly Review Press.

Lewis, W.A. 1951. "Issues in land settlement policy". *Caribbean Economic Review* 3, nos. 1 and 2.

Lewis, W.A. 1977. *Labour in the West Indies: The Birth of a Workers Movement with Afterword by S. Craig*. London: New Beacon Books.

Lipton, M. 1974. "Towards a theory of land reform". In *Agrarian Reform and Agrarian Reformism,* edited by D. Lehman. N.p.

Litvak, I., and C. Maule. 1975. "Foreign corporate social responsibility in less developed countries". *Journal of World Trade Law* 9, no. 2.

Liverpool, H. 1990. *Kaiso and Society*. Trinidad: Juba Publications.

Lobdell, R. 1988. "British officials and the West Indian peasantry 1842–1938". In *Labour in the Caribbean,* edited by M. Cross and G. Herman. Warwick Caribbean Studies Series. London: Macmillan.

Mandle, J. 1973. *The Plantation Economy: Population and Economic Change in Guyana. 1838–1960*. Philadelphia: Temple University Press.

Mandle, J. 1977. "Problems of the non-capitalist path of development in Guyana and Jamaica". *Politics and Society* 7, no. 2.

Mangru, B. 1987. *Benevolent Neutrality: Indian Government-policy and Labour Migration to British Guiana 1854–1884*. London: Hansib.

Manley, R. 1982. *Guyana Emergent. The Post-independence Struggle for Non-dependent Development*. Cambridge, MA: Schenkman.

Marshall, A. 1955. "Report on local government in British Guiana". May. Georgetown.

Marx, F. 1965. "Organized labour in British Guiana". In *The Caribbean in Transition: Papers on Social, Political and Economic Development,* edited by F.M. Andic and T.G. Matthews. Rio Pedras, Puerto Rico: Institute of Caribbean Studies, University of Puerto Rico.

Matthews, L., and G. Danns. 1980. "Communities and development in Guyana: A neglected dimension in nation-building". IDS, University of Guyana, Seminar paper.

McCormack, M. 1979. *Land Settlement in Guyana: Inventory and Legal Basis: A Compilation of Existing Information*. IICA/ OAS Misc. Publication, Series no. 199 (March).Washington, DC: IICA/OAS.

Melville, P. 1997. *The Ventriloquist's Tale*. London: Bloomsbury.

Miles, R. 1987. *Capitalism and Unfree Labour: Anomaly or Necessity?* London and New York: Tavistock.

Miller, L E. 1918. *In the Wilds of South America: Six Years of Exploration in Colombia, Venezuela, British Guiana, Peru, Bolivia, Argentina, Paraguay and Brazil*. New York: Scribner.

Miller. n.d. "Survey of animal husbandry, feeding, management and veterinary services in the West Indies: Report on British Guiana". *Development and Welfare in the West Indies Bulletin* 19A.

Mintz, S. 1985. "Epilogue: the divided aftermaths of freedom". In *Between Slavery and Free Labour. The Spanish-speaking Caribbean in the 19th Century,* edited by M. Fraginals. Baltimore: Johns Hopkins University Press.

Mitchell, I., and H. Lucius. 1979a. "Cooperative transformation process: Adaptation strategies and programmes". *Review of International Cooperation* 72, no. 4.

Mitchell, I., and H. Lucius. 1979b. "Cooperative development growth: an integrated structural model". *Annals of Public and Cooperative Economy* 2.

Mittelholzer, A.S. 1973. "Potato production in the Guyana highlands". Georgetown, Guyana. Mimeo.

Mittelholzer, E. 1955. *My Bones and My Flute*. London: Longman Caribbean Writers.

Momsen, J. 1987. "Land settlement as an imposed solution". In *A Paradox in Caribbean Attitudes to Land: Land and Development in the Caribbean*, edited by J. Besson et al. Warwick Caribbean Studies Series. London: Macmillan.

Moore, B. 1975. "The social impact of Portuguese immigration into British Guiana after emancipation". *Journal of Latin American and Caribbean Studies*, no. 19 (December).

Moore, B. 1987. *Race, Power and Social Segmentation in Colonial Society. Guyana after Slavery 1938–1891*. New York: Gordon and Breach.

Moore, B. 1995. "The culture of the colonial elite in nineteenth century Guyana". In *The White Minority in the Caribbean*, edited by H. Johnson et al. London: James Currey.

Naraine, S.S. 1971. "A study of land use, including land tenure, land reform, valuation and land taxation in Guyana". Georgetown, Guyana.

Nath, D. 1950. *A History of Indians in British Guiana*. London: Thomas Nelson and Sons.

Nath, D. 1976. *A History of Guyana*, Vol. 3. London: D. Nath.

Nathan Associates Inc. 1974. "Guyana's food crop system: An analysis for development planning". 30 June.

Nathan Associates Inc. 1980. "The income and production of Guyana rural farm households: An analysis based on the 1979 Guyana Rural Farm Household Survey". Prepared for USAID (January).

Nelson, J. 1989. *Fragile Coalitions: The Politics of Economic Adjustment. ODC vs Third World Policy Perspectives* (No. 12). New Brunswick, NJ: Transaction Books.

Ner, B., et al. c. 1970. *On the Economics of Self Management: The Kibbutz and the Yugoslav Enterprise*. N.p.

New World Associates. 1963. "The long-term economic, social and cultural programme". *New World Quarterly* 1, no. 1.

New World Associates. 1966. "Working notes towards the modification of Guyana". *New World Quarterly*. Independence Issue (May).

Newman, P. 1960. "The economic future of British Guiana". *Social and Economic Studies* 9 (September).

Newman, P. 1961. "Epilogue on British Guiana". *Social and Economic Studies* 10.

Newman, P. 1964. *British Guiana. Problems of Cohesion in an Immigrant Society*. Oxford: Oxford University Press.

Norwood, Y. 1956. *Man Alone! Adventures in the Jungles of British Guiana and Brazil*. London and New York: T.V. Boardman.

Nunes, F. 1989. *Plantation to Cooperative: Managerial Issues in the Castle Bruce Transition*. Working Paper 26. Mona, Jamaica: Institute of Social and Economic Research.

Odle, M. 1975. *Conflicting Attitudes Towards Public Enterprises in the Caribbean*. New Delhi: Lok Udyog.

Odle, M. 1976. *The Evolution of Public Expenditure: The Case of a Structurally Dependent Economy: Guyana*. Mona, Jamaica: Institute of Social and Economic Research.

Optima Technical Services. 1991. "Guyana agricultural sector water control". Prepared for IDB (March). Government of Guyana: Agricultural Sector Programme.

Oxaal, I., et al., eds. 1975. *Beyond the Sociology of Development*. London: Routledge.

Payne, G. 1976a. "Report on survey of settlers along the Linden-Soesdyke Highway, Long

Creek, Dora and Moblissa". Mirev Planning Unit, Ministry of National Development. Mimeo.

Payne, G. 1976b "What aspects of cooperatives are recommended for new settlements?" Mirev Planning Unit, Ministry of National Development. Mimeo.

Payne, G. 1977. "Report on survey of Black Bush Polder settlement and some areas of the Corentyne coast". Undertaken by the Research Dept., 13–18 March. Mirev Planning Unit, Ministry of National Development. Mimeo.

Payne, G. n.d. (c. 1977). "Report on a survey of Kaituma, North West District". Mirev Planning Unit, Ministry of National Development. Mimeo.

Pearse, A. 1972. "Peasants and the revolution: the case of Bolivia. Parts I and II". *Economy and Society* 1, nos. 3 and 4.

People's National Congress. 1975. "Declaration of Sophia". Address by the leader of the PNC. Georgetown, Guyana.

Persaud, B. 1976. "Agricultural development problems of small states". *Commonwealth Secretariat* (September).

Pierce, P. 1984. *Non-capitalist Development: The Struggle to Nationalize the Guyana Sugar Industry*. Ottowa, NJ: Rowman and Allanheld.

Platteau, J. 1992. "Land reform and structural adjustment in sub-Saharan Africa: controversies and guidelines". A report prepared for the FAO, Rome. FAO Economic and Social Development Paper, no. 107

Post, K. 1978. *Arise Ye Starvelings: The Jamaican Labour Rebellion of 1938 and its Aftermath*. The Hague: Martinus Nijhoff.

Potter, L. 1975. "Internal migration and resettlement of East Indians in Guyana, 1870–1920". PhD thesis, McGill University.

Potter, L. 1979a. "Coastal interior settlements in Guyana: Development, problems and prospects". Fifth Commonwealth Conference on Development and Human Ecology, Georgetown, Guyana.

Potter, L. 1979b. "Resources, regional systems and development strategies in Guyana". Geography Association Seminar, Trinidad.

Potter, R., and D. Conway, eds. 1997. *Self-help Housing, the Poor and the State in the Caribbean*. Kingston, Jamaica: The Press, University of the West Indies.

Pryor, F. 1982. "The plantation as an economic system". *Journal of Comparative Economics* 6, no. 3 (September).

Quamina, O. 1987. *Mineworkers of Guyana: the Making of a Working Class*. London: Zed Books.

Ramphal, S. 1983. "Some in light and some in darkness: the long shadow of slavery." *Third World Foundation Monograph* 12.

Ramphal, S. 1985. "Caribbean alternatives". Address by Commonwealth Secretary-General to mark the opening of the Centre for Caribbean Studies, University of Warwick, 9 May.

Ramsahoye, F.H. 1966. *The Development of Land Law in British Guiana*. New York: Ocean.

Reno, P. 1964. *The Ordeal of British Guiana*. New York: Monthly Review Press.

Rhodes-Checci. 1967. "Feasibility study and report on modernizing storage and processing for Guyana rice", Vols. 1 and 2. United Founders Towers, Oklahoma.

Richardson, B. 1975. "Plantation infrastructure and labour mobility in Guyana and Trinidad". In *Migration and Development*, edited by Sofa and Du Toit. The Hague: Martinus Nijhoff.

Robertson, A. 1976. "Report of trip to Black Bush Polder". Mirev Planning Unit, Ministry of National Development. Georgetown.

Rodney, W. 1966. "Masses in action". *New World Quarterly*. Independence Issue.

Rodney, W. 1979. *Guyanese Sugar Plantations in the Late Nineteenth Century: A Contemporary*

Description from the Argosy. Georgetown, Guyana: Release Publishers.

Rodney, W. 1981a. *A History of the Guyanese Working People, 1881–1905*. Baltimore: Johns Hopkins University Press.

Rodney, W. 1981b. "Guyana: the making of the labour force". *Race and Class* 22, no. 4.

Rohlehr, G. 1990. *Calypso and Society in Pre-independence Trinidad*. Trinidad and Tobago: Gordon Rohlehr.

Ruthenberg, H. 1966. "African agricultural development in Kenya, 1952–65". Berlin: IFO, Instel. fur wertschefts fasching. Af. Stadien.

Sallahuddin. 1994. *Guyana the Struggle for Liberation, 1945–1992: Dr Cheddi B. Jagan the Indomitable Architect*. Georgetown, Guyana: Guyana National Printers.

Satchell, V. 1990. *From Plots to Plantations: Land Transactions in Jamaica, 1866–1900*. Mona, Jamaica: Institute of Social and Economic Research.

Sattaur, O. 1990. "Guyana's coast at high tide". *New Scientist* 125, no. 1710 (31 March).

Saunders, K., ed. 1984. *Indentured Labour in the British Empire 1834–1920*. London: Croom Helm.

Schuler, M. 1988. "Plantation labourers, the London Missionary Society and emancipation in West Demerara, Guyana". *Journal of Caribbean History* 22, nos. 1 and 2.

Shahabuddeen, M. 1978. *Constitutional Development in Guyana, 1621–1978*. Georgetown, Guyana: Guyana Printers.

Shahabuddeen, M. 1981. "Nationalisation of Guyan's bauxite: The case of Alcan". University of Guyana, Georgetown.

Shahabuddeen, M. 1983. *From Plantocracy to Nationalization: A Profile of Sugar in Guyana*. Georgetown, Guyana: Guyana Printers.

Shahabuddeen, M. 1984. "Slavery and histigraphical rectification". Guyana Commemoration Commission, Georgetown.

Shahabuddeen, M. 1986a. "The nationalisation of Guyana's bauxite: The case of Alcan". Georgetown, Guyana.

Shahabuddeen, M. 1986b. *Long Through the Night: Two Speeches on the Human Condition in Southern Africa and Colonial Guyana*. Georgetown, Guyana: Ministry of Foreign Affairs.

Shanin, T., ed. 1971. *Peasants and Peasant Societies*. London: Penguin Modern Sociology.

Shinebourne, J. 1986. *Timepiece*. Leeds: Peepal Tree Press.

Silverman, M. 1980. *Rich People and Rice: Factional Politics in Rural Guyana*. Monographs and Theoretical Studies in Sociology and Anthropology in Honour of Nets Anderson 16. Lieden: E.J. Brill.

Singh, K. 1987. "The abolition of Indian indentureship and response of the planter interests in Trinidad". *Journal of Caribbean History* 21, no. 1.

Smith, R. 1962. *British Guiana, R.I.I.A.*, London: Oxford University Press.

Smith, R. 1969. "The origins of pork-knocking in Guyana". *Studies in Caribbean Anthropology*. Montreal: McGill University.

Smith, R. 1977. Introduction. In *The Stratification System and Occupational Mobility in Guyana: Two Essays*, edited by S. Graham and D. Gordon. Mona, Jamaica: Institute of Social and Economic Research.

Soloman, P., and T. Friedman. 1982. *Life and Death on the Corporate Battlefield: How Companies Win, Lose, Survive*. New York: Signet.

Spackman, A. 1975. "The role of private companies in the politics of empire: A case study of bauxite and diamond companies in Guyana in the early 1920s". *Social and Economic Studies* 24, no. 3.

Standing, G., and F. Sukdeo. 1977. "Labour migration and development in Guyana".

International Labour Review 116, no. 3 (November–December).

Stavenhagen, R. 1973. "Changing functions of the community in underdeveloped countries". In *Underdevelopment and Development: The Third World Today*, edited by H. Bernstein. Harmondsworth: Penguin.

Stern, N. 1989. "Peasant economy". In *The New Palgrave Economic Development*, edited by J. Eatwell et al. New York and London: Norton.

Sukdeo, I. 1978. "Labour mobility in land development schemes". ILO Labour Mobility Project, IDS, University of Guyana.

Sukdeo, F., et al. 1978. "Report on agrarian reform in Guyana for the World FAO Conference". Presented by Chairman of Research Committee, Rome, July.

Taylor, C. 1984. "The journal of an absentee proprietor". *Journal of Caribbean History* 18.

Taylor, J. 1979. *From Modernization to Modes of Production. A Critique of the Sociologies of Development and Underdevelopment*. London: Macmillan.

Thomas, C.Y. 1965. "Monetary and financial arrangements in a dependent monetary economy: A study of British Guiana 1945–62". Mona, Jamaica: Institute of Social and Economic Research.

Thomas, C.Y. 1969. "Sugar economics in a colonial situation: A study of the Guyana sugar industry". *Ratoon Studies in Exploitation* 1.

Thomas, C.Y. 1979. "Agrarian change in a plantation economy: the case of Guyana". In *Agrarian Systems and Rural Development*, edited by D. Ghai et al. London: Macmillan.

Thomas, C.Y. 1983. "State capitalism in Guyana". In *Crisis in the Caribbean*, edited by F. Ambursley and R. Cohen. London: Heinemann.

Thomas, C.Y. 1984. *A Study of the Mode of Sugar Production in Guyana*. Los Angeles: University of California; and Mona, Jamaica: Institute of Social and Economic Research.

Thompson, T.S. 1976. "Interim Report: A perspective on the development of Sebai (a village settlement in the north west district of Guyana)". Ministry of National Development, Georgetown, Guyana.

Thorner, D., et al. 1987. *A.V. Chayanov on the Theory of Peasant Economy*. Madison: University of Wisconsin Press.

Tuma, E. 1968. "Harmony and conflict in agrarian reform". World Conference of Rural Sociology, The Netherlands.

USAID. 1975. "Food crop production/marketing loan/grant: First interim review". Georgetown, Guyana.

Van Lier, R. 1987. *Frontier Society: A Social Analysis of the History of Suriname*. The Hague: Martinus Nijhoff.

Veramallay, A. 1976. "An evaluation of water resource development in Guyana: With application to selected drainage and irrigation projects". PhD diss., Iowa State University at Ames.

Vining, J.W. 1976. "Site development and settlement scheme failure in Guyana". *Journal of Tropical Geography* 42.

Warriner, D. 1969. *Land Reform in Principle and Practice*. Oxford: Oxford University Press.

Waugh, E. 1934. *Ninety-two Days: A Journey in Guiana and Brazil*. Dockworth, UK: Penguin.

Webber, A. 1988. *Those That Be in Bondage. A Tale of Indian Indentures and Sunlit Western Waters*. Wellesley: MA: Calaloux Publications.

Will, H. 1968. "The Colonial Office and problems of constitutional reform in Jamaica, Trinidad and British Guiana, 1880–1903". PhD diss., University of London.

Williams, E. 1970. *From Columbus to Castro: The History of the Caribbean 1492–1969*. London: André Deutsch.

Williams, D. 1985. "Ancient Guyana". Ninth Series of the Edgar Mittelholzer Memorial

Lectures. Department of Culture, Georgetown Guyana.

Wilson, H.H. 1929. "Reports: colonization activities". *Agricultural Journal of British Guiana* 2.

Woldemariam, Y. 1976. "Report on Long Creek settlement". Mirev Planning Unit, Ministry of National Development. Mimeo.

Young, A. 1958. *The Approaches to Local Self-government in British Guiana*. London: Longmans.

INDEX

www.ingramcontent.com/pod-product-compliance
Lightning Source LLC
Chambersburg PA
CBHW070404270326
41926CB00014B/2700